# ORIGINS OF
# ICELANDIC
# LITERATURE

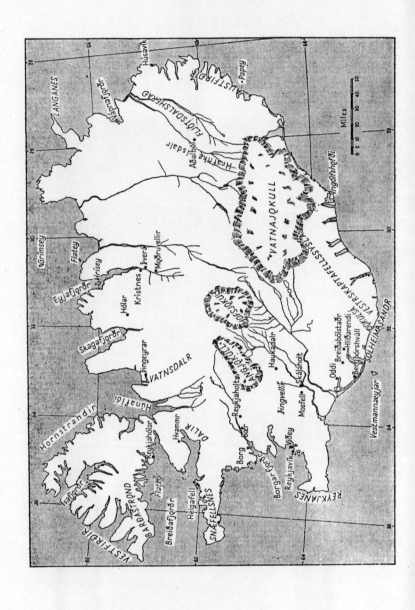

# ORIGINS OF ICELANDIC LITERATURE

BY

G. TURVILLE-PETRE

OXFORD
AT THE CLARENDON PRESS

*Oxford University Press, Ely House, London W. 1*

GLASGOW NEW YORK TORONTO MELBOURNE WELLINGTON
CAPE TOWN IBADAN NAIROBI DAR ES SALAAM LUSAKA ADDIS ABABA
DELHI BOMBAY CALCUTTA MADRAS KARACHI LAHORE DACCA
KUALA LUMPUR SINGAPORE HONG KONG TOKYO

ISBN 0 19 811114 2

*First published 1953*
*Reprinted 1967 (from corrected sheets of the First Edition)*
*1975*

*Printed in Great Britain*
*at the University Press, Oxford*
*by Vivian Ridler*
*Printer to the University*

# PREFACE

MANY books and papers have been published in the last fifty years about the origins of various branches of Icelandic literature, and in particular about the origins of 'Kings' Sagas' and 'Icelanders' Sagas'. Much of this work has been valuable, although often speculative and controversial. In this book I have attempted to avoid controversy and guess-work, although I may not always have succeeded. The origins of the classical prose can perhaps be discerned best if Icelandic literature of pre-classical ages is considered. It is plain that the greatest 'Kings' Sagas' and 'Icelanders' Sagas' were written in the thirteenth century, but it is well known that much poetry was composed and much prose was written in Iceland before that century. The origins of the classical sagas may thus be found, in part at any rate, in the prose and poetry of preceding ages, such as I have attempted to describe here.

I have discussed the prose of the twelfth century in some detail, for the sagas of the thirteenth century cannot be dissociated from it. Nearly all the prose written in the twelfth century was written in the interest of the ecclesiastical and secular powers, but in Iceland at that time these powers could not be sharply distinguished. Bishops were often drawn from chieftainly families; chieftains took clerical orders.

I have not discussed oral sagas or their form. For the existence of such sagas in twelfth-century Iceland has not yet been proved and, even if they existed, it will never be possible to show what they were like. At least it can be said that the sagas which we know are not in oral form, and that their usually polished style is the outcome of generations of training in literary composition.

I have refrained from speaking in general terms about the value of sagas as sources of history. Some sagas undoubtedly preserve much historical fact, and a great proportion of it comes from works, whether lost or extant, written early in the twelfth century, from the histories of Sæmundr and Ari, from genealogical lists, and

perhaps from lost annals. Perhaps no less of the history contained
in the sagas is derived from scaldic poetry handed down orally,
some of it as old as the tenth century, or even as the ninth, and
from tales which went with it.

Valuable as they may be as sources of history, sagas are read and
enjoyed chiefly as art and, in all probability, that was how most of
their authors intended that they should be read.

This book is not a handbook of early Icelandic literature but,
as its title suggests, a study of the literature in its older stages.
Some branches of this literature have been neglected in most works
on the subject, more especially the poetry of the eleventh and
twelfth centuries, as well as the lives of the saints and homilies.
These will help to show how closely the literature of Iceland was
linked with that of Europe.

In original form much of this literature must have reached the
Icelanders in Latin but, as S. Þorlákr sadly regretted, the learning
of the Icelandic clergy left much to be desired, and they needed
versions of standard works in Icelandic. It is still possible to
identify the authors of some of the Icelandic versions of Latin
texts, such as Gunnlaugr Leifsson, author of the metrical version
of the 'Prophecies of Merlin'. The Benedictine traveller, Nikulás,
should also be considered as well as Gizurr Hallsson and Kygri-
Bjǫrn, author of a *Maríu Saga*. The part played by such scholars
in developing Icelandic literature has not yet been fully appreciated. This book is by no means definitive, for much work
remains to be done on the origins of Icelandic literature.

I would like to thank many friends both in Iceland and in England
who have helped me with advice and criticism. A. Campbell has
read through the manuscript more than once; J. R. R. Tolkien has
also made many useful suggestions. Sigurður Nordal has been
most generous with his advice, and the reader will see how much
I owe to his published works. I would also like to thank Einar Ól.
Sveinsson, with whom I have had fruitful discussions during
many years, and I may mention the help and kindness shown to me
by Jón Jóhannesson, by Björn Sigfússon, Librarian of the University of Iceland, and by Kristján Eldjárn, Curator of the National

Museum in Reykjavík. Joan Turville-Petre has given me patient
assistance at every step, and Gervase Mathew has helped me much
in the last stages.

I wish finally to thank Miss G. Feith for the trouble which she
has taken in preparing the Index, and the Press for the great care
with which they have produced this book.

G. T.-P.

OXFORD
*January* 1953

# CONTENTS

# LIST OF PLATES

# ABBREVIATIONS

*Saga-Book*   Saga-Book of the Viking Society for Northern Research.

ONOI   Finnur Jónsson, *Den oldnorske og oldislandske litteraturs historie*, ed. 2, 1920–4.

*Skjald.*   *Den norsk-islandske Skjaldedigtning*, ed. Finnur Jónsson, 1912–15.

# I
# PAGAN ICELAND

## 1. THE DISCOVERY AND SETTLEMENT OF ICELAND

ICELAND was the last land in which viking Norsemen made a permanent settlement, but nowhere did their heroic traditions live so long and so vigorously as they did there. Styles of poetry used by the Norsemen of the Dark Ages and of the Viking Age flourished in this poor, isolated island after they had been forgotten elsewhere. But Iceland was not merely the storehouse of northern tradition. Its poets and prose authors did not only preserve and develop literary forms of their forefathers; they also devised new forms, and the literature of Iceland thus became the richest and most varied of medieval Europe.

It was not until the latter decades of the ninth century that Norse seamen first sighted Iceland, and when they did so, it was by accident rather than by design. Early Icelandic historians wrote of a Norwegian, Naddoðr, who was driven to the coasts of Iceland by the winds, and of a Swede, Garðarr, whose ship drifted from the Pentland Firth to the south-east coast of Iceland.[1]

Reports about the new country spread rapidly and, before long, Norse chieftains saw prospects of settling there. The first to attempt this was Flóki, who sailed from Norway and set up house on Barðaströnd in the west of Iceland. His settlement was a failure, for he and his men were better seamen than farmers. They spent the summer pursuing shoals of fish with which the fjords of Iceland teemed, and neglected the harvest so that they had no hay to feed their stock when winter came. Before he left Iceland in the following spring, Flóki climbed a mountain ridge and looked down into a fjord filled with pack-ice. For this reason he called the land Iceland, as it has been called ever since.[2]

These first voyages were probably made about the year 860, but no permanent settlement was established in Iceland until ten or

[1] See *Landnámabók*, ed. Finnur Jónsson, 1900, pp. 4 and 130; cf. G. Turville-Petre, *The Heroic Age of Scandinavia*, 1951, ch. ix.
[2] See *Landnámabók*, loc. cit.

fifteen years later. The first successful settler was Ingólfr, a man
of western Norway. It is commonly believed that he set up house
in Reykjavík, the site of the modern capital, about the year 874.
According to Ari Þorgilsson, one of the oldest of the Icelandic
historians, the settlement of the country occupied some fifty or
sixty years, reckoning from the time when Ingólfr came to Iceland
until 930, when the island was fully peopled. These dates have
been revised by modern historians, and cannot be considered precise, but they give a rough indication of the period when most of
the settlers reached Iceland.[1]

The story of the settlement of Iceland is told in most detail in
the *Landnámabók* (Book of Settlements), which will be discussed in
a later chapter. Although we cannot believe all the details given
by the authors of this book, we may be satisfied that their story is
true in outline. They name the original settlers of each district
of Iceland, together with their descendants and, in many cases,
their ancestors. They often tell us where and how these settlers
had lived before they came to Iceland. The authors of the *Landnámabók* thus help us to understand both the material and spiritual
culture of the Icelandic people.

We learn from the *Landnámabók*, and from other works of its
kind, that most of the settlers came from Norway, and especially
from southern and western Norway, and their civilization was that
of the Norwegians.

The sources suggest that settlers reached Iceland in greatest
numbers during the last fifteen or twenty years of the ninth century. Many of them were said to be chieftains of western Norway,
who abandoned the hereditary estates on which they had lived as
independent rulers rather than submit to the tyranny of Haraldr
Finehair. Haraldr was the first prince of Norway to subject the
whole country to his authority, and he finally broke the resistance
of his rivals in the battle of Hafrsfjǫrðr, fought about 885.[2]

---

[1] See *Víga-Glúms Saga*, ed. G. Turville-Petre, 1940, Introduction, § iv, and
works to which reference is there made.

[2] See G. Turville-Petre, *The Heroic Age of Scandinavia*, pp. 116 ff. and especially H. Koht, *Innhogg og Utsyn*, 1921, pp. 34 ff.; Guðbrandur Vigfússon and
F. York Powell, *Corpus Poeticum Boreale*, ii, 1883, pp. 487 ff.

Not all the settlers of Iceland came from Norway itself. A considerable proportion came from the Norse colonies in the British Isles, and especially from those in Ireland and the Hebrides. These men were descendants of Norsemen who had left their homes a generation or two earlier and had gone to live in the Celtic lands. The Norse colonists had frequently married Celtic women, or taken Celtic concubines, and their children were mixed in culture as they were mixed in blood.

The story of Helgi the Lean, one of the most illustrious of the settlers of Iceland, may be quoted as an example. Helgi was the son of Eyvindr austmaðr ('ostman'), a prominent Norseman (or Gautr), who had settled in Ireland. Helgi's mother was called Rafarta (Irish *Rafertach*), and she was said to be the daughter of an Irish king, Kjarvalr. Modern historians sometimes identify Kjarvalr with Cearbhall, King of Ossory, who died in 887. Helgi was brought up partly in Ireland and partly in the Hebrides; he was partly Christian and partly pagan. He believed in Christ, but he preferred Þórr to be his guide at sea, and used to invoke Þórr when the issue was of great moment. Helgi took possession of a large district of northern Iceland, and he called his home Kristnes (Christ's Headland), as it is called to this day. Many of the foremost Icelanders were descended from Helgi, and such men as he must have exercised a considerable influence on the civilization of the new country.[1]

The story of Helgi is one of a number which show that the first chieftains of Iceland included men of mixed race, creed, and culture. Further evidence of this may be seen in the Irish names borne by several famous Icelanders of the tenth century. Examples are Njáll, Kormákr, Kjartan. Irish nicknames were also current among the Icelanders of the first century, and these must have significance. The thralls and servants of the Icelanders are often described as Irishmen, and they are called by such foreign names as Dufþakr, Dufan, Melkólfr. A number of places in Iceland are also called by names of Irish origin, or else suggest that Irishmen

---

[1] On Helgi see my edition of *Viga-Glúms Saga*, p. 52 and works to which reference is there made.

once lived in those places. Examples are Minþakseyrr (cf. Irish *menadach*, a kind of meal), Brjánslœkr, Patreksfjǫrðr, Dufgusdalr, Íragerði, and perhaps Dímon.

The Icelandic language shows comparatively slight traces of Celtic influence. But before conclusions are drawn from this fact, it must be realized that Icelandic is the purest of Germanic dialects, and that the Icelanders have always resisted the influence of foreign languages. Moreover, Celtic languages have contributed little to the vocabulary of those languages with which they have been brought into contact in historic times, although they have sometimes influenced the syntax. Among the loan-words from Irish in Icelandic are several interesting ones. The Irish word *gealt* (geilt), 'a raving lunatic', is common in Icelandic, although it is used only in the dative, and only in the expression *verða at gjalti* 'to become a lunatic', 'to go mad with terror'. Native speakers of Icelandic have forgotten the meaning of *gjalti*, as Guðbrandur Vigfússon showed in his *Icelandic–English Dictionary* (1874), when he said that *gjalti* was an old dative of *gǫltr* (hog), and that the phrase *verða at gjalti* had originally meant 'to be turned into a hog'. Among other loans from Irish may be counted *púst*, also written *súst* (a flail), from Irish *súiste*; *skjaðak* (sourness of stale beer), which must derive from the Irish adjective *sceathach* (vomiting, emetic, vapid, nauseating); *slavak* (a kind of chickweed), from Irish *sleabhac* (laver, sloke); *tarfr* (a bull), from Irish *tarbh*.

A greater number of words which appear to be of Irish origin are found in Icelandic poetry than in the prose, and some of these were probably never used in daily speech. Examples are *lind* (pool, Irish *linn*), *korki* (oats, Irish *coirce*), *bjǫð* (land, world, Irish *bith*, *bioth*). There are other words of Latin origin, which must have come to Icelandic through the medium of Irish, such as *bagall* (crozier, Irish *bachall*, Latin *baculus*), *bjannak* (Irish *beannacht*, Latin *benedictio*).[1]

As already remarked, most of the settlers of Iceland came from Norway, and particularly from the south-west of that country. The dialect spoken by the Icelanders in the Middle Ages differed little

[1] Cf. F. Fischer, *Die Lehnwörter des Altwestnordischen*, 1909, pp. 18 ff. and *passim*.

from that of south-western Norway, and their culture was predominantly that of Scandinavia. But the culture of the Scandinavians was by no means pure for, throughout their history, the Norsemen had been susceptible to the influences of Europe. Foreign influences had never been stronger than they were in the Viking Age, the ninth century, when Norsemen raided, traded, and established colonies in countries east of the Baltic and south of it, in the Frankish Empire and in the British Isles. The Norsemen who invaded Russia were mainly Swedes, and those who established colonies in England were mainly Danes. The Norsemen who left the strongest mark on Ireland and the Hebrides were Norwegians. C. Marstrander[1] has studied the forms of loan-words borrowed by the Irish from the Norsemen, and he concludes that a great proportion of them are to be traced to the dialects of western and southern Norway. He suggests that the Norse invaders of Ireland came largely from these regions. If this is so, the Norwegians who settled in Iceland were among those whose contacts with the Celts were closest. The Norse colonies in the Celtic lands and the settlement of Iceland appear to be two forms of the same viking movement in the west. Norsemen who had lived in the Celtic lands would sometimes move on to Iceland as their prospects in the Celtic lands declined during the last years of the ninth century. Some of the intellectual and imaginative qualities which distinguish the Icelanders from other Scandinavians may be traced to their early contacts with the Celts.

The chieftains who settled in Iceland lived as sovereign rulers and, during the first decades, there was no central government or administration in Iceland. Chieftains took the title of *goði* (pl. *goðar*) or 'priest'; their subjects were those who attended sacrifice in their temples and, we may suppose, meetings at which matters of common interest were discussed. The limits of the *goði*'s jurisdiction were not territorial; his liegemen were those who enjoyed his protection and supported him in return.[2]

---

[1] *Bidrag til det norske sprogs historie i Irland*, 1915, pp. 128 ff.
[2] See Aa. Gregersen, *L'Islande, son Statut à travers les Âges*, 1937, ch. iii and *The Heroic Age of Scandinavia*, ch. x.

It was not long before the chieftains of Iceland felt the need of some form of central government. About the year 927 they sent an emissary, Úlfljótr, to Norway to draw up a code of law which could be applied to the whole country. Úlfljótr modelled his code on that current in the western districts of Norway, the Gulaþing. It was made law in Iceland about the year 930.

Under the law of Úlfljótr, the *Alþingi*, or General Assembly, was established. It met annually at Þingvellir, in the south-west of the island, under the presidency of the Law-speaker (*lǫgsǫgumaðr*). One of the chief duties of the Law-speaker was to recite the laws, which were then unwritten, and would quickly have been forgotten unless they were heard frequently. The Law-speaker was elected by the *goðar* for three years, but he could be re-elected for further terms, and frequently was.

The powers of the *Alþingi* were both legislative and judicial, and it was controlled solely by the *goðar*. At this time there were probably thirty-six *goðar* in Iceland, and the *Alþingi* was an agreement in which they took part, not an authority above them.

There was no police force, army, or other executive body, and it is plain that all authority, civil and religious, was in the hands of the *goðar*. They alone could enforce the laws of the *Alþingi* and the judgements delivered by it, or they could resist these laws and judgements if their interests were better served by doing so.

The office of *goði* would normally pass from father to son, although it could be bought, sold, and even divided. The political system of Iceland was thus aristocratic, and bore no resemblance to the democratic systems introduced in Europe in later times.

The Constitution was altered slightly about the year 965, when the land was divided into four administrative districts or Quarters. Some further changes were made about the year 1005, and the total number who took part in the *Alþingi* with the rights of *goðar* was then increased to forty-eight. But in essentials the system of government remained unchanged until the year 1262, when Iceland was subjected to the Crown of Norway.

The absence of central executive authority gave scope to lawless men, whose faith was in their own might. Violent deeds provoked vengeance, and much of the history of early Iceland is that of blood-feuds between one family and another. It is the more remarkable that the Icelanders of the Middle Ages were a nation of literary artists and scholars. In this introductory chapter I hope to show what was the cultural heritage which the settlers of Iceland brought with them, and in later chapters I shall discuss changes in taste, interest, and ideals which occurred after the conversion of the Icelanders to Christianity.

## 2. THE EDDAIC POETRY

Scandinavians of the Viking Age, as indeed of earlier ages, had excelled as visual artists, as is proved by their sculpture, metalwork, and tapestry. But the Icelanders of early times showed little talent in these arts, partly, no doubt, because their volcanic stone was unfit for carving, they had little timber, and no natural source of metal. From the first, the Icelanders found artistic expression in words, and it was the art of poetry and perhaps of story-telling, rather than of sculpture and metal-working, that the settlers brought with them.

It is recognized that the greater part of the early poetry of Scandinavia has perished. Practically none of it survives except in the Icelandic manuscripts of the thirteenth and later centuries, and this poetry must have lived orally in Iceland for many generations before it was written down. In its present form it is, therefore, Icelandic, and the study of Scandinavian poetry is the study of Icelandic poetry.

The oldest of this poetry is preserved in a manuscript now called the *Elder Edda*, written about 1270, and in a few smaller manuscripts of rather later date.[1] Both linguistic and literary evidence show that some of the poetry contained in these manuscripts is very ancient, and that it originated at a period earlier than the settlement of Iceland.

Two classes of poetry are commonly distinguished in the *Edda* and in the other manuscripts of its kind. These are the mytho-

[1] Unless otherwise stated, I quote from the edition of G. Neckel, *Edda*, i–ii, 1927.

logical lays and the heroic. The distinction is not precise but, on the whole, it may be said that the authors of the mythological lays describe the world of gods, and those of the heroic lays the world of men.

### 3. The Heroic Lays

The heroic lays may be considered first, for theirs is probably the older class, and they represent a form of poetry which was at one time current among all Germanic tribes from the Black Sea to Greenland. Heroic lays comparable with those found in the Icelandic manuscripts are preserved in Old English and in Old High German. Many of the heroes depicted in poetry of this kind are based upon historical characters, although others are the creation of legend and of the authors of the lays.

It is held widely that this form of poetry was used first by the Goths when they dwelt in south-eastern Europe in the first century A.D.[1] The oldest historical person described in existing lays is the King of the Goths Jǫrmunrekkr (Ermanaric), who died in A.D. 375. It is improbable that legends about Jǫrmunrekkr would long survive his death as formless oral tales, and we may consequently suspect that lays about him were composed within a few years of his lifetime. This is not to say that existing poetry about Jǫrmunrekkr is as old as the fourth century, but it may suggest that it derives ultimately from poetry of that date.

While there can be little doubt that heroic lays were known among Germanic peoples in the fourth century, there are reasons for believing that heroic lays of some kind were popular among them at a much earlier date. There is evidence that lays about Gothic heroes older than Jǫrmunrekkr were once current, and Tacitus, writing about A.D. 100, alludes to songs about the Cheruscan hero, Arminius (died A.D. 19), which were remembered nearly a century after the hero's death.[2] We cannot be sure that these songs of Arminius resembled the heroic lays of later times, although this is not improbable.

[1] Cf. A. Heusler, *Die altgermanische Dichtung*, 1923, pp. 149 ff.; J. de Vries, *Altnordische Literaturgeschichte*, i, 1941, pp. 32 ff.
[2] Tacitus, *Annals*, ii. 88.

The heroic lays were probably designed, in the first place, to be declaimed in the halls of the chieftains and, on occasion, they were accompanied with the harp. Among the oldest, or at least the most archaic heroic lays surviving today are the Old High German 'Lay of Hildebrand' and the Old English 'Fight at Finnsburh'.[1] Only fragments of these are preserved, but they are sufficient to show that, at one time, the English and the continental Germans cultivated lays like those which we know from the Icelandic manuscript.

The heroic lays of the Germanic tribes differed in many ways from epics, with which they might naturally be associated. The difference is not only in length, but also in scope and in choice of subject. The life-story of a hero could not be told in an early heroic lay, but the poet would concentrate on one or two incidents in it. It thus resembled the epic only as the short story resembles the novel. The poets were moved most deeply by tragic situations and by moral conflict. Thus, in the 'Lay of Hildebrand', in its original form, it was told how Hildebrand and his son, Hadubrand, met on the battlefield on opposite sides, and how Hildebrand was obliged to kill his son or else suffer the stigma of a coward and a traitor. Loyalty is one of the dominant motives, and the poets were often inspired by conflicts of loyalty. In the *Atlakviða* it was told how Guðrún butchered her own sons in order to avenge her brothers on her husband, Atli. It was these same brothers who had treacherously instigated the murder of Guðrún's first husband, Sigurðr, the 'jewel among princes'. The story shows how much stronger were the claims to loyalty of blood-relatives than those of husbands and lovers. No less sacred were the bonds between men who had sworn oaths of foster-brotherhood.

It was not the aim of the heroic poets to depict character in detail. They did not treat their subjects objectively, as the authors of the family sagas did, striving to make characters complete and living.[2] The heroic poets appealed rather to the emotions. The figures whom they described typified virtues, vices, and failings which the early Germanic peoples admired, feared, and despised.

[1] Ed. Bruce Dickins, *Runic and Heroic Poems*, 1915, pp. 64 and 78 ff.
[2] Cf. A. Heusler, op. cit., pp. 156 ff.

In no other sources are heroic ideals expressed so clearly and so magnificently as they are here.

The types described are comparatively few. One of them is the young and valiant hero, of whom Sigurðr is the foremost example. He was loyal, and so brave that he faced the dragon Fáfnir alone. He was dexterous in arms and on horseback, but his weakness was in his innocence and lack of guile. He did not perceive the treachery of the smith, Reginn, with whom he had lived for many years, until, accidentally tasting the blood of the dragon's heart, he understood the speech of the birds, and heard what they were saying about Reginn. Sigurðr's downfall resulted from this innocence. He understood nothing of the guile of his wife's brothers as they plotted his murder.

The story of the youths Hamðir and Sǫrli, told in the *Hamðismál* (Words of Hamðir), most clearly shows the northern concepts of fate and of bravery. The outcome of battle and the moment of death are predetermined, but the heart of the warrior is independent of fate, and his bravery enables him to face death rejoicing in the fame which will survive him. As Hamðir and Sǫrli fell in the hall of the Goths, which they had invaded against overwhelming odds, Hamðir cried out:

> Well have we battled;    like eagles on a bough
> under foot we trample    Goths fallen in fight.
> Fame shall be ours,    die we early or late;
> nightfall none sees    when the Norns have spoken.[1]

Beside the brave and guileless youth stands the cruel and cunning tyrant. Jǫrmunrekkr and Atli (Attila) are striking examples. Among the most memorable verses in heroic poetry are those of the *Hamðismál*, in which Jǫrmunrekkr is described as he learns that Hamðir and Sǫrli have come to attack him in his castle:

> Chuckling, Iormunrekk    his chin-beard stroked,
> with wine wanton,    he welcomed the fray;
> his dark locks shook he,    at his white shield did look,
> in his hand upholding    the horn all-golden.

---

[1] Translation of B. Philpotts, *Edda and Saga*, 1931, p. 64.

'Most happy were I      if behold I might
Hamthir and Sorli      my hall within:
bind them would I          with bow-strings long,
the good sons of Guthrun      on gallows fasten.'[1]

The same Jǫrmunrekkr had caused his young wife, Svanhildr, to
be trodden under foot by horses, and had hanged his own son.
Atli has qualities like those of Jǫrmunrekkr. It is told in the
*Atlakviða* (Lay of Atli) how Atli deceitfully lured the Burgundian
princes into his castle with promises of gifts and entertainment,
and then murdered them brutally. Vǫlundr (Wayland), the crafty
smith, is of the same stamp. He used his cunning to seduce the
king's daughter, Bǫðvildr, and invited the king's young sons to see
his treasures, so that he might butcher them.

The weak and foolish contrast with the forceful figures like these.
They are the instruments of evil and the dupes of cunning.
Gutthormr, according to the 'Fragmentary Lay of Sigurðr', was
incited by his wiser brothers to murder Sigurðr, but they must feed
him on the flesh of the wolf and the serpent before he had the
heart and the wits to carry out the deed:

> Some a wolf did steak,      some a worm did bake,—
> of the grim beast gave they      Gutthorm to eat.[2]

Women play an important part in several of the lays, and their
characters are often complicated. Grímhildr, the mother of Gunnarr and Guðrún, was a counterpart to Atli. She gave Sigurðr a
drugged drink, so that he should forget the oaths which he had
sworn to Brynhildr, and marry her own daughter, Guðrún. After
the death of Sigurðr, she gave Guðrún another poisoned drink, so
that she might forget him and marry Atli. Psychology is developed
most fully in the descriptions of the rival women, Brynhildr and
Guðrún. According to some of the poems, Brynhildr was torn
between love and hatred of Sigurðr. She hated him because,
through no fault of his own, he had deceived her, and she instigated
his murder, whereupon she was heart-broken and threw herself
on to the funeral pyre beside him. The conflict in Guðrún's heart

---

[1] Translation of L. M. Hollander, *The Poetic Edda*, 1928, p. 380.
[2] Translation of L. M. Hollander, op. cit., p. 286.

has already been mentioned. These spiritual conflicts arise partly
from the difficulty, which poets must have felt, in combining con-
flicting versions of the story. It was hard to explain why Guðrún,
whose husband had been killed by her brothers, should afterwards
be married to Atli, most especially if, as the poets had said, Atli
was the brother of the hated Brynhildr. Originally the story of the
Burgundians and Atli must have been distinct from that of
Sigurðr and Brynhildr. Poems such as the 'Short Lay of Sigurðr',
the 'First' and 'Second' Lays of Guðrún, in which the most
elaborate studies of psychology are found, are generally believed
to be of comparatively late date.

The motives used in the heroic lays were drawn largely from
history and, as I have said, the heroes can sometimes be identified
in the historical records. Thus, prototypes of Gunnarr and his
father, Gjúki, can be found in the history of the Burgundians of
the fifth century, while prototypes of other heroes appear in the
history of the Franks of the sixth century. But, to identify these
heroes in history is of little help in interpreting the lays for, in
them, the political history of the Dark Ages is personified, and no
room is left for armies and tribal movements. The defeat of the
Burgundians by the Huns in the year A.D. 437 appears in the lays
of the *Edda* as a family quarrel, in which the chief characters are
Gunnarr and his brother-in-law, Atli. Men who, in history, were
divided by several generations often appear in the lays together.
The Gothic king Jǫrmunrekkr (Ermanaric), who died in 375, is
made contemporary with Gunnarr (Gundicarius), who died in 437.
The Frankish queen, Brunehild, who died in 613, is probably the
prototype of Brynhildr who, in the lays of the *Edda*, is said to be
the wife of Gunnarr.

Heroes of the lays were known to all Germanic tribes, and
lays about Jǫrmunrekkr, Atli, Gunnarr, Sigurðr, and even about
Vǫlundr the Smith, must have been recited among all of them at
one time or another. It would be hard to believe that legends about
these heroes spread from tribe to tribe as formless oral tales. In the
earliest times, the lays themselves must have been carried by
travellers—whether professional poets, soldiers, or tradesmen—

from land to land, and translated, or adapted from one dialect into another.[1]

Heroic lays of continental origin were probably heard in Denmark and in southern Sweden as early as the sixth century A.D. The poets of these lands were thus moved to sing of the heroes of their own nations. No eastern Scandinavian lays of this period are preserved, although some of them must have been known to the English author of *Beowulf* in the eighth century, and were used by him as sources. Other lays of eastern Scandinavia were known to the Danish historian, Saxo Grammaticus (died *c.* 1216), and he retold their substance in his *Gesta Danorum*. The authors of the Icelandic Heroic Sagas (*Fornaldar Sǫgur*) must also have known lays about eastern Scandinavian heroes as late as the fourteenth century. Some of the lays still preserved in the *Edda*, those of Helgi Hundingsbani and of Helgi Hjǫrvarðsson, probably descend from originals composed in Denmark in the ninth century or the tenth.[2]

Many scholars believe that the cult of the heroic lay came to Norway later than to other Germanic lands,[3] although there can be little doubt that poetry of this kind was composed there as early as the eighth century. No heroic lay survives in a Norwegian manuscript, but a number of those found in the Icelandic manuscripts must have been composed in Norway, and some of them were perhaps the work of Norwegian colonists in the British Isles.

Among the oldest lays which survive today may be counted the *Hamðismál*, the *Atlakviða*, the 'Battle of Goths and Huns', and perhaps the *Vǫlundarkviða*, whose authors use a narrative technique and a metrical system like those of the 'Lay of Hildebrand' and the 'Fight at Finnsburh'. They may well be the work of Norwegians who lived between the eighth and tenth centuries,

---

[1] Cf. A. Heusler, op. cit., pp. 152 ff.; J. de Vries, op. cit., i. 34 ff.; G. Neckel, *Die altnordische Literatur*, 1923, pp. 80 ff.

[2] On the heroic lays of Denmark see J. de Vries, op. cit., i. 62 ff.; H. Schneider, *Germaniscne Ⅱeldensage*, ii, 1933, pp. 299 ff.; A. Olrik, *The Heroic Legends of Denmark*, translated by L. M. Hollander, 1919; and my *Heroic Age of Scandinavia*, pp. 44 ff.

[3] Cf. Heusler, op. cit., p. 151; H. M. Chadwick, *The Heroic Age*, 1912, pp. 99–100; for another view see de Vries, op. cit., i. 57–58.

although their form must have altered in some degree during centuries of oral transmission.

It is not known for how many centuries lays about traditional Germanic heroes continued to be composed in Norway. One of them, the *Fáfnismál* (The Words of the Dragon, Fáfnir)[1] was remembered and quoted by King Sverrir (died 1202), but it is unlikely that poetry of this kind was much admired by educated Norwegians after their people had adopted Christianity, early in the eleventh century.

It was in Iceland that the heroic lay survived and developed, and it was one of the most important and fruitful elements in the civilization which the settlers of Iceland brought from Norway. Although designed, originally, to be declaimed in the halls of the Germanic princes, the heroic lay flourished in the farm-houses of Iceland as it never had elsewhere. The traditional poetic forms continued to be used by the Icelanders, and the same heroic stories continued to inspire them throughout the Middle Ages. An Icelandic poet of the twelfth or thirteenth century rehandled the story of Hildebrand, and the verses which he left supplement the Old High German fragment. It is from the Icelandic relics, and not from the German ones, that we learn that Hildebrand had killed his son. Changes of taste, which reflected changing conditions in Europe, inspired new poems, in which new sympathies and sentiments were expressed, while the traditional stories were retold in similar poetic forms. The three 'Lays of Guðrún' and the 'Short Lay of Sigurðr' are assigned by many to Icelandic poets of the eleventh or twelfth centuries, although characters portrayed in them had appeared already in the *Atlakviða* and the *Hamðismál*, poems of a much earlier period. The *Hamðismál* and the *Atlakviða* represent an austere pagan civilization, while the 'Lays of Guðrún' and the 'Short Lay of Sigurðr' have more to do with the Christian Middle Ages.

## 4. THE LAYS OF THE GODS

Some of the mythological lays found in the Icelandic manuscripts can be little younger than the oldest heroic lays found there.

[1] See *Flateyjarbók*, ed. G. Vigfússon and C. R. Unger, ii, 1862, p. 686.

Like the oldest heroic lays, some of the mythological ones must be older than the settlement of Iceland. But, while the heroic lays represent a branch of literature which was, at one time, common to all Germanic peoples, there is nothing to show that mythological lays comparable with those of the *Edda* were known among Germanic tribes other than those of Scandinavia, and nothing to suggest that those which we now possess originated among peoples other than the Norwegians and Icelanders.

Several kinds of mythological lays may be distinguished in the *Edda* and in the kindred manuscripts. Some of them are didactic, and could almost be considered as treatises on pagan legend and belief. The *Vafþrúðnismál* (Words of Vafþrúðnir) is a good example of a lay of this kind. It is cast in the conventional form of a dialogue between Óðinn and the giant Vafþrúðnir, whom Óðinn visited in disguise. The god and the giant enter a contest of wits, on which each wagers his head. Óðinn asks the giant many questions, which are answered readily and lucidly. The giant tells of the origin of the earth, of the sun and the moon, the winds and the gods. He even predicts the *Ragnarǫk* (Fall of the Gods) and the manner of Óðinn's death. But in the end, the giant forfeits his head for Óðinn defeats him, and discloses his own identity with his last question: 'What did Óðinn whisper into the ear of his son (Baldr) as he was laid on the funeral pyre?' Only Óðinn knows the answer to this.

The *Grímnismál* is another didactic poem, in which Óðinn appears, disguised as the vagrant Grímnir (the Masked One), in the castle of an earthly king, Geirrøðr. The king laid hands upon him, and placed him between two fires. As the raging flames singed his cloak, Óðinn was relieved by the king's young son, who brought him a horn full of drink. Óðinn then discoursed on Valhǫll and the homes of the gods, Ullr, Freyr, Baldr, and others. Later he spoke of the World Tree, Yggdrasill, and finally he gave a list of his own names, for Óðinn had many names as he had many disguises. When Óðinn disclosed his identity, the cruel king, Geirrøðr, fell on his sword and was killed.

The *Hávamál* consists of strophes of various ages and about various subjects; they were probably put together under the title *Hávamál* (Words of the High One, Óðinn) by the antiquarian who collected and wrote them down in the thirteenth century. Five or six distinct poems can be distinguished in these 164 strophes. They are all assigned by the scribe to Óðinn, and it is plain that many of them were conceived originally as spoken by him.

A great part of the *Hávamál* consists of advice about social conduct and of words of proverbial wisdom. The tone of these passages is cynical and suspicious and it is commonly believed that they originated among Norwegian peasants of the Viking Age, when men were violent and often treacherous. Nevertheless, sentiments like those of the *Hávamál* were often expressed by the Icelandic heroes of the family sagas and by Icelandic chieftains of the Middle Ages. Neither the literature nor the history of medieval Iceland can be properly understood without a knowledge of poetry of this kind.

It is said in the *Hávamál* that a man should always be on guard against his enemies; one out in the field must not move a step from his weapons, and one who has saved money must not stint himself or keep it for his loved ones, lest his enemies seize it. A man must learn to conceal his emotions, and simulate affection for those whom he mistrusts. But despite such cynicism, friendship and loyalty are valued highly. A man shall be a friend to his friend, and to this one's friend as well. One without friends is like a lone pine-tree withering on a barren hill. Cautious as a man should be, he must also be brave, and fear nothing for his life. The coward thinks that he can live for ever if only he can keep out of battle, but old age will give him no peace, even though the spears spare him. In these passages of the *Hávamál* there is little mysticism, and no faith in superhuman powers or in life after death. A greater misfortune can hardly befall than death, for even a lame man can sit a horse, a one-armed man can drive a herd of cattle, a deaf man can wield a spear; it is better to be blind than to be burnt on the funeral pyre; a corpse is of no use to anyone. Nothing transcends death but good repute. Cattle die, kinsmen die, and man dies himself, but good repute may live for ever. This was the thought which sprang to the minds of Hamðir and Sǫrli when they were killed in the castle of Jǫrmunrekkr, and to Norse heroes of succeeding ages at the time of death. When Gunnarr of Hlíðarendi was struck down after he had fought alone against overwhelming odds, the leader of his assailants said: 'his defence will be remembered so long as this land is peopled.'[1]

There are more obscure and more mysterious passages in the *Hávamál* than those already quoted. Óðinn discourses upon charms and upon magic, and especially upon the runes and their power, and he tells how he discovered them. He says:

> It is true that I hung     on the windy tree
>      for nine full nights,
> gashed with a spear     and given to Óðinn,
>      myself to myself,
> upon that tree     of which none knows
>      of what roots it rises.

> They brought me not bread     and not the beaker,
>      downward I glared,
>      grasped the rune-staves,
> shrieking I grasped them,     and sank back thence.

The sacrifice of Óðinn to himself has puzzled many readers, and has not been explained fully. It is commonly held to represent a kind of initiation, in which the god suffers a symbolic death, to be reborn fortified with the knowledge which belongs to the dead.[2] Óðinn is the god of the dead, and especially of the hanged. Such were his powers of necromancy that he could make the victims of the gallows talk. These passages of the *Hávamál* show what the runes meant for the pagan Norsemen and, to a lesser extent, for the Norsemen of the medieval period. They were not intended for writing historical or literary records, nor even in the first place for inscribing on stone monuments, but rather to work spells.

The mythological poems mentioned so far are cast in artistic form and, in many passages, they rise to heights of great poetic beauty, but the chief purpose of these poems is to teach, whether it be to teach rules of conduct or pagan beliefs about gods, giants,

---

[1] *Brennu-Njálssaga*, ed. Finnur Jónsson, 1908, ch. lxxvii.
[2] Cf. A. G. van Hamel, *Óðinn hanging on the Tree* in *Acta Philologica Scandinavica*, vii, 1932, pp. 260 ff.

and elves. There are, however, other poems, whose purpose is to tell stories about the gods, and these resemble the heroic lays in many ways. We may suspect that their authors had learnt from the heroic poets. The *Skírnismál* (Words of Skírnir) is a lay of this class and, as a love-story, it stands alone in Norse literature. It is told in it how Freyr was so presumptuous as to sit in Hliðskálf, the seat of Óðinn, from which all the mythical worlds could be seen. As Freyr gazed into Jǫtunheimar (the world of the giants), he beheld Gerðr, daughter of Gymir, a maiden of such beauty that Freyr was sick with the love of her. The god sent his brave messenger, Skírnir, to court the maiden on his behalf. Skírnir took Freyr's horse, and his magic sword which fought by itself, together with the golden apples of eternal youth (?), and other treasures with which to win the favour of Gerðr. His perilous journey is described in a few telling phrases, of which I quote the following, spoken by Skírnir to his horse:

> It is dark without      and time for us to fare
> over the dewy hills
> over the demon tribe;
> both of us shall prosper      or both shall perish
> at the hands of the mighty monster.

After the hazards of the journey, Skírnir reached the castle of Gymir, the father of Gerðr. He courted her, first with promises of gifts, but since these were of no avail, and Gerðr refused to be Freyr's wife, Skírnir used threats. He would cut off her head with Freyr's magic sword, and her father's head as well; he would place her under spells; she should live with a three-headed giant, or else have no husband at all, and be gnawed by desire until she withered like a crushed thistle at the end of the harvest. Finally, Gerðr gave way, and agreed to meet Freyr in the grove Barri.

Scholars have seen an ancient fertility myth in the *Skírnismál*.[1] The fertility god, Freyr, is said to symbolize the sun; his messenger, Skírnir, whose name is associated with the adjective *skírr* (bright), represents a ray of sunshine. The name of Gerðr is compared with

[1] On Freyr and Skírnir see J. de Vries, *Altgermanische Religionsgeschichte*, ii, 1937, pp. 257 ff.

the noun *garðr* (field, 'yard'), and she symbolizes the cornfield held
fast in the clutches of the frost-giants, the demons of winter. *Barri*,
the name of the grove where the god and the giantess meet, is
thought to be related with the Old Norse *barr* and with other
words meaning 'corn, barley'. This interesting interpretation of the
names and motives underlying the *Skírnismál* may well be correct.
But the *Skírnismál* has to be read as a poem, made all the more
valuable because it contains a love-story of a kind rare in early
Norse literature. The mythical origin has no more relevance to the
poem than has the history of the Goths to the *Hamðismál*. It is
doubtful whether the authors of either of them considered the
origins of the stories which they retold.

Þórr is the hero of the *Þrymskviða*, which is one of few tales of
humour in Eddaic poetry. It is told in the *Þrymskviða* how Þórr
was robbed of his hammer by the giant Þrymr, who refused to
restore it unless the gods would give him their fairest goddess,
Freyja, as his wife. Freyja was enraged at the suggestion that she
should be married to a giant. If the hammer were to be recovered,
Þrymr must be deceived, so Þórr, the most masculine of the gods,
was disguised as Freyja, and decked out as a bride. He set forth for
the world of the giants, with Loki disguised as his serving maid.
The hammer was brought, and Þórr showed who he was, when he
seized it and plunged it into their heads.

The *Þrymskviða* displays brilliant narrative skill and dexterity,
besides licence in the use of metrical forms. These metrical forms,
as well as certain features of style, have been said to indicate a late
date of composition.[1] It has been suggested that the poem originated, not in the pagan period, but among Icelandic Christians of
the twelfth century, who could afford to laugh at the gods. This
suggestion should be accepted with reserve, for the metrical liber-
ties could be explained in other ways. It does not follow that those
who told humorous tales about the gods had ceased to believe
in them.

The god Baldr is the subject of the *Baldrs Draumar* (Baldr's
Dreams), which inspired Thomas Gray's beautiful *Descent of Odin*.

---

[1] See J. de Vries, *Altnordische Literaturgeschichte*, ii. 133 ff.

The *Baldrs Draumar* is not found in the *Edda*, but in a manuscript of rather later date. Although slight, it is one of the most interesting of the mythological lays. It contains lyrical passages such as are rarely found in early Norse poetry, although less rarely than is sometimes supposed. The gods were disturbed in mind because their favourite, Baldr, had had dreams portending disaster. Óðinn, as usual in disguise, saddled his horse and rode down to the world of the dead, until he reached the castle of Hel, the death-goddess. He stopped at the eastern gate, by the grave of a sibyl, who had long been dead. Using his powers of necromancy, he called her from her rest with mighty, magic songs, and forced her, reluctant as she was, to answer the questions which he put to her. As she rose from her tomb, the sibyl said:

> What is the man,      to me unknown,
> That has made me travel      the troublous road?
> I was snowed on with snow,      and smitten with rain,
> and drenched with dew;      long was I dead.[1]

She told Óðinn that the benches and the platforms of the Underworld were decked with gold and with bracelets and that the mead stood ready brewed to welcome Baldr. She told him how Baldr would be struck down by the mistletoe, and how Óðinn would beget a son to take vengeance for Baldr. The sibyl perceived, from his last question, that the necromancer was none other than Óðinn. She told him to be off and hurry home, for Loki had broken loose and the *Ragnarǫk* was at hand.

The author of the *Baldrs Draumar* appears to be influenced by the *Vǫluspá* (Sibyl's Prophecy), for several of the phrases used in the *Vǫluspá* are echoed in the *Baldrs Draumar*, and the themes of the two poems resemble each other. If this is so, there can be little doubt that the *Baldrs Draumar* was composed in the Christian period and that, like the *Vǫluspá*, it is an Icelandic poem.

Like the heroic lays, the mythological ones show great differences in style, taste, and interest, and they must differ greatly in age. The *Vǫluspá*, the greatest of all the mythological poems, appears to be the work of an Icelandic poet, who lived towards the

---

[1] Translation H. A. Bellows, *The Poetic Edda*, 1926, p. 197.

end of pagan domination, when a new religion, with new symbolism and eschatology, was drawing near.[1] We cannot say how many
of the lays about gods were composed in Iceland after Christianity
had been made the religion of that land, but we know that the
Christian Icelanders cherished the religious traditions of their
pagan ancestors. Were this not so, they could not have preserved
lays about pagan gods through two centuries of Christianity, until
they were written down in the thirteenth century. The pagan lays
must have been recited regularly throughout this long period. If
the early Christians did not think it wrong to recite such lays, they
would not think it wrong to make others on similar subjects. For
reasons which will be discussed in a later chapter, the conflict
between paganism and Christianity was less bitter in Iceland than
in other northern lands. The Icelanders took care to preserve that
which was best in their pagan culture.

## 5. The Verse-forms of the *Edda*

There are few countries in Europe in which the interest in poetic
form has been so great as it has in Iceland. The forms of the
Eddaic lays should be considered, however briefly.

The poetry of the *Edda* is alliterative like all early Germanic
poetry. The alliteration is not, as it became in Middle and Modern
English, and in much of the Irish poetry, a decorative device to be
employed at will, but it is essential to the metrical structure. The
lines of most of the narrative poems of the *Edda* are bound by
alliteration in pairs, and the unit thus formed is often called the long
line. Each short line contains two heavily stressed syllables, and the
alliteration must be distributed among the four stressed syllables
of the long line. According to the rule generally followed, either
or both of the stressed syllables in the first short line may carry
alliteration, but in the second short line, only the first stressed
syllable may carry it, and it is obliged to do so. This syllable thus
forms a fixed point in the unit of the long line.

The Icelandic scholar, Snorri Sturluson, who wrote a treatise on
prosody early in the thirteenth century, describes the alliterating

[1] See Ch. II below.

syllables of the first and second short lines almost as if they were the 'props' and the 'pillar' of a building. He calls those in the first short line the *stuðlar* (cf. *styðja*, 'to prop, support'), and that in the second short line the *hǫfuðstafr* (cf. *stafr*, 'letter', also 'post, pillar'). Snorri tells us that the *hǫfuðstafr* dominates in recitation (*sá stafr ræðr kveðandi*),[1] and he seems to imply that it is stressed more heavily than any other syllable in the long line.

A few examples will illustrate the ways in which alliteration is most commonly used in Eddaic poetry:

(1) Úti stóð *G*uðrún    *G*júka dóttir.
(2) *S*oltinn varð *S*igurðr    *s*unnan Rínar.

All initial vowels alliterate together, and *j* is treated as a vowel:

(3) *E*k man *j*ǫtna    *á*r um borna.

Combinations of s (sk, sp, st) are kept distinct in most poems:

(4) *St*jǫrnur þat né vissu    hvar þær *st*aði áttu.

but *sv* is treated as *s* followed by a vowel:

(5) *S*undr hǫfum *S*igurð    *s*verði hǫggvinn.

The metre used in most narrative poems of the *Edda* differs little from that of the 'Lay of Hildebrand', the 'Fight at Finnsburh', and of other narrative poems of the Anglo-Saxons and continental Germans. In origin, this was an accentual and not a syllabic metre, for it depended, not upon the number of syllables in the line, but upon the number, position, and strength of the stresses. Most lines of Norse heroic poetry can be classified according to the grouping of stressed and unstressed, long and short syllables, and they fall into the types A–E (F, G), which were discovered by E. Sievers, and applied to Old German, English, and Norse poetry alike, as is well known to students of early Germanic literature.[2] But since some of the lines of the *Edda* cannot easily be assigned to these types, a greater number of them should be allowed.

---

[1] Snorri Sturluson, *Edda*, ed. Finnur Jónsson, 1926, p. 149.

[2] *Altgermanische Metrik*, 1893. See also Sievers's papers in *Beiträge zur Geschichte der deutschen Sprache und Literatur*, v, 1878, pp. 449 ff. and vi, 1879, pp. 265 ff.

The so-called 'Five-type' theory of Sievers has lasting value, but it is a grammatical rather than a metrical theory. It shows how stressed and unstressed, long and short syllables are most commonly grouped together in Germanic poetry, but it is of little help in reading the lines or in measuring their length. In the past the doctrines of Sievers have led editors of the *Edda* to somewhat ruthless emendation of the lines, following principles in which scholars no longer believe.[1] A more practical guide in reading the lines of the *Edda* may be found in another theory, whose most able exponent was A. Heusler.[2] This theory is less dogmatic than that of Sievers and, while it helps in reading the lines, it seldom shows whether, or how, they should be emended.

According to Heusler's analysis, each normal short line is of equal metrical value, and it is divided into two feet or bars, each of which is metrically equal, regardless of the number of syllables which it contains. The greater the number of syllables, the more quickly they must be spoken. Using musical terminology, Heusler gives the foot the value of four crotchets, and the foot always contains one fully stressed syllable, with which it begins. The intervals between the fully stressed syllables are, therefore, equal. All syllables placed before the first main stress are considered to be anacrusis. The theory allows for subsidiary stress and for rests. If they are scanned in this way, the lays of the *Edda* will be found to have a regular and insistent rhythm rather like that produced by Icelandic *rímur* and Faeroe ballads.

It was remarked above that the metre of Old Norse poetry was originally accentual, and not syllabic. In this it resembles the early poetry of other Germanic peoples. A normal short line of *Beowulf* may vary between four and twelve syllables, and in the Old Saxon *Heliand* the variation is even greater. Similar freedom in packing the lines with unaccented syllables is found in several lays of the

---

[1] The most conservative text is that of G. Neckel, quoted above. Among the texts which have been emended most ruthlessly on metrical grounds may be mentioned those of B. Sijmons, *Die Lieder der Edda*, 1906, and of Finnur Jónsson, *Sæmundar Edda*, 1905 and 1926.

[2] *Deutsche Versgeschichte*, i, 1925; cf. the same author's *Die altgermanische Dichtung*, pp. 30 ff.; Heusler's views are conveniently summarized by J. C. Pope, *The Rhythm of Beowulf*, 1942, pp. 20 ff.

*Edda*, which have been counted among the oldest, e.g. in the *Hamðismál* (str. 28) where we read:

> Af væri nú haufuð,    ef Erpr lifði,
> bróðir okkarr inn boðfrœkni,    er vit á braut vógum;

and in the *Atlakviða* (str. 8):

> Hvat hyggr þú brúði bendu,    þá er hon okkr baug sendi,
> varinn váðum heiðingia?    hygg ek, at hon vornuð byði.

Lines comparable with these could be quoted from the 'Battle of the Goths and the Huns' and from the *Volundarkviða*. But in narrative lays which are considered younger than these less liberty is allowed, and there is less variation between line and line. In such poems as the 'First Lay of Guðrún', the *Helreið Brynhildar* and the *Grípisspá*, a great proportion of the lines consist of four syllables, of which two are stressed and two unstressed. So general is this tendency to count the syllables in Old Norse poetry, that it is said of many of the lays that they are in a metre whose lines consist normally of four syllables, sometimes of five, and less commonly of six. This metre is called the *Fornyrðislag* (Old Story Metre). The Norse poets also devised another metre, in which the lines normally consisted of five syllables, sometimes of six, and less commonly of seven. This was called the *Málaháttr* (Speech Metre), and it is used in the Greenland *Atlamál* (Words of Atli). The lines of the *Málaháttr* did not differ radically from those of the *Fornyrðislag*; each of them contained two main stresses, and there was an equal interval of time between them. But the rhythmical effect of the two metres could be very different, as anyone who has slight knowledge of the Norse language will appreciate by reading the following examples:[1]

*Fornyrðislag*

> Þá |grét |Guðrún,    |Gjúka |dóttir,
> svá at |tár |flugu    |tresk í |gognum,
> ok |gullu |við    |gæss í |túni,
> |mærir |fuglar,    er |mær |átti.
> (First Lay of Guðrún, Strophe 16.)

---

[1] I indicate the beginning of each foot, which coincides with the main stress, by a perpendicular stroke.

*Málaháttr*

|Grimm vartu, |Guðrún,   er þú |gøra svá |máttir,
|barna þinna |blóði   at |blanda mér |drykkju;
|snýtt hefir þú |syfjungum   sem þú |sízt |skyldir,
|mér lætr þú ok |sjálfum   |millum ills |lítit.

(*Atlamál*, Strophe 85.)

As they began to count syllables in their lines, the poets of the *Edda* departed farther from the Germanic tradition in combining their short lines in groups of eight, forming a unit called in English a strophe, and in Icelandic a *vísa* or *erendi*. There is nearly always a deep caesura after the fourth line of the strophe, and the half-strophe is, in most instances, metrically and syntactically complete. The metrical unit is, therefore, the half-strophe of four lines rather than the full strophe of eight lines. In some of the more archaic lays the strophes vary in length, and this suggests that the strophe was a Norse innovation in Germanic verse, and that its introduction was gradual. The origin of the strophic form is obscure. If traces of it could be seen in the early poetry of the Germans or Anglo-Saxons, it might be concluded that both the strophic and the unstrophic forms were known among the ancient Germanic peoples. But attempts to find strophes in early English and German poetry have not been successful,[1] and it is therefore probable that the strophic form used in the lays of the *Edda* arose from some external influence. The immediate influence which gave rise both to this strophic form and to the syllabic tendencies is probably to be sought in the measures of the scalds (see p. 31 below).

A third metre used by the poets of the *Edda* should be mentioned. This was the *Ljóðaháttr* (cf. *ljóð*, 'song', especially 'magic song').[2] It is the most irregular of Norse metres and in it lines of different length and form are combined in strophes. The *Ljóðaháttr* is most often divided into strophes of six lines which, in their turn, are divided into half-strophes of three lines. As is the case in the *Fornyrðislag*, the half-strophe of the *Ljóðaháttr* is metrically complete, and the pattern of the first half is repeated in the second.

---

[1] See G. Neckel, *Beiträge zur Eddaforschung*, 1908, pp. 1–21; cf. R. W. Chambers, *Widsith*, 1912, pp. 174–6.

[2] On the *Ljóðaháttr* see especially Heusler, *Versgeschichte*, i. 230 ff.

The first and second lines each have two main stresses, and these
two lines alliterate like the short lines of the *Fornyrðislag*. The third
line is often called the 'full' line, and it generally contains a greater
number of syllables than either of the other two. The full line is not
bound by alliteration with any other. In its typical form it contains
two syllables which carry main stress, and these alliterate with each
other. In some instances the full line may contain three heavily
stressed syllables, but scholars often disagree about its scansion.
The *Ljóðaháttr* was much used in mythological poetry, and
especially in that of the didactic rather than of the narrative kind.
The *Hávamál* provides some of the best examples of the *Ljóðaháttr*, and the following strophe will serve to show its metrical
form:

|Baugeið |Óðinn      hygg ek at |unnit |hafi:
      hvat skal hans |tryggðum |trúa?
|Suttung |svikinn     hann lét |sumbli |frá,
      ok |grœtta |Gunnlǫðu

(*Hávamál*, Strophe 110.)

## 6. THE LANGUAGE OF THE SCALDS

Besides the Eddaic poetry there was another cultural heritage
which the settlers of Iceland brought from Norway. This was the
scaldic, or court poetry. It was used, in the first instance, for the
glorification of the princes and for their entertainment. The *Edda*
and the collections related to it contain lays of very diverse subject
and taste, but these lays have much in common. Emotions are expressed in them, and stories are told simply and directly. The verse-
forms, in which they are composed, are not intricate, and the lays
are seldom encumbered with obscure imagery. To succeed as an
Eddaic poet it was necessary chiefly to be born a poet, for the
technique could be mastered quickly. But it was not sufficient to
be born a poet in order to master the scaldic art. A long training
was necessary before scaldic poetry could be made, or even understood. This is the poetry of the professional, and not of the amateur.

Scaldic poetry bears little resemblance to any other kind of
poetry known in Germanic. If the scaldic poets were sometimes

lesser artists than the Eddaic poets, they were the more accomplished craftsmen, and their work was the jewellery of literature. It is descriptive rather than narrative, and yet the poets drew liberally on the stories of Germanic gods and heroes, and chased them, as if they were precious stones, in their rich descriptions of princes and battles and voyages at sea.

The scaldic poets achieved their effects largely by means of 'kennings'. The kenning is a device common to all European poetry, and it is often used in prose and in daily speech. English speakers commonly refer to the 'clothes horse', and sometimes talk of a camel as the 'ship of the desert'. A poet of any nation might refer to the west wind as the 'breath of Autumn's being'. Old English poets favoured such expressions. The author of *Beowulf* called the sea the 'whale road' (*hronrad*) or the 'gannet's bath' (*ganotes bæð*), and the hart the 'moor-stepper' (*hæðstapa*). In these expressions one aspect or function of the object to which the poet alludes is emphasized. The sea may properly be described as the 'gannet's bath', and the hart is in fact the 'stepper of the moor'. The lays of the *Edda* contain many expressions like these, and the scaldic poets also used them. Loosely, at any rate, they may be regarded as kennings, but they are rudimentary ones, and are not far removed from normal speech.

Sometimes the poets of the *Edda* and the Old English poets resort to more abstruse expressions than those mentioned, and when they do so, they draw nearer to the figurative diction which characterizes the poetry of the scalds. The author of the *Beowulf* refers to the sun as the 'jewel of the sky' (*heofones gim*), and to the sword as the 'battle-light' (*beado-leoma*). The sun is not a jewel, nor is the sword a ray of light, although it may look like one as it flashes in battle. It is one of the characteristics of the scaldic poets that they used far-fetched expressions of this kind much more frequently than did the poets of the *Edda* or the Old English poets.

Attempts have often been made to define the kenning, but definitions cannot be fully satisfactory, because the word 'kenning' and others of related meaning have been used by modern, and even by medieval commentators, for many different classes of poetical and figurative expression.[1] It is plain that every kenning consists basically of two elements, both of which are nouns. In one of them the object is named, and in the other it is qualified. Expressions like *bróðir Býleists* (brother of Býleistr, Loki), *Hǫrða gramr* (Lord of the Hǫrðar, King of Norway) are sometimes said to be kennings, as are *baugbroti* (ring-breaker, ring-giver, prince), *sauða týnir* (sheep-destroyer, fox), *Fáfnis bani* (slayer of Fáfnir), and, with better reason, *hreinbraut* (reindeer's road, land), *hjǫrlǫgr* (sword-sea, blood).

Under the definition of the kenning given by Snorri Sturluson in his treatise, the *Skáldskparmál*,[2] none of these expressions could be counted as kennings, except perhaps the last two. Snorri's definition of the kenning is still helpful, and less confusing than the later ones. While it has the advantage that it excludes some kinds of expression which are falsely called kennings, it may also exclude some for which this term could reasonably be used. Snorri writes:

'. . . if we name Óðinn or Þórr or Týr, or one or another of the gods or elves, and to each one that we mention, we add the name of a property of another god, or allude to some of his deeds, then the latter becomes the owner of the name, and not the former, whose name was given. Just as when we say Victory Týr, or Hanged Men's Týr, or Cargoes' Týr, these are names for Óðinn.'

Snorri's definition might be expressed in more general terms. If one object is named, and the property or quality of another object is added, the allusion applies to the second object which was not named, and not to the first which was named. Therefore, when we say 'jewel of the sky' we do not mean a jewel, for there is no jewel in the sky. We mean the sun, because the sun is in the sky and, in its relation to the sky, the sun is rather like a jewel. This implies that the typical kenning involves a simile or metaphor, and that it is descriptive. The object named should be something like the object which the kenning denotes, although the likeness is often

---

[1] For a detailed description of the kenning see R. Meissner, *Die Kenningar der Skalden*, 1921, especially Introduction, pp. 1–20. The most lucid summary of the problem is that of Einar Ól. Sveinsson, *Skírnir*, cxxi, 1947, pp. 15 ff.

[2] *Edda*, ed. Finnur Jónsson, 1926, pp. 74 ff.

remote. Men are often called 'trees of battle'. Men are not trees, and trees do not engage in battle, but men may look rather like trees as they sway in battle, just as trees sway in the storm.

Most of the kennings which have been mentioned so far are of the simplest type, and they might be used in many kinds of poetry. They each include the names of two objects, which may at first sight appear incongruous, but their meaning is easily perceived from the relationship of these two objects to each other. A third object is thus suggested, and this is the meaning of the kenning.

Most of the kennings mentioned depend on the correlation of two objects observed in the world of nature. It was characteristic of the scalds that they drew the components of their kennings as liberally from mythology and from heroic legend as they did from nature. The poets of the *Edda* rarely did this, and the Old English poets hardly at all. Such a practice implies an intense 'literary' culture. Not only the poet but also his audience must be trained in mythology and heroic legend. The allusion to the myth or legend enriches the picture which the poet gives.

The kennings which Snorri cites, in the extract quoted above, are mythological kennings. In each of them Týr is named, and a characteristic of Óðinn, or an incident from the life of Óðinn, is added to Týr's name. That is how we know that the kenning belongs to Óðinn and not to Týr, e.g. Óðinn was especially the god of the hanged, because with his necromancy he could make the victims of the gallows talk. Objects other than gods are often denoted by kennings in which gods' names are used. The sea stands in the same relationship to the sea-gods as land does to other gods or to men. Meiti is the name of a sea-god and the sea may, therefore, be called 'Meiti's land' or 'plain' (*Meita vǫllr*). The waves on the sea are like hills and slopes on land; they are therefore called 'Meiti's slopes' (*Meita hlíðir*).

Sometimes kennings may be based on an allusion to a single event in mythological or heroic legend. Óðinn once hanged himself, and so he is not only the god of the hanged, but he is himself the 'gallows load' (*galga farmr*). The treasure of the Niflungar was immersed in the Rhine, and since gold glitters like fire, all gold might be called 'Rhine fire' (*Rínar bál*), or similarly 'Rhine gravel' (*Rínar grjót*). Sigurðr's horse, Grani, carried the gold from the dragon's lair, and this legend was generalized in the kenning for gold, 'Grani's burden' (*Grana byrðr*). Before he was killed, the dragon, Fáfnir, lay on his gold, and so all gold may be called 'Fáfnir's bed' (*Fáfnis setr*).

All the kennings mentioned so far consist of two elements and no more. These two elements were called by R. Meissner the *Grundwort* and the *Bestimmung*. The expressions 'basic word' and 'determinant' have been used in English as equivalents for these terms.[1] In the basic word the object is named, and in the determinant it is qualified. Thus, in *Meita vǫllr*, the *vǫllr* or 'plain' or 'field' is named, and the determinant *Meita* (Meiti's) shows what kind of 'plain' or 'land' is denoted by the kenning. Numerous poetical words with different associations may fill the place both of the basic word and of the determinant, and by such means great variation is obtained.

Even further variation is obtained by constructing kennings of more than two elements. In such cases one of the two elements of the kenning is replaced by a complete kenning, which itself consists of two elements. The whole kenning thus consists of three elements, and it is said by Snorri to be *tvíkennt* (doubled). Needless to say, this process may be extended, and as many as five or even six complete kennings are sometimes used to designate one object. In almost every case it is the determinant which undergoes the elaboration caused by the introduction of component kennings. The basic word nearly always remains fixed, and stands as a fixed point in the whole constellation of kennings.

Because of the custom of wearing bracelets, glittering gold is often called 'fire of the arm'. Falconry called forth the kenning 'land' or 'resting-place of the hawk' for 'arm'. A word which means 'fire' may thus be combined with a kenning which means 'arm', and the whole kenning means 'gold', e.g. *hauka fróns leygr* (hawk's land's flame), *hauka klifs hyrr*. Since gold is thought to be present

[1] See H. van der Merwe Scholtz, *The Kenning in Anglo-Saxon and Old Norse Poetry*, 1927, pp. 39–40.

in the sea, a word for 'fire' combined with a kenning for 'sea' also means 'gold', and this kenning for 'sea' may be made up of two complete kennings, e.g. 'elk of the fjord' is a kenning for 'ship'; the 'land' or 'plain of the ship' is 'sea', hence *fjarðar elgs vangs fúrr* may be rendered 'the fjord elk's plain's fire', and this means 'gold'.

The language of kennings sometimes approaches that of riddles, and thus loses much of its aesthetic value. When the force of the kenning is spent, it becomes stereotyped and conventional. These tendencies may be noticed among the Christian scalds of the twelfth century. Nevertheless, the great variation provided by myth, legend, and language enables skilful poets to avoid the stereotyped, and to endow scenes which would otherwise be trite and dull with a vivid brilliance. A great number of the scaldic poems commemorate battles, and the poet has to say that the sword struck against the shield. If the sword is called 'Óðinn's grey rainbow' and the shield the 'stormy sky of the valkyrie',[1] the bald statement may be worth making.

As is shown by the last example, the scalds were sometimes interested in the expressions which they chose, rather than in the subject with which they dealt. In such cases, the artistry is in the picture created by the kenning, and not in the meaning which it gives.

## 7. THE MEASURES OF THE SCALDS

The scalds differed from the poets of the *Edda* not only in choice of expression, but also in the poetic forms which they used. They established formal conventions of which other Germanic poets had known nothing, and they devised new metres, which made their verse sound altogether different from that of the early English and German poets.

Scaldic poetry is invariably strophic and, with few exceptions, the strophe consists of eight lines. Like the Eddaic strophe (see p. 25 above), the scaldic strophe is nearly always broken by a caesura after the fourth line, and the formal unit is the half-strophe rather than the strophe.

---

[1] See *Skjald*, B, ii. 108.

Mention has already been made of the tendency to limit the
number of syllables allowed in the line, which was observed in the
lays of the *Edda* in a greater or smaller degree. In following this
tendency the poets of the *Edda* departed from the Germanic tradition of accentual verse. The scalds carry this syllabic tendency
further, and in their metres, the number of syllables allowed in
each line is fixed within narrow limits.[1]

Whereas the English and German poets hardly used more than
one verse-form, the poets of the *Edda* used three. The scalds never
tired of experiment, and they devised about a hundred different
forms of verse. Only a small proportion of these were commonly
used, and the majority of them were probably designed as models,
upon which young poets could exercise their skill.[2]

The favourite scaldic metre, and perhaps the oldest, was the
*Dróttkvætt* or Court Metre. Like most of the others, the *Dróttkvætt*
consists of a strophe of eight lines. Each strophe consists of two
half-strophes, each of which is syntactically and metrically complete. Each normal line consists of six syllables, and three of these
are stressed and three unstressed. Every line ends in a trochee,
consisting of a long stressed syllable, followed by a short unstressed
one. Each pair of lines is bound by alliteration. This alliteration
must fall on the first stressed syllable of the second line of the
pair. The following pair of lines will illustrate the rule generally
observed:

> Þél høggr *st*órt fyr *st*áli
> *st*afnkvígs á veg jafnan.

The *Dróttkvætt* and the metres related to it were removed even
farther from the Germanic tradition by the introduction of internal rime and consonance, which were called *aðalhending* and

---

[1] Snorri Sturluson (*Edda*, edition quoted above, *Háttatal*, pp. 152–3) explains
that a line, which would normally contain six syllables, may have seven or even
eight if they are sufficiently 'quick', or fewer than six if they are 'slow'. This is
*leyfi* (licence). Cf. Heusler, *Versgeschichte*, i. 286 ff.

[2] About the middle of the twelfth century, the Orkney Jarl Rǫgnvaldr, col-
laborating with an Icelander, made the *Háttalykill* (Key to Verse-forms), in
which two strophes were given in each form. See *Háttalykill enn forni*, ed. Jón
Helgason and A. Holtsmark, 1941. Snorri, in his *Háttatal*, follows the conventions established by the *Háttalykill*.

*skothending* respectively. The *aðalhending* consists of full syllabic rime between two syllables of one line:

gram reki bǫnd af lǫndum.

The *skothending* consists of correspondence between two syllables whose vowels differ, but whose post-vocalic consonants are identical:

Svá skyldi goð gjalda.

The scalds, especially the earlier ones, exercised some liberty about the positions to which they assigned the *aðalhending* and the *skothending*, and on occasion they dispensed with them altogether. But in the stricter forms of *Dróttkvætt*, *skothending* was used in the first line of the pair, and *aðalhending* in the second. Both the *skothending* and the *aðalhending* should fall on the last stressed syllable of their respective lines. A half-strophe will serve to illustrate all these complexities of rime and alliteration as they are commonly used in the *Dróttkvætt*:

Áðr grindlogi Gǫndlar
gellr í hattar felli
opt vák mann of minna
meir nǫkkurum þeira.

Many of the scaldic verse-forms are variations and elaborations of the *Dróttkvætt*. One example is the resounding *Dunhenda*, in which the last stressed syllable of the first line is repeated as the first syllable of the second line:

Þýborna kveðr þorna
þorn reið áar horna,
sýslir hann of sína
síngirnð Qnundr, mína.

The metre *Hrynjandi* (Jingling) may also be regarded as a development of the *Dróttkvætt*. Its normal line consists of eight syllables, and it has the appearance of a line of *Dróttkvætt*, to which an additional trochee has been added at the end:

Mínar biðk at munka reyni
meinalausan farar beina;
heiðis haldi hárar foldar
hallar dróttinn yfir mér stalli.

Some of the scaldic metres resemble the Eddaic *Fornyrðislag*
more closely than they do the *Dróttkvætt*. The *Kviðuháttr* is like
the stricter forms of *Fornyrðislag*, with the difference that instead
of having four syllables in each line, its lines alternate between
three syllables and four:

> ok dáðsæll
> deyja skyldi
> Ála dolgr
> at Uppsǫlum.

In the *Tøglag* the measure of the *Fornyrðislag* is combined with
the internal rimes of the *Dróttkvætt*:

> Uggðu Egðir
> ǫrbeiðis fǫr
> svans sigrlana
> sǫkrammir mjǫk.

From what has been said it will be plain that, both in diction
and in form, the scalds departed far from the Germanic tradition
of poetry, and that scaldic verse-forms are the product of an artistic
revolution. It may be interesting to consider when this revolution
took place, and what its causes were.

## 8. The Origins of Scaldic Poetry

The first poet to whom credible tradition assigns poetry in
scaldic form was Bragi Boddason, nicknamed the Old.[1] Little is
known about Bragi's life, but stories and genealogical lists in which
he figures suggest that he was a native of south-western Norway.

The chief surviving work ascribed to Bragi is the *Ragnarsdrápa*,
of which nine strophes and eleven half-strophes survive. In this
poem Bragi describes the figures of gods and of heroes painted
on a shield which had been sent to him by a certain Ragnarr
Sigurðarson. This Ragnarr is sometimes identified with the
famous Ragnarr loðbrók, although he was more probably another
chieftain.

---

[1] On Bragi see Finnur Jónsson, *ONOI*, i. 414; L. M. Hollander, *The Skalds*,
1945, pp. 25 ff.; J. de Vries, op. cit. i. 91 ff. and references given there; Sigurður
Nordal, *Íslenzk Menning*, i, 1942, pp. 235–7.

The surviving strophes of the *Ragnarsdrápa* are in the *Dróttkvætt* and it is remarkable that, as Bragi uses it, the *Dróttkvætt* bears all the features which distinguish it from the Eddaic verse-forms. Bragi uses the allusive scaldic diction, the free word-order, the strophe of eight lines and the half-strophe of four, and the line of six syllables, furnished with internal rime and consonance. The chief formal difference between the work of Bragi and that of the later poets is that Bragi inserts internal rime and consonance less regularly than the later poets do.

The *Ragnarsdrápa* shows that the scaldic technique, or at least the technique *Dróttkvætt*, was perfected by the time Bragi composed it. This can be explained in two ways. We might suppose that the technique originated many generations before Bragi's time and, in this case, that all the earlier, fumbling attempts to perfect it have been forgotten. Alternatively, we may suppose that Bragi himself devised the *Dróttkvætt*, and perhaps other scaldic forms as well, and that it was he who revolutionized the form and diction of poetry.[1]

In favour of the second alternative we may remember that this poet, Bragi, shared his name with the Norse god of poetry, for the god of poetry was also called Bragi. It is hard to doubt that the poet and the god were really one and the same.[2] Since 'Bragi' is recorded as a personal name, and since men rarely bear the names of gods, it is easier to believe that the historical poet Bragi was revered by later generations as a god, rather than that the god was later thought to have been a man, and that existing verses were ascribed to the god.

If Bragi was the founder of the scaldic system, it is necessary to consider his age, although little can be said about this with certainty. It is said that he made poetry in honour of a certain Bjǫrn of Haugr. In some sources this Bjǫrn is described as King of the

[1] The first alternative is preferred by de Vries, op. cit. i. 70 ff.; A. Heusler (*Deutsche Versgeschichte*, i. 300) and Sigurður Nordal (op. cit. i. 236–7) incline to the second alternative.

[2] J. de Vries (*Algermanische Religionsgeschichte*, ii. 312–13) holds that the god and the poet are distinct. E. Mogk (*Reallexikon der germanischen Altertumskunde*, ed. J. Hoops, i, 1911–13, pp. 306–7) and Sigurður Nordal (op. cit., loc. cit.) identify them.

Swedes. Consequently, modern scholars have identified Bjǫrn with
Bernus, who was King of the Swedes when S. Anskar visited them
about the year 830, and have supposed that Bragi was in his prime
about that time. But although some of the medieval writers said
that Bjǫrn was King of the Swedes, it appears that the older ones
regarded him as a man of Norway, and probably of western
Norway. Moreover, Bjǫrn cannot be so old as the Bernus whom
Anskar knew. According to the *Landnámabók*, a son, or a nephew,
of Bjǫrn settled in Iceland, and this was probably about the end
of the ninth century. This suggests that Bjǫrn was born about the
middle of that century, or a few years earlier.[1]

Other genealogies in which Bjǫrn figures do not give a clear
indication of his age, but if the generations in them are counted, it
looks as if he was born about 830–40. This was the conclusion
of Guðbrandur Vigfússon, but it has been disregarded by most
modern scholars.[2]

The little evidence available suggests, therefore, that Bragi
was the founder of the scaldic system of prosody, and that
he founded it in Norway during the second half of the ninth
century.

However great his inventive genius, it is improbable that Bragi
could have devised the elaborate scaldic diction and verse-forms
unless he knew some kind of poetry other than the traditional
Germanic. If foreign models for the new technique are to be sought,
they should be sought first in the western lands, for Norway's
foreign contacts in the ninth century were chiefly with the west,
and especially with England and the Celtic lands.

If the features which distinguish scaldic poetry from other Germanic poetry are considered, a similarity between them and certain
features which characterize the highly artificial styles of Irish poets
may be noticed. Like the scalds, the Irish use kennings based upon
myth or legend, such as *gabra Lir* (Ler's horses, the sea-gods
horses, waves), and occasionally double kennings, such as *búar*

---

[1] On Bjǫrn of Haugr see Jón Jóhannesson in *Afmælisrit Dr. Einars Arnórs-
sonar*, n.d., pp. 1–6.

[2] Guðbrandur Vigfússon and F. York Powell, *Corpus Poeticum Boreale*, ii,
1883, pp. 2 ff.

*maige Tethrai* (the cattle of the field of Tethrae, cattle of the field of the sea-god, fish).

A. Heusler, who studied Germanic poetry more deeply than any other scholar of recent times, was struck by the non-Germanic qualities of the scaldic verse-forms. He did not believe that they could have developed from the traditional Germanic forms without some external stimulus. This was to be found chiefly in Irish poetry, and partly in Latin poetry current in the western lands in the ninth and tenth centuries.[1]

Originally, it is said, Irish poetry was like early Germanic poetry, accentual and alliterative. But under the influence of hymns and other popular poetry in Latin, Irish poetry gradually became syllabic, and that composed between the eighth century and the sixteenth is nearly all syllabic.[2] Its measure is determined less by stress than by the number of syllables in the line and by the form in which the line ends. In these things Irish syllabic poetry resembles scaldic poetry.

Irish syllabic poetry is invariably strophic and its strophes consist, for the most part, of four lines. They thus resemble the half-strophes of the favourite scaldic measure, the *Dróttkvætt*. The Irish poets also used internal rime and consonance, although not according to the rules which the scalds followed. Like the scalds, the Irish poets were conscious and 'professional' artists, and they experimented endlessly with different measures.

The affinity between Irish and scaldic poetry cannot be discussed further in this book, but I must reserve the subject for a monograph which I hope to publish soon.[3] It is hard to escape the conclusion that the scalds were influenced by the technique of the Irish poets, although perhaps superficially. Perhaps the Irish poets

---

[1] Heusler, *Die altgermanische Dichtung*, pp. 28 ff. and *Deutsche Versgeschichte*, i. 284 ff.

[2] On Irish verse-forms see especially K. Meyer, *Über die älteste irische Dichtung*, i–ii, 1913–14, and the same scholar's *Hail Brigit*, 1912, p. 7; R. Thurneysen, *Revue Celtique*, vi. 309–47, and *Irische Texte*, iii, pt. i, 1891, pp. 138–68. For summaries of Irish metrics see K. Meyer, *Primer of Irish Metrics*, 1909, and E. Knott, *Irish Syllabic Poetry*, 1934, Introduction.

[3] *Ireland and the Poets of Iceland*, paper delivered to the Oxford University Celtic Society, 28 May 1951.

taught the scalds that poetry could take many different forms, and that every form could be analysed and given a name. Perhaps they also taught the scalds that words could be twisted and used in various combinations to give meanings far removed from those of normal speech. Above all, the Irish poets taught their Norse colleagues to regard poetry as a professional craft, and as one for which substantial reward might be expected.

## 9. THE SCALDS OF THE TENTH CENTURY

Poems in the traditional Germanic style of the *Edda* and in the new scaldic style flourished side-by-side, and those who practised the new art remembered the old. In one way, the scaldic poetry was dependent upon the Eddaic. No one could understand the scaldic kennings unless he knew the myths and legends to which the scalds alluded. These myths and legends lived in their most coherent form in the Eddaic lays. One reason why the modern reader finds much of the scaldic poetry obscure is that the Eddaic lays which survive are only a small proportion of those which inspired the diction of the scalds.

In the ninth and tenth centuries the Norse princes were the chief patrons of the scalds. Most of the older scaldic poetry is panegyric, and it is designed to praise these princes and to immortalize their achievements. Several of them are themselves remembered as scalds. Haraldr Finehair (died about 940–5?), the first ruler of all Norway, was said to be the author of existing verses in scaldic form. He favoured none of his followers as he did his poets, and they occupied the highest place in the court after the king himself.

The foremost of Haraldr's poets was Þorbjǫrn Hornklofi, who made the *Haraldskvæði* (Lay of Haraldr), also called the *Hrafnsmál* (Words of the Raven), which occupies an important place in the history of Norse poetry. It is commonly regarded as a scaldic poem because, like many scaldic poems, it was made by a poet whose name is remembered, to celebrate the deeds of a contemporary prince. The diction and syntax of this poem are mixed, for in some passages Þorbjǫrn uses the abstruse kennings of the scalds, but in others he resorts to the more direct expressions of the Eddaic poets. The metrical forms which he uses are those of the *Edda*; the *Málaháttr* is combined with the *Ljóðaháttr*. The outer frame of the *Hrafnsmál* also resembles that of some of the Eddaic lays, for it is a dialogue between a valkyrie and a raven, who had followed the young king ever since he came out of his egg. The raven rejoices in the carrion which Haraldr has left on the battlefield, and he praises his prowess in war. Several strophes are devoted to the battle of Hafrsfjǫrðr, the greatest of Haraldr's victories. In other strophes the poet describes the splendour of the court and the generosity of the king. He rewards his warriors with splendid swords, with weapons from southern lands and bondwomen from the east. His scalds are no less richly endowed; they wear golden bracelets and red cloaks, and carry swords chased with silver. Only the jesters (*leikarar*, *trúðar*) earn the contempt of the poet, for they were probably foreigners, whose profession was new to Norway. One of them disports himself with a crop-eared dog, and they make the king laugh with every kind of foolish trick. They are fit for nothing but a kick.

The *Eiríksmál* is a poem in the same style as the *Hrafnsmál*, but it is more solemn and serious. It was made by a poet whose name has been forgotten, on the order of Queen Gunnhildr to commemorate her husband, Eiríkr Bloodaxe, who was killed in England about the year 954. Like Þorbjǫrn Hornklofi, the author of the *Eiríksmál* uses Eddaic verse-forms, chiefly the *Ljóðaháttr*. His diction and syntax are also closer to those of the Eddaic poets than to those of the scalds. This poem is also in the form of dialogue, for Óðinn and the fallen warriors are heard conversing in Valhǫll, as they prepare to welcome the dead Eiríkr. Óðinn sends Sigmundr and Sinfjǫtli, heroes of the Vǫlsung legend, to welcome the Norse king. He has need of Eiríkr to defend his castle, for none can tell when the *Ragnarǫk* will come and the wolf Fenrir fall upon gods and heroes.

The only other great poem in this mixed Eddaic-scaldic style is the *Hákonarmál*, made by Eyvindr, nicknamed Skáldaspillir (the Plagiarist), to commemorate Hákon the Good, who was killed in battle against the sons of Eiríkr Bloodaxe about the year 962. This is the most ambitious poem of the three, although not the most original, for the influence of the *Eiríksmál* and of several of the lays of the *Edda* can be seen in its lines. As in the *Hrafnsmál*, the Eddaic metres *Málaháttr* and *Ljóðaháttr* are combined in the *Hákonarmál*. The theme is like that of the *Eiríksmál*, for Óðinn sends his valkyries to bring Hákon home from the battlefield, and the poem is in the form of dialogue. Hákon, who was brought up in England, had been a Christian in his youth, but had conformed with pagan custom when he was King of Norway. The pagan poet praises him as the guardian of the temples and the friend of the gods; in the translation of William Morris and Eiríkr Magnússon:

> Now it was wotted
> how well the King
> had upheld holy places,
> whereas all powers
> and all the god-folk
> bade Hakon welcome home.

The poem ends with lines which recall the *Hávamál*:

> Now dieth wealth,
> die friends and kin,
> and lea and land lie waste.
> Since Hakon fared
> to the heathen gods
> are many a folk enthralled.[1]

The first generation of settlers in Iceland included few poets, or at least few whose names are remembered. But the second generation included Egill Skalla-Grímsson (about 910–90), the greatest of all the scalds. The story of Egill's life is told in the *Egils Saga*, and many of his verses are found in its text. The verses ascribed to Egill include three long sequences, each comprising twenty strophes or more. Two of these are in the metre *Kviðuháttr* (see p. 34 above). The third, the *Hǫfuðlausn* (Head-ransom), is in a scaldic form, which Egill probably devised himself. It is modelled on the Eddaic *Fornyrðislag*, but it is smoother and stricter than the

---

[1] *The Stories of the Kings of Norway*, translated by William Morris and Eiríkr Magnússon, i, 1893 (= The Saga Library, iii), p. 193.

metre in most lays of the *Edda*. Moreover, Egill enriched the simple *Fornyrðislag* with end-rime, linking the lines in couplets and some-times in greater units. The rimes are sometimes of one syllable, and sometimes of two, and sometimes they resemble the rimes of the Irish measure *Debide*, in which stressed syllables are rimed with unstressed ones, as in the following example:

> Vasat villr staðar
> vefr darraðar
> of grams glaðar
> geirvangs raðar.

These lines were skilfully translated by L. M. Hollander:[1]

> Did the shower-of-darts
> strike shield-ramparts
> of the prince's array
> as he plunged in the fray.

The subject of the *Hǫfuðlausn* and the circumstances under which it was composed are also interesting as they are described in the *Egils Saga*. For reasons which are left obscure, Egill came to York when his arch-enemy, Eiríkr Bloodaxe, was ruler there (about 948). Egill fell into the hands of Eiríkr and redeemed his head with this poem in praise of the prince whom he despised. It was said that he composed it in a single night.

Egill was before his time in using end-rime regularly, for Norse poets rarely used it, except as an occasional embellishment, before the twelfth century. It is generally held that, in introducing end-rime at the end of his lines, Egill was influenced by poetry in Old English. This is unlikely, for only one poem in which end-rime is used with such sustained regularity survives in Old English, and this poem is of uncertain date, and hardly less unique than the *Hǫfuðlausn* itself. The source can hardly be Irish or Welsh vernacular poetry, for the rules which governed end-rime in the poetry of these languages differed from those which Egill observed. Egill's model is more probably to be found among the Latin hymns current in the British Isles in the tenth century. In some of the hymnal forms, end-rime was well established by this time.

---

[1] *The Skalds*, 1945, p. 69.

It is believed that it was first perfected by the Irish Latinists, from whom it passed to the poets of western Europe.[1] It may be remembered that, although pagan at heart, Egill was marked with the Cross (*prímsignaðr*) as a catechumen while in England.[2] This would give him the right to attend church and to listen to the hymns chanted there. The interest of the *Hǫfuðlausn* is in its unusual poetic form, rather than in its content. The sentiments expressed are conventional. The king is praised, as many others were, for his generosity and bravery, but the poet is not sincere.

Two other long poems are assigned to Egill, and they are composed in the *Kviðuháttr* (see p. 34 above). The first of them is the *Sonatorrek* (the Irreparable Loss of his Sons). This is a more personal poem than the *Hǫfuðlausn*, and there can be no doubt of the poet's sincerity. He describes how he was overcome by sorrow at the death of two of his sons. The circumstances under which this poem was made are also described in the *Egils Saga*. One of Egill's sons, Gunnarr, had died of fever in early youth, and another, Bǫðvarr, who was his father's favourite, was drowned off the coast of Iceland, near his home. Egill was overwhelmed with grief and shut himself in his bed-closet, resolved to starve to death, but his daughter, Þorgerðr, with resourceful cunning, persuaded him to live and make the memorial poem. The *Sonatorrek* is a passionate and tragic poem. If it were possible, Egill would carry his sword against the sea-god Ægir and his wife, Rán, and avenge his son. He has no joy left but in poetry.

Some of Egill's finest work is to be found in his occasional strophes, composed in the *Dróttkvætt* and in variants of it. Unruly and rebellious as he was, Egill succeeded best under the strict discipline of such measures. At times he could depict nature as no other scald could do, as in the following strophe, in which he describes a storm at sea:

> The angry troll of tree-trunks
> the tempest's chisel wieldeth,
> around the bull of bow-sprits
> beats a file of breakers;

[1] Cf. F. J. E. Raby, *A History of Christian Latin Poetry*, 1927, pp. 22 ff. and 135 ff.     [2] *Egils Saga Skalla-Grímssonar*, ed. Sigurður Nordal, 1933, ch. 1.

the freezing wolf of forests
files the swan of the sea-god,
grinds the beak of the galley,
grimly batters the forecastle.[1]

With the same controlled energy, Egill cursed Eiríkr Bloodaxe and
his Queen Gunnhildr, who had seized his property and driven him
from Norway. L. M. Hollander[2] reproduces Egill's curse in its
original metre:

May the powers repay the
prince and drive him from his
realm, for wroth are at the
robber all gods and Odin:
put to flight th' oppressor
of people, Freyr and Niord, the
foe of free men, who de-
filed the holy thing-meet!

The more famous Icelandic scalds of the tenth and eleventh centuries practised their art abroad, and lived much of their lives on
the favours of foreign princes. By the end of the tenth century, the
Icelanders had nearly supplanted the native scalds in the halls of
the Norwegian princes. It had become conventional for Norwegian
and even for Danish princes to employ Icelandic scalds. Among
the foremost of the Icelandic court poets was Einarr Skálaglamm,
the younger contemporary and friend of Egill. Einarr is remembered chiefly for his verses in praise of Jarl Hákon Sigurðarson
(died 995), most of which are included in the sequence *Vellekla*
(Gold Dearth). The *Vellekla* is a valuable source of history. The
poet tells how Hákon defended the Danavirki for Haraldr Gorms-
son against the invading forces of the German Emperor in 974. The
passages in which Einarr describes the religious practices of
Hákon and his affection for the pagan gods are especially interesting. The sons of Eiríkr Bloodaxe, who ruled Norway before
Hákon, had been Christians in name, and they had torn down the

[1] See *Egils Saga*, ch. lvii. The 'troll of tree-trunks' (Icelandic *vandar jǫtunn*)
is 'the wind'; the 'bull of bow-sprits' is the 'ship'. The waves of the sea are depicted as a huge file cut with a chisel. The 'wolf of forests' is the 'enemy of
forests', the 'wind'; the 'swan of the sea-god' is the 'ship'. Cf. Nordal's interpretation ad loc.                                           [2] Op. cit., p. 58.

temples and interfered with the sacrifices, until the gods were so angry that the harvests failed. When Hákon came to rule, he restored the temples and promoted sacrifice. The gods returned to receive the offerings and the grass grew again luxuriantly.

Sigvatr Þórðarson (*circa* 995–1045) left Iceland and joined the court of S. Ólafr about 1015, soon after Ólafr was made King of Norway. Sigvatr became the friend and counsellor of the saint, a great part of whose life is recorded in his verses. In a sequence called the 'Viking Verses' (*Víkinga Vísur*), Sigvatr celebrated the exploits of S. Ólafr's youth, when he had fought as a viking in the Baltic countries, in England and on the Continent. Sigvatr had not witnessed these battles himself, and his verses about them have greater value as history than as poetry. Sigvatr's *Austrfararvísur* (Verses on a Journey to the East) are more valuable as poetry, and the circumstances under which they were composed are also interesting. About the year 1019, S. Ólafr sent Sigvatr on a diplomatic mission to Rǫgnvaldr, Jarl of Gautland. The most permanent result of the mission was this series of verses, in which Sigvatr told of his adventures on the journey and described the inhospitable, heathen peasants, whom he met in the dense forests of Gautland.

Óttarr Svarti (the Black) was a nephew of Sigvatr, and a typical court poet of the period. He is heard of first at the court of the King of the Swedes, Ólafr Eiríksson (died about 1022). He came later to S. Ólafr of Norway. Accused of making a love-poem about Ástríðr, the Queen of S. Ólafr, he redeemed his head with a *Hǫfuðlausn* (Head-ransom), a poem in praise of S. Ólafr, of which a number of strophes survive. As a source for the history of S. Ólafr's career, Óttarr's *Hǫfuðlausn* is an important supplement to the poetry of Sigvatr. Óttarr also made a sequence of strophes in praise of King Knútr the Great, of which a number are preserved.

The court poets are the best known of the Icelandic scalds, but there were others of a less professional kind. In the sagas about Icelandic heroes, strophes in *Dróttkvætt* and other scaldic forms are frequently quoted. Scaldic strophes undoubtedly formed the historical basis of some of the sagas of Icelanders, just as they did of many of the sagas about the kings of Norway. It could be argued reasonably that those sagas which contain historical truth owe a great proportion of it to scaldic poetry, which was composed by or during the lifetime of the heroes whose lives are related. It has recently been shown that the *Hrafnkels Saga*, one of the most perfect of the sagas of Icelanders, contains little historical truth, and it is noticeable that this saga contains no scaldic verse. But it cannot be concluded, because a saga contains little or no scaldic verse, that its author did not use such verse as a source.

We cannot always be satisfied that verses found in the sagas about Icelanders are correctly ascribed to the scalds of the tenth and eleventh centuries, who are said to have composed them. In some instances they must have been made by later poets, and attached by tradition to the well-known heroes of the saga-age. Sometimes the authors of the sagas, working as artists rather than as historians, would compose verses to illustrate their sagas. Nevertheless, few who read the sagas doubt that a proportion of the verses quoted in them are correctly ascribed to the men whose lives are depicted in those sagas. The verses thus show how important a part of daily life poetry used to be among the Icelanders of the saga-age.

Just as an Icelandic court poet could commemorate S. Ólafr's part in the battle of Ringmere (1010), and another could describe his last battle, at Stiklastaðir (1030), so an Icelandic farmer could commemorate a local brawl or a scene at the *Alþingi*, using the same complicated poetic forms. Such events were not of great political moment, and consequently the artistic value of the work of these peasant poets is sometimes overlooked by readers who are not natives of Iceland. The three love-poets, Kormákr, Hallfreðr, and Gunnlaugr, are remembered rather for the romantic stories of their lives than for the poetry attributed to them. These three also practised as court poets abroad.[1] Þórarinn Svarti (the Black) is a more homely poet, and his story is told in the *Eyrbyggja Saga*,[2] where he appears as an antagonist of the chieftain Snorri goði

---

[1] See Hollander, op. cit., pp. 116 ff.
[2] Ed. Einar Ól. Sveinsson, 1935. On the verses, see the editor's Introduction, Section 1.

(died 1031). Seventeen strophes are ascribed to Þórarinn in the *Eyrbyggja Saga*, and in them he describes a fight in which he was engaged after he had been falsely accused of theft. In two of the strophes, Þórarinn relates how a Scottish (Irish) merchant, called Nagli, accidentally involved in this Icelandic feud, lost his head in the heat of battle, and fled to the brink of a cliff, where Þórarinn rescued him:

> Nagli gave the geese of
> Grímnir a poor dinner:
> screaming the gold-hoarder
> scaled the rugged cliff-tops. . . .

> Guardian of the spear-path
> groaning ran from battle;
> keeper of the helmet
> hoped not for men's mercy;
> necklace-breaker fearful,
> fleeing to the headland,
> almost dropped in terror
> to the sea beneath him.[1]

Víga-Glúmr (died about 1003), the hero of the saga which bears his name,[2] was not only a ruthless and avaricious peasant, but he was also a considerable poet. In his youth he had dealt hardly with those who encroached upon his ancestral property. In his old age, after swearing an ambiguous oath in order to acquit himself of manslaughter, he was driven from his estates in disgrace. He looked back sadly to his great days, when he had cleared his lands of his enemies:

> With staves of storms of Óðinn's
> sticks I cleared the land, like
> warriors of old I made my
> way, my fame was widespread.

---

[1] 'Geese of Grímnir' are 'Óðinn's geese', i.e. 'ravens'; the Icelandic text has 'corpse-geese' (*nágǫglum*), which gives the same meaning. To feed ravens is to slaughter men. The 'spear-path' is the 'shield'; 'guardian of the shield' is 'warrior', 'keeper of the helmet' the same. 'Necklace-breaker' is 'man', more literally 'generous man'. For the Icelandic text and interpretation see Einar Ól. Sveinsson's edition, ch. xix.

[2] *Víga-Glúms Saga*, ed. G. Turville-Petre, 1940.

Wafter of the war-god's
wand, I hurled with slaughter
the broad earth and its boundaries
bounteous from my keeping.[1]

[1] 'Óðinn's sticks' are 'swords', whose 'storm' is 'battle', whose 'staves' are 'warriors', 'men'. The 'war-god's wand' is 'Óðinn's wand', the 'spear', whose 'wafter' is the 'warrior', 'man', to whom the verse is addressed. The original has a rather more complicated kenning: *Valþognis Várar skíðs bendir* 'bender of the plank of Óðinn's valkyrie', 'bender of the sword or spear'. For a more detailed interpretation of this strophe see my edition of the *Víga-Glúms Saga*, p. 81.

# II

# THE CONVERSION OF ICELAND

THE Icelanders must have known something about Christianity since the beginning of their history. A considerable number of the settlers had been baptized before they came to Iceland, and had lived among Christians in the British Isles.[1] Their descendants lapsed into paganism, and there were few but pagans in Iceland for about a hundred years,[2] but the thoughts and civilization of Christian Europe exercised a growing influence throughout this period. Icelanders, like other Scandinavians, would sometimes visit the British Isles, Germany, and even more distant lands. Sometimes they travelled as vikings, but no less often as merchants, mercenary soldiers, and poets, taking part in the lives of the foreign peoples.

The poet Egill Skalla-Grímsson was a typical example of a cosmopolitan Icelander of the tenth century,[3] and another was Ólafr the Peacock, the son of an Icelandic chieftain and an Irish princess who had been sold into slavery.[4] Ólafr was reared in Iceland, but as a young man he sailed to Ireland, where he visited his mother's relatives. Another man, called Hrafn, had spent many of the latter years of the tenth century in Limerick, and had earned the nickname 'Limerick-farer'. His countrymen heard him tell tales about the Land of White Men (*Hvítra manna land*), or Ireland the Great, a mythical land said to lie in the Atlantic Ocean, three days west of Ireland.[5] Several stories are told in sagas about Icelanders who were entertained by chieftains abroad, especially in England and

---

[1] See above, pp. 3 ff., and especially Björn M. Ólsen, *Um kristnitökuna árið 1000*, 1900, pp. 1–7.

[2] See *Landnámabók*, ed. Finnur Jónsson, 1900, pp. 125 and 231.

[3] See above, pp. 40 ff.

[4] See *Laxdœla Saga*, ed. Einar Ól. Sveinsson, 1934, chs. xiii and xxi.

[5] See *Landnámabók*, pp. 41 and 165; also *The Vinland Sagas*, ed. Halldór Hermannsson, 1944, p. 41. For the identification of the Land of White Men in Irish sources, see E. Hogan, *Onomasticon Goedelicum*, 1910, s.v. *Tír na fer fionn*.

in the Celtic lands. Although these stories may not be accurate in detail they are probably based upon genuine tradition.

Pagan Scandinavians were often tolerant of the religious beliefs of others, and the Norse hierarchy of gods was ever changing, as new gods came to live side-by-side with the older ones. An illustrative story is told about the Swedes at the time of S. Anskar. When their pagan leaders heard that the saint was coming to preach to them (*circa* 850), they drew up a message purporting to come from the gods and addressed to the king and his people. The gods had said that they would willingly accept a new member in their hierarchy, but they would prefer that he should be a former king of the Swedes rather than Christ. They were unwilling to accept Christ as one of themselves because he was a foreigner.[1] Some of the early Icelanders found less difficulty than the Swedes had done in combining Christianity with pagan beliefs, and not all of them considered the two religions incompatible. Already the settler, Helgi the Lean, had numbered Þórr and Christ among his patrons,[2] and the poet, Egill Skalla-Grímsson, was marked with the Cross while in England, but returned to Iceland and died a pagan death.[3]

Unlike Christianity, northern paganism was not dogmatic.[4] Neither its tenets nor its rules of conduct were clearly defined, and it offered none but shadowy promises of life after death. Its gods were to be propitiated, rather than worshipped or loved, and it was wise to bring sacrifices to them, for they could grant favours in exchange. It was dangerous to insult the gods, for they had power to take revenge. Neither the gods nor the religious system were closely concerned with morals. Although the pagan Icelanders had a strict and in many ways an admirable moral code, their morals had little to do with their religious beliefs.

The fundamental distinction between paganism and Christianity was in the conception of the deities. The one religion was

---

[1] Rimbert, *Vita Anskarii*, ch. xxvi (in *Monumenta Germanica historica, Scriptores*, ii, 1829, p. 711); cf. K. Maurer, *Die Bekehrung des norwegischen Stammes zum Christenthume*, i, 1855, pp. 32–33.

[2] See above, p. 3.         [3] See above, pp. 40 ff.

[4] The general characteristics of Norse paganism are described best by Sigurður Nordal, *Íslenzk Menning*, i, 1942, pp. 153–232. The most detailed account is that of de Vries, *Altgermanische Religionsgeschichte*, ii, 1937.

dominated by a single god, who was all-powerful and all-good; but the other knew no supreme god. None of its gods were all-powerful, for like men they were the playthings of an impersonal fate. Like men they were also partly good and partly bad. By the end of the pagan period some of the gods had assumed attributes of Christ. Óðinn was depicted hanging on a tree, and his side was pierced with a spear.[1] Baldr was thought of almost as a Messiah, who would return to the world after death and restore it,[2] but Baldr could not be equated with Christ, for he was not omnipotent. Northern paganism had, thus, more in common with atheism than with Judaism and Christianity. The supreme power for the pagans was fate, which was impersonal, and so indifferent to the affairs of men that it was useless to offer sacrifice to it, or to invoke it in any other way.

It is not surprising that people whose religious beliefs were so ill defined as those of the Icelanders should take no pains to propagate them, and should seldom defend them with violence, for they did not believe that salvation depended upon them. Those who had adopted Christianity, and understood the force of its teaching, were more easily roused. Consequently, it was only pagans, and never Christians, who lost their lives in religious controversy. But the early protagonists of Christianity in Iceland were not generally ruthless in their methods, and tolerance was met by tolerance.

Records of the period of transition from paganism to Christianity are more detailed than those about earlier periods in the history of Iceland, but in reading them it is often hard to distinguish history from legend and fiction. The conversion was the most memorable event in the history of Iceland since the settlement and, for this reason, many facts about it were recorded. But, for the same reason, the more tendentious historians of the thirteenth century made the period of the conversion a favourite field for embroidery, and artistic saga-writers made tales about it. Before any such story in the profuse literature of Iceland can be accepted as history, the author's source must be considered. He may have

---

[1] The *Hávamál* in *Edda*, ed. G. Neckel, 1927, str. 138.
[2] See *Völuspá* in *Edda*, str. 62.

derived it from a reliable record written at an early date, but his source might be folk-lore, or he may have borrowed his motives from international hagiography and romance; he may even have invented the story.

Icelandic historians began early to write of the conversion. Sæmundr Sigfússon (1056–1133) probably dealt with it in his 'History of the Kings of Norway', but this book is lost.[1] Lists of genealogies were probably written before the end of the eleventh century, and these may have contained notes about the conversion. It is not known how early the Icelanders began to make annals, but they probably did so early in the twelfth century.[2]

The oldest account now known is that written by Ari Þorgilsson (1067–1148) in the 'Book of the Icelanders' (*Íslendingabók*). Ari also wrote other and more detailed works than this book,[3] and they included details not to be found there. These other works of Ari do not survive as separate documents, but much of their content has been incorporated in the books of later historians, such as those of Oddr Snorrason, Gunnlaugr Leifsson, Snorri Sturluson and others. It is often difficult to know when these later historians are following the lost works of Ari, and when their source is a less reliable one.

It is commonly said that the first attempt to convert the Icelanders was made between the years 981 and 985, and the fullest accounts are to be found in the *Þorvalds Þáttr Víðfǫrla* (Tale of Þorvaldr the Far-traveller) and in the *Kristni Saga* (Saga of Christianity).[4] The first of these was written by Gunnlaugr Leifsson early in the thirteenth century,[5] and the *Kristni Saga* was probably put together from older books by Sturla Þórðarson towards the end of that century.[6] Although they cannot be counted reliable, these works need not be dismissed as wholly fictitious.

---

[1] See Ch. III below.
[2] See N. Beckman in *Alfræði íslenzk*, ii, 1914–16, Introduction, pp. cxxiii ff.
[3] See Ch. IV below.
[4] Both published in *Biskupa Sögur*, i, ed. Jón Sigurðsson and Guðbrandur Vigfússon, 1858, and in *Kristni Saga*, ed. B. Kahle, 1905.
[5] Cf. Kahle, op. cit., Introduction, pp. xvi–xix; Finnur Jónsson, *ONOI*, ii. 399.
[6] Cf. Jón Jóhannesson, *Gerðir Landnámabókar*, 1941, pp. 70–71.

The story of this first mission contains many points of interest. It was initiated by an Icelander called Þorvaldr, who was brought up at Giljá, near the shores of the Húnaflói. Like others destined to be heroes, Þorvaldr showed little promise in childhood, and was despised as a 'ne'er-do-well'. In early years he sailed to Denmark, where he took service under Sveinn Forkbeard (died 1014), who was at that time leader of a viking band. Þorvaldr fought bravely at his master's side and earned his esteem. Although he was still a pagan, Christian charity was innate in Þorvaldr's heart, for he gave up his share of the booty to ransom prisoners and to relieve those in distress. His travels brought him to Germany, where he came to know a bishop called Frederick, by whom he was baptized. Þorvaldr persuaded the bishop to accompany him to Iceland and to join him in preaching to the people. They worked for about four years in the island, chiefly in the north, the region of Þorvaldr's home. Picturesque tales are told of the bishop proving his spiritual strength against elemental wights and berserks. The missionaries were not persecuted at first, and were even allowed to advocate their cause at the Assembly. As might be expected, leading pagans spoke against them and, as tempers rose, pagan poets began to lampoon them in obscene doggerel. Þorvaldr could not endure these insults, and he slew two of the slanderers, although against the will of the bishop. The missionaries now grew unpopular, and fled the country.

Þorvaldr never returned, but instead he made a pilgrimage to Jerusalem, and came later to Byzantium. Extravagant tales were told of his achievements in the east. The Emperor of Byzantium was so struck with his nobility and piety that he appointed him his deputy, and said that all the kings of Russia should be subject to him. Before his death, Þorvaldr built a monastery at a place called Drǫfn, said to lie in the neighbourhood of Polotsk. This was called Þorvaldr's monastery, and Þorvaldr himself is buried there.

These edifying and entertaining tales of Þorvaldr and Frederick have undoubtedly some foundation in history. Although Ari records no details about them in the 'Book of the Icelanders', he once names Frederick, as the only bishop who came to Iceland in pagan times.[1]

It cannot be told how widespread or how deep were the results of this mission. It is said that several of the chieftains were baptized, and among them Þorvaldr's father, Koðrán. One of the converts built a church at Áss in Hjaltadalr and another, Máni, withdrew from the society of men to live as a hermit. Other well-known men, like Eyjólfr Valgerðarson, showed their sympathy with Christianity, and allowed themselves to be marked with the Cross. Some, who did not accept the new religion, abandoned pagan practices and declined to contribute to the upkeep of the temples. At any rate, the Icelanders must have learnt much about Christian teaching while they listened to the words of the bishop and heard them interpreted in their own language by Þorvaldr.

Little is known about religious thought in Iceland for the next ten or fifteen years, although the period is much favoured by sagawriters, who depict it as one when men's minds were disturbed by doubt. After Njáll had heard of King Ólafr Tryggvason, and of his efforts to convert the people of Norway, he would sometimes withdraw from other men and mumble to himself in solitude.[2] Those in the toils of spiritual conflict would see visions, or have other occult experiences. One man, Þiðrandi Síðu-Hallsson, was killed mysteriously by the attendant spirits of his pagan family. These attendant spirits appeared as women clothed in black and armed with swords.[3] Even the trolls and elemental beings, whose existence depended upon pagan superstition, were shaken in their age-old beliefs. A cairn-dweller appeared to a certain Þorsteinn Oxfoot in a dream, and advised him to adopt the new religion, only regretting that he could not do it himself. He asked Þorsteinn, if ever he had a son, to call him by his own name, Brynjarr. The cairn-dweller's name might then enjoy the benefits of baptism, even though he himself were denied them.[4] Þorhallr, a farmer of southern Iceland, once looked from his bed through the window,

---

[1] *The Book of the Icelanders*, ed. Halldór Hermannsson, 1930, ch. viii.

[2] *Brennu-Njálssaga*, ed. Finnur Jónsson, 1908, ch. c.

[3] See *Flateyjarbók*, ed. Guðbrandur Vigfússon and C. R. Unger, i, 1860, pp. 419–21.     [4] See *Flateyjarbók*, i. 253–5.

and saw all the mounds and hillocks opening, and their troll-like inhabitants packing their bags and preparing to leave. Shortly afterwards, Christianity was adopted in Iceland.[1] Although many of these stories were probably invented by clerks of the twelfth and thirteenth centuries, some of them may well preserve memories of the spiritual experiences of men who waited for Christianity, and were torn between loyalty to the traditions of their ancestors and the claims of the new religion.[2]

The spiritual conflict of a convert from paganism is nowhere more clearly described than in the *Hallfreðar Saga*.[3] This is one of the older sagas of Icelandic heroes, and it contains many verses which are ascribed to the Icelander Hallfreðr, nicknamed 'the troublesome poet' (*vandræðaskáld*). Both the language and style of these verses suggest that the traditional ascription to Hallfreðr is correct, and they are generally accepted as his work.[4] If so, the *Hallfreðar Saga* must have great value as history, for the verses are its core. As literature, they do not rank with the best of scaldic poetry, but they have much human interest, because in them Hallfreðr expresses his religious sympathies and doubts.

The main theme of the *Hallfreðar Saga* is the growth of affection and friendship between the poet Hallfreðr and King Ólafr Tryggvason (995–1000). Under the king's influence, Hallfreðr became a Christian, but his conversion was not easy, and perhaps not deep, for he did not hate but rather mourned the gods whom he deserted:

Hallfreðr never disparaged the gods, although others spoke ill of them. He said that there was no need for a man to abuse the gods, even though he believed in them no longer. On one occasion he uttered this verse within the hearing of the King:

> Warmly once I worshipped
> wise Óðinn of Hliðskálf;
> the ways of men are other
> than all I learnt in childhood.

---

[1] *Flateyjarbók*, i. 421.  [2] Cf. Maurer, op. cit. i. 226 ff.
[3] Edited by Einar Ól. Sveinsson, *Íslenzk Fornrit*, viii, 1939.
[4] On the verses see Einar Ól. Sveinsson, Introduction to *Íslenzk Fornrit*, viii, pp. lviii ff.

The King said: 'this is a wicked verse, and you must atone for it', and then Hallfreðr uttered another verse:

> All the world once worshipped
> the weather-god in poems,
> I call to mind the custom
> my kinsmen glorious practised.
> Well pleased Óðinn's power
> the poet, loth am I to
> hate the glorious husband
> of Hlín, though Christ I serve now.[1]

It was not until he had been severely rebuked by the king that Hallfreðr abjured the pagan gods in this verse:

> May Freyr and Freyja loathe me
> —lately I left Njǫrðr's temple—
> hate me Þórr the mighty,
> monsters worship Óðinn;
> I crave Christ's gentle mercy,
> cruel is the saviour's anger;
> he rules with God the Father,
> the great, who reigns above him.

Even after this, Hallfreðr went to pagan Sweden, where he married a non-Christian woman and reverted to his evil ways, until King Ólafr appeared to him in a dream and brought him back to the fold. Hallfreðr died of illness at sea while still a young man, and in his last verse he showed that, for him, Christianity had triumphed over paganism. He would have died without fear were it not for the fear of Hell. The doctrine of eternal punishment was a powerful weapon in the hands of missionaries, and those who read the *Lucidarius*[2] will realize how ruthlessly this weapon was used by medieval Christians. Scandinavian pagans had nothing to rival it.

The author of the *Vǫluspá* (Sibyl's Prophecy)[3] most probably lived at a time when men were turning from their traditional beliefs to the new religion. This is the most profound of the lays in

---

[1] The 'weather-god' (Viðrir) is Óðinn; Hlín (also called Frigg) is the wife of Óðinn.      [2] See Ch. V below.

[3] Edited in *Edda*, ed. G. Neckel, i. 1–15. The best critical text and the most valuable discussion of the poem will be found in Sigurður Nordal's edition, *Vǫluspá*, 1923. I quote from Nordal's text.

the *Edda*, and none of them was better known or more influential in the Christian Middle Ages. Snorri Sturluson quoted nearly half its strophes in his 'Prose Edda', and many of his chapters are based upon it. The monk Gunnlaugr (died 1218) freely borrowed lines from it when he made his version of the 'Prophecies of Merlin' in Icelandic,[1] and the Austin Canon, Gamli, echoed it when he described the Last Day in his poem the *Harmsól* (The Sun of Sorrow).[2] It was plagiarized in the so-called 'Short Vǫluspá',[3] the work of an inferior poet who probably lived in the twelfth century. The influence of the *Vǫluspá* appears first in a memorial lay, which Arnórr Jarlaskáld made in honour of the Orkney Jarl Þorfinnr, who died in 1064. Arnórr says:

> Bjǫrt verðr sól at svartri
> søkkr fold í mar døkkvan . . .[4]

recalling Strophe 57 of the *Vǫluspá*, in which the *Ragnarǫk* (the gods' Doomsday) is described:

> sól tér sortna
> søkkr fold í mar . . .

This shows that the *Vǫluspá* is older than Arnórr's memorial lay, and it is now generally believed to date from the last years of the tenth century.

It is often difficult to decide whether a poem of the *Edda* originated in Norway, Iceland, or elsewhere, but the *Vǫluspá* can hardly be other than an Icelandic poem. Its Icelandic origin is shown in many things, and especially in the scenery which the poet describes. He knew great sandy beaches and wall-like rocks, and had seen volcanoes in eruption. But, although observant of nature, he described the mistletoe as a beautiful, slender tree towering above the plain. In other words, the scenery which this poet knew was that of volcanic, treeless Iceland, not of wǫoded Scandinavia.[5]

There is no poem in all Germanic literature of such scope. In little more than sixty strophes the poet tells the story of the cosmos

---

[1] See Ch. VII below.                                    [2] See Ch. VI below.
[3] Cf. Finnur Jónsson, *ONOI*, i. 203–6.
[4] Cf. E. Noreen, *Den norsk-isländska poesien*, 1926, p. 89; Ch. VI below.
[5] Cf. Sigurður Nordal, *Vǫluspá*, 123–5 and references there given.

from the beginning almost to the end, and the theme is no less than that of *Paradise Lost* and *Paradise Regained* together. The poem is placed in the mouth of a sibyl, who addresses it both to men and to gods and especially to Óðinn. She first proves her wisdom by telling of the time when the universe began. She remembers the primeval giants who fostered her, and the days when there was nothing but a huge void, until three gods, Óðinn and his two brothers, lifted land from the sea and fashioned the earth. With two other gods, Óðinn then found two inanimate tree-trunks washed on the sea-shore and engendered them with life, and the race of men descended from these. The sibyl describes the golden age of the youthful gods. Playing with golden draughtsmen, they were industrious, joyful, and innocent, until three maidens came to their city bent on the errand of the wicked trolls (*jǫtnar, þursar*). Yet another wicked woman came to the city of the gods, and she was called Gullveig; a name which probably means 'Gold-Power', and symbolizes the corrupting influence of gold. The gods riddled Gullveig with spears, and burnt her three times, but she lives to this day. The youthful innocence of the gods was now past; avarice and treachery were enkindled in their hearts. They engaged in wars and broke their covenants. Their happiness and welfare declined with their morals. Misfortunes were precipitated by Loki, a traitor in the tribe of the gods. Loki guilefully induced the pathetic blind god, Hǫðr, to strike Baldr with the mistletoe, and Hǫðr thus became the instrument of Baldr's death. Baldr, the son of Óðinn, was the best loved and purest of gods. The treacherous Loki was bound in chains, but he will break them when the gods' Doomsday (*Ragna-rǫk*)[1] draws near. Wolf-like monsters will be born and reared, only for the destruction of gods and men. The wolf, Garmr, who waits for the *Ragnarǫk*, in chains like Loki, will free himself. Meanwhile, men will grow cruel; they will ignore the most sacred family ties, slaughter their own kindred and indulge in whoredom. The beautiful ash-tree, Yggdrasill, which upholds the world, will shiver and creak, and its limbs will catch fire. The monstrous enemies of

[1] On the meaning of *Ragnarǫk* see H. Gering and B. Sijmons, *Kommentar zu den Liedern der Edda*, i, 1927, p. 58.

gods and men will approach from different points of the compass, Loki among them. Foremost of the enemies will be Surtr, the Black, and after him the mysterious sons of Múspell.[1] The gods will die, partly to expiate their crimes, but they will die like heroes. Óðinn will be killed by the monstrous wolf, but his son Víðarr will avenge him. Last of all Þórr will fight against the serpent who surrounds the world. He will strike the beast and step back dying, but not dismayed. When Þórr falls the end will be near. The sun will turn black, and the stars vanish from heaven; smoke and flames will gush forth, playing against the firmament, while the earth itself sinks into the sea.

After the tragedy, the world will rise again, as if refreshed from the sea. Some of the gods will meet once more and their golden draughtsmen will be found. Unsown fields will bear corn. Baldr will be reconciled with Hǫðr, who unwittingly slew him, and these two will come back to live in the sanctuaries of the gods. Just men will live in the castle Gimlé, which, tiled with gold, will shine more brilliantly than the sun. Lastly, the mighty one, who rules all, will come to his godhead. The poem ends with an obscure strophe, in which reference is made to the flying dragon, who carries corpses in his wings. In this strophe the poet seems to warn his audience that the forces of evil will survive the chastening fire of *Ragnarǫk*.

There has been more controversy about the *Vǫluspá* than about any lay in the *Edda*. This controversy cannot be reopened here, but some prevailing opinions about the poem must be mentioned. It has been said that the *Vǫluspá* is not a single poem at all, but a scrap-book containing fragments on mythological subjects derived from various sources. If this is correct, it was wrong to summarize the *Vǫluspá* as I have done, for the outline given implied a continuous sequence of events, and a unity, which no poet intended. E. Noreen[2] was among those who denied the unity of the *Vǫluspá* most emphatically. He rightly pointed out that some scholars have given way to their own subjective prejudices in attempting to

---

[1] On the sons of Múspell see Gering and Sijmons, op. cit. i. 298, and A. Olrik, *Ragnarök*, translated into German by W. Ranisch, 1922, pp. 68 ff.

[2] Op. cit., pp. 87 ff.

interpret the *Vǫluspá*. Indeed, the interpretations of most, if not of all, scholars are partly subjective. It would be too much to hope that even the bare summary given above is objective in every detail. No one would agree with every sentence in it.

This implies that, like most mystical poets, the author of the *Vǫluspá* used symbols and images which have different meanings for different readers, and must have been obscure even for his contemporaries. Snorri Sturluson was the most accomplished critic of Eddaic poetry in the Middle Ages. The interpretations which he gave of many passages in the *Vǫluspá* remain unchallenged, but it is evident that he did not understand every strophe in it. One reason for obscurity is in the corruption of the text, for some strophes have been interpolated, and a few have been lost between the date of composition and the thirteenth century, when the poem was first written. But the chief difficulty lies, not in corruption, but in the visionary symbolism of the *Vǫluspá*.

Most scholars recognize the unity of this poem, but they fail to agree on certain fundamental questions. The chief of these is whether the *Vǫluspá* should be regarded as a pagan or as a Christian monument. Finnur Jónsson[1] hardly allowed for the presence of Christian influences in it. He said that the poem gave a faithful picture of pagan beliefs, and in this lay its unique significance and value. B. M. Ólsen[2] regarded the *Vǫluspá* rather as a Christian monument, and yet he admired it no less than Finnur Jónsson did. The truth must lie somewhere between these two extreme views.

A. Olrik[3] attempted to distinguish the Christian from the pagan elements, and many of his conclusions are irrefutable. He studied the non-Christian legends of Europe and compared them with the Christian ones, especially as they were known in western countries in the tenth century, and he recognized elements of various religious cults in the *Vǫluspá*.

Thus, according to Olrik's method, the story of Óðinn's death in his struggle with the wolf (*Vǫluspá*, strophe 53) might be

[1] *ONOI*, i. 130–3.
[2] *Tímarit hins íslenzka bókmenntafjelags*, 1894, pp. 79–89; *Um kristnitökuna árið 1000*, 1900, pp. 60 ff.; *Skírnir*, 1912, 372–5.
[3] Op. cit., pp. 110 ff.

regarded as a part of the pagan heritage, and so could the avenge-
ment of Óðinn by his son Víðarr (strophe 55). Both of these
motives were known widely in pagan times, and there was no
Christian legend from which they derive. The wolf born to swallow the sun (strophe 40) had no counterpart in Christian legends
of the end of the world, but he was a well-known figure in non-
Christian myth. The chained wolf, whose bonds will break when
the *Ragnarǫk* draws near (strophes 49, &c.), could not be associated with any Christian legend, but figures like him could be
found in non-Christian eschatology in the north and elsewhere.
Not only the wolf, but the demoniacal god, Loki, will also break
his chains at the approach of the *Ragnarǫk* (see strophe 51, cf.
*Baldrs Draumar*, 14). The bound Loki, the fallen god, could not
altogether be dissociated from the bound Satan, the fallen angel
of Apocrypha, who lies chained in Hell, and will free himself at
the time of Antichrist.[1] The ringing horn, with which Heimdallr
will announce that *Ragnarǫk* is at hand (strophe 46), perhaps
originated in the symbolism of *Revelation* (viii–ix). The magnificent castle Gimlé, in which just men will live after death, must
somehow be associated with the New Jerusalem.

Olrik laid emphasis on the artistic qualities of the *Vǫluspá*, and
he showed how the author's conception of the cosmos, and
especially of the *Ragnarǫk*, differed from the popular beliefs of his
day. Many people might fear that a monstrous wolf would one day
break loose and swallow the sun, and that another wolf would
swallow Óðinn, but this did not imply that they had a coherent
conception of the *Ragnarǫk*, or that they could describe it in logical
sequence, as the author of the *Vǫluspá* did. Snorri's conception of
the tragedy of *Ragnarǫk*, and consequently our own, were derived
chiefly from the *Vǫluspá*.

The author of the *Vǫluspá* was an individual rather than a representative of his age. Unlike his contemporaries, he had little
interest in the grotesque motives of pagan mythology. He did not
say, as others did, that the world was fashioned out of the flesh and
blood and bones of a giant. He knew that the world and the cosmos

[1] See A. Olrik, op. cit., p. 89 and *Viking Civilisation*, 1930, pp. 40–41.

had not always existed, but he left their origin obscure, as many a philosopher would do. While he often used grotesque motives, typical of northern folk-lore, he modified them. He knew of the apprehension that the sun would be swallowed by a wolf (strophe 40), but he made little of it. He supposed rather that the sun would turn black, and the heavenly bodies would vanish during the *Ragnarǫk* (strophe 57). This poet did not say that, in avenging Óðinn, Víðarr would tear the jaws of the wolf asunder, or that this beast's jaws would extend from the earth to the sky. Instead, he described Víðarr as a hero, who would stab the wolf to the heart (strophe 55). In other words, this poet regarded the fate of gods and men as a natural evolutionary and devolutionary process. Such views would accord better with Christian teaching than the cruder and more grotesque ones typical of northern paganism.

It is not necessary to suppose that Christian influences reached the author of the *Vǫluspá* directly, through books or missionary teachers. It is improbable that he would distinguish between the pagan and Christian motives in his poem. The truth is more probably that pagan mythology and symbolism became more strongly coloured by Christian beliefs as Christianity drew nearer to the northern shores, and intercourse between Christians and pagans grew more frequent. This implies that the *Vǫluspá* originated towards the end of the pagan period in Iceland. This might be shortly before the year 1000, when Christianity was legally adopted in Iceland, or shortly after that year, when pagan beliefs and sympathies still lingered. It has several times been suggested that the author of the *Vǫluspá*, in his apprehension of the *Ragnarǫk*, was influenced by the Christian apprehension that the millenium was nearly complete, and that the world would end in the year 1000, or else in 1033. There are reasons for believing that pagans shared this popular dread.[1] Ólafr Tryggvason and his agent Þangbrandr[2] were perhaps inspired, in their missionary zeal, by a certainty of

---

[1] Cf. Guðbrandur Vigfússon and F. York Powell, *Corpus Poeticum Boreale*, i, 1883, p. lxvii; Nordal, op. cit., pp. 125–9; F. Paasche, *Kristendom og kvad*, 1914, p. 14 ff.　　　　　　　　　　　　　　[2] See below, pp. 65 ff.

impending doom. Whether Christian or pagan, the author of the *Vǫluspá* may also have feared that the end was at hand.

It would be difficult to assign the *Vǫluspá* to any 'class' or type of poetry. For, whichever the class to which it is assigned, it rises far above that class. Yet the poem cannot be dissociated altogether from other prophetic poetry which flourished in the early Middle Ages. In many lands prophecies used to be expressed in poetry, and they were sometimes delivered as if they were visions seen in a trance. The Greenland witch, Þorbjǫrg, whose story is told in the *Eiríks Saga Rauða*[1], apparently spoke in a trance. It is not certain that this woman spoke in poetry, but it is known that poems of a kind called *varðlok(k)ur*[2] were chanted by an attendant, in order to stimulate or control her prophetic powers. The sibyl, to whom the poet attributes the *Vǫluspá*, seems also to speak in a trance. She alludes to her vigil beneath the open sky, during which Óðinn had spoken to her (strophe 28). At the end of the poem she is said to 'sink' (*søkkvask*), just as if she had been propped on pillows, as Þorbjǫrg was. Indeed, the ecstatic tone of the *Vǫluspá* might lead to the suspicion that it was composed in an abnormal state of mind.

Prophetic visions, described by poets in trances, were especially popular in Wales, where poetry of this kind was probably cultivated as early as the tenth century.[3] Giraldus Cambrensis, in the *Description of Wales*, describes the practices of the inspired poets, the *awenyddion*. Whether genuine or not, the *Prophecies of Merlin* were undoubtedly intended by Geoffrey of Monmouth to represent a prophetic vision such as the *awenyddion* would relate. It was not fortuitous that, when Gunnlaugr Leifsson translated the *Prophecies of Merlin* into Icelandic verse,[4] he chose the metre of the *Vǫluspá*, and freely borrowed its lines. Gunnlaugr thereby showed to which class of poetry he would assign the *Vǫluspá*.

Visions of the Christian Doomsday are preserved in poetry and

[1] *Eiríks Saga Rauða*, ch. iv, ed. by Halldór Hermannsson, *The Vinland Sagas*, 1944.
[2] On the meaning of *varðlok(k)ur* see D. Strömbäck, *Sejd*, 1935, pp. 124 ff.
[3] Cf. Ifor Williams, *Lectures in early Welsh Poetry*, 1944, pp. 7 ff.
[4] See below, Ch. VII.

prose both in Latin and in the vernacular languages. One of the best-known examples is the *Prophecy of the Sibyl Tiburtina*,[1] which bears some similarity to the *Vǫluspá*. M. E. Griffiths[2] quotes a Welsh poem found in a manuscript of Llanstephan, in which fifteen signs of doom are enumerated, and some of them are reminiscent of the *Vǫluspá*: the sea will rise like a wall, buildings will fall, stones and rocks will hit each other, men shall come from their hiding places and be as madmen, the stars and the heavenly signs will fall, and the world will burn. Early English homilists described Doomsday and the time of Antichrist in symbols very similar to those last quoted.[3]

If the influence of prophetic poetry of the Christian nations is to be seen in the *Vǫluspá*, this need not imply that the author of the poem was himself a Christian. The pagans believed that all things were transitory, and their philosophy was pessimistic. The gloomier side of Christian belief would not be slow to inspire them. There is no evidence to show whether the author of the *Vǫluspá* was formally pagan or Christian, but the importance of this question should not be over-emphasized. His thoughts and sympathies were pagan. Like the pagans, he recognized the faults of the gods, but he respected them none the less. He admired Þórr for his heroism (strophes 26, 56), and he shared in Frigg's grief at the death of her son and husband (strophes 32–33, 53). If this poet were converted to Christianity, it would not be to blaspheme the gods, like Hjalti Skeggjason.[4] He would rather regret that he must leave their temples. Like Hallfreðr, he owed his poetry and his culture chiefly to the pagan religion. But the author of the *Vǫluspá* was a greater poet and a deeper thinker than Hallfreðr. In strophe 65 of the *Vǫluspá* the poet says:

> Then to his godhead
> the great one will come,
> the mighty descend,
> the master of all . . .

[1] See Migne, *Patrologia Latina*, vol. xc, col. 1181.
[2] *Early Vaticination in Wales*, 1937, p. 45.
[3] *Der Vercelli-Codex*, cxvii, ed. M. Förster, 1913, pp. 51, 59; *The Blickling Homilies*, ed. R. Morris, 1874–80, pp. 93 ff.   [4] See below, pp. 67 ff.

This defective strophe appears only in one manuscript of the *Vǫluspá*, and that a late one, viz. the *Hauksbók*.[1] Some critics have attempted to exclude it from the poem, but there are good reasons to suppose that it was part of it in its original form.[2] Nowhere does the poet express his religious convictions so clearly as he does in these four lines. After describing the fates of his favourite gods, he finds solace in the conception of an almighty and eternal God who rules all. In this, the poet is separated widely from his poly-theistic ancestors, to whom such a conception was alien. Pagan though he was in training and sympathy, the poet of the *Vǫluspá* had come to share that belief in an almighty god, which distin-guished Judaism and Christianity from the religions native to Europe. But this does not show that the author of the *Vǫluspá* would have regarded himself as a Christian, whatever judgement we might pass upon him.

Like the author of this poem, many Icelanders must have realized in the last decades of the tenth century that the pagan religion could not survive. Its doom was sealed when Ólafr Trygg-vason seized the throne of Norway in 995. This king was not con-tent to convert the people of Norway alone. He was no less concerned for those of the islands in the north Atlantic, who were linked with Norway by bonds of race and culture. Ólafr was remembered as the apostle, not only of Norway, but also of Orkney, Faeroe, Greenland, and Iceland, and among those who followed him at the beginning of his reign was a Christian Icelander, Stefnir Þorgilsson. In 996 the king ordered this man to go to Iceland and to preach to the people anew,[3] but Stefnir had no success and, in his anger, he resorted to violence, breaking down temples and destroying idols. He returned to Norway in 997.

The first results of Stefnir's mission were to strengthen pagan opposition, and a rigorous law against blasphemy was introduced. Those who blasphemed or insulted the gods were to be prosecuted

---

[1] On the manuscripts of the *Vǫluspá* and their relationship see Nordal's edition, pp. 1–5.

[2] See B. M. Ólsen, *Tímarit*, 1894, pp. 85–86; Nordal, op. cit., pp. 106–9.

[3] See *Flateyjarbók*, i. 286 ff.; *Kristni Saga*, ed. B. Kahle, ch. vi; further K. Maurer, op. cit. i. 373–82.

by their own relatives, for Christianity was branded as a stain on family honour (*frænda skǫmm*).[1] Hitherto, the Icelanders had been remarkable for their tolerance. Both godless men and Christians had lived unmolested among them.

King Ólafr was not discouraged by Stefnir's failure, but busied himself by proselytizing eminent Icelanders who came to Norway, using both threats and kindness. Among those who were baptized in Norway while Iceland was still a pagan country was Hallfreðr, who was mentioned above. Others were Kjartan and Bolli, heroes of the *Laxdœla Saga*.[2] In 997 the king sent a second mission to Iceland, and it was led by a German priest called Þangbrandr. Some details about Þangbrandr's work in Iceland are given by Ari in the *Íslendingabók*.[3] Ari writes:

King Ólafr, son of Tryggvi . . ., introduced Christianity into Norway and into Iceland. He sent to this country a certain priest, called Þangbrandr, who preached Christianity to the people, baptising all who received the faith. Hallr Þorsteinsson of Síða received baptism early, as well as Hjalti Skeggjason of Þjórsádalr and Gizurr the White, son of Teitr . . ., and many other chiefs; but there were more who spoke against Christianity, and refused to adopt it. Now after he had stayed here a winter or two, Þangbrandr went away, and had then killed two men or three in this land, because they had slandered him. And when he returned to Norway, Þangbrandr told King Ólafr all that he had suffered here, and said that there was no prospect that Christianity would yet be adopted in this land. The King was very angry at this, and because of it, he intended to have our countrymen who were then in Norway maimed or killed.

These simple sentences may be accepted as history. Ari, who was born about 1067, was a skilful and scrupulous historian, and he had good opportunities to learn facts about Þangbrandr's mission. From now on the story of the Icelanders might be said to pass from legendary folk-lore to history. But the Icelandic writers of the thirteenth century were too imaginative and creative to leave these

[1] On the implications of this law see K. Maurer, op. cit. i. 376–9; B. M. Ólsen, *Um Kristnitökuna*, pp. 23 ff.
[2] See *Kristni Saga*, ed. Kahle, ch. xi; *Flateyjarbók*, i. 312 ff.
[3] *The Book of the Icelanders*, ed. Halldór Hermannsson, 1930, ch. vii.

bare bones of history uncovered. Chapters about Þangbrandr's mission are found in several later sources, and the fullest of them are contained in the 'Greater Saga of Ólafr Tryggvason'[1] and the *Kristni Saga*. Such texts show how a few dry facts could be used as the basis for vivid and exciting stories.

In these later texts the character of Þangbrandr is painted in lurid colours. According to the 'Greater Saga of Ólafr Tryggvason', with which the *Kristni Saga* agrees closely, Þangbrandr was the son of Vilbaldus, Count of Bremen, and he had been a clerk of Albertus, Bishop of Bremen. He had the bearing of a soldier, rather than of a priest, and became the friend of King Ólafr while Ólafr was still a pagan. After he had been outlawed for killing a man in a duel, he took refuge with Ólafr, and later accompanied him as chaplain while he Christianized Norway. The king gave him a church with some revenues on the island of Morstr, but these were not sufficient for his extravagant tastes. He supplemented his income as a viking, and plundered the heathens of Norway. It was partly to expiate his crimes that the king sent him to Iceland.

Þangbrandr came first to the east coast of Iceland, where he stayed as the guest of the chieftain Síðu-Hallr. The heathen's heart was stirred when he heard the tinkling bells, saw the flickering candles and smelt the incense. He was no less moved when he heard Þangbrandr preach about S. Michael, whose feast he was celebrating. Hallr recognized that the glory of the God served by such angels must be beyond human understanding. He would not, at first, consent to baptism, for he feared its results. But after Þangbrandr had baptized two bedridden old women, and Hallr saw that their health was not worse, but rather better, he was himself baptized in a neighbouring stream.

The pagan Icelanders were alarmed by Þangbrandr's early successes, and they engaged their most skilful magician, Galdra-Heðinn, to work such a spell that he would be swallowed alive in the earth. As the missionary rode by the south coast the earth opened, and his horse sank into it, but Þangbrandr dismounted in

[1] See *Flateyjarbók*, i. 114–15, 151, 229, 363, 421–6; cf. *Kristni Saga*, chs. viii, ix.

time. He went on to the Assembly, where he preached and made
many converts. But after magic had failed, pagan poets began to
satirize Þangbrandr, as they had satirized Frederick and Þorvaldr
several years earlier. Þangbrandr and his companion, Guðleifr,
slew two poets as well as a foreign berserk and, in 999, Þangbrandr
returned to Norway and told the king of his adventures.

It will be noticed that the stories of Þangbrandr and of Þorvaldr
resemble each other in several ways. In fact, both of them probably owe their existing form largely to Gunnlaugr, the monk of
Þingeyrar (died 1218).[1] It is plain that they were intended, not as
records of history, but as imaginative descriptions of the fortunes
of missionaries in pagan Iceland. They are historical romances and,
although tendentious, they probably give as fair a picture of the
period as it was possible to give, after all but the barest facts had
been forgotten.

If not successful, Þangbrandr's mission led indirectly to the
conversion of Iceland. The story of how the Icelanders finally
agreed to adopt the Christian religion is told in the *Íslendingabók*.[2]
Ari's story is nowhere so detailed as it is in this passage. Among
those whom Þangbrandr converted were Hjalti Skeggjason and
Gizurr the White. These men reached Norway shortly after Þangbrandr had returned to the king and had incited him against the
Icelanders. They persuaded him not to persecute the Icelanders
then in Norway. Gizurr had especial claims on the king's favour,
for he was his distant cousin. Gizurr and Hjalti undertook to
return to Iceland as missionaries, and they assured the king that,
with their support, the Icelanders would accept Christianity.
Together with a priest, called Þormóðr, they reached Iceland in
time to take part in the Assembly at the end of June, A.D. 1000.
They landed on the Vestmannaeyjar, and proceeded to Þingvellir.
They were allowed to address the Assembly, and for a time passions ran high. The rival parties, those who preferred to adhere to
established custom, and those who favoured Christianity, declared
each other outside the law, and each party elected its own Law-
speaker (President). But moderation prevailed on both sides and,

[1] See below, Ch. VII.        [2] See below, Ch. IV.

instead of coming to blows, the two parties agreed to abide by the decision of the pagan Law-speaker, Þorgeirr, a man of proved integrity.

It is interesting to read how Þorgeirr reached his decision. He retired to his tent, and threw a cloak over his head, and spoke to none for a day and a night. When he arose, he addressed the Assembly from the Law-rock (*lǫgberg*). He spoke of the disasters which would befall if the Christians and the pagans were each to have their own code of law. He illustrated his contention with a parable about ancient kings in Norway and Denmark, who quarrelled until their own subjects were obliged to make peace between them. Þorgeirr decided that all Icelanders should be Christians in name, and should submit to baptism. But he tempered this decision, and ordained that those who wished might still observe their traditional rites and customs, so long as they did so in private. These traditional practices included sacrifice to the gods, consumption of horse-flesh, and the exposure of new-born children. It was several years before these were forbidden, and the last traces of paganism were obliterated.

The ease and unanimity with which the Icelanders accepted Christianity is remarkable. It is even more remarkable that organized paganism never revived in Iceland. Ólafr Tryggvason's work was, thus, more thorough in Iceland, which he never saw, than it was in his own country. When his namesake, Ólafr the saint, became King of Norway (about 1014), he found that, although the people of the coastal districts were nominally Christians and baptized, they knew nothing of Christian law. Meanwhile, the people of the interior had reverted to full paganism.

The differences in the history of the conversion of Norway and of Iceland seem to imply that, in those days, religious tradition was stronger among the Norwegians than it was among the Icelanders. This would not be altogether surprising. The ancestors of the Icelanders had been uprooted from their homes in the ninth century and early in the tenth. Their wanderings had brought them into close contact with the Christians of the British Isles. Christian influences were probably stronger in pagan Iceland than they were in pagan Norway, at any rate than they were in the interior of Norway.

Although Iceland had first been organized almost as an ecclesiastical state, in which the *goðar*, the pagan priests, wielded supreme power, the chief functions of these *goðar* were temporal and not religious, as could be illustrated from many sagas. The priestly functions of the *goðar* had nearly been forgotten by the time of the conversion, and it is not difficult to see why their authority survived the transition to Christianity. As Christians, the *goðar* were hardly less powerful than they had been as pagans. This shows that, however great the spiritual importance of the conversion, it was not, as in some lands, a social and cultural revolution. This may help to explain why the traditions of pre-Christian Scandinavia survived the conversion in Iceland, as they could not survive in Norway or in any other northern land.

# III

# THE FIRST CENTURY OF CHRISTIANITY

IT would be hard to determine how immediate and how deep were the results of the Conversion. Social conditions do not appear to have altered greatly at first. Ruthlessness and violence, always dangers under a political system so loosely organized as that of the Icelanders, were more than usually rife in the first decades of Christianity. Ari says[1] that many chieftains were convicted and outlawed for manslaughter and assault while Skapti was Lawspeaker (1004–30), and it is told elsewhere that many lived as vikings and robbers during the days of Bishop Ísleifr (1056–80).[2] These statements are supported by several sagas; it was said that Njáll and his sons were burnt to death at Bergþórshváll about the year 1010, and that at least one eminent Christian took part in that cruel deed.[3] Not a few of the tragedies which supplied motives for the sagas of Icelandic heroes were believed to have taken place in the first Christian decades.

The conversion did not bring any immediate change in the system of government, for the Icelanders continued to be governed by the *Alþingi*, or rather by the *goðar* who controlled that Assembly. Some *goðar*, whose office had originally been associated with pagan belief and ritual, now became leaders of the Church, and their influence was hardly less than before. Snorri goði (died 1031) is a good example. He lived, in those days, at Helgafell (Holy Hill), which had been revered as a holy place in pagan times, and no family had worshipped Þórr more ardently than that from which Snorri descended. Yet, according to the *Eyrbyggja Saga*, Snorri was among the first of pagan chiefs to replace his temple with a church.[4]

---

[1] *The Book of the Icelanders*, ed. Halldór Hermannsson, 1930, ch. viii.
[2] *Hungrvaka*, ch. ii, in *Kristni Saga*, ed. B. Kahle, 1905.
[3] *Brennu-Njálssaga*, ed. Finnur Jónsson, 1908, chs. cxxvii ff.
[4] See *Eyrbyggja Saga*, ed. Einar Ól. Sveinsson, 1935, ch. xlix. On the early churches in Iceland see K. Maurer, *Die Bekehrung des norwegischen Stammes zum Christenthume*, 1855–6, ii. 456 ff.

In course of time, Helgafell became nearly as holy for the Christians as it had formerly been for the pagans. Many other prominent chiefs did the same as Snorri, for clerks had told them that the doors of Paradise would be opened to as many of their friends as they could accommodate in their own churches.[1] So rapidly did churches spring up throughout the land that the Icelanders seemed to follow the advice which S. Gregory gave to S. Augustine: temples were not to be destroyed, but rather sprinkled with holy water; idols were to be taken down and replaced by altars.[2] Before long there were too many churches in Iceland for the clerks to serve.

However little their social system and conduct were altered, the Conversion brought the Icelanders into touch with European civilization in a way which they had not been before. Those who preached to them and first taught the *Pater Noster*, the *Credo* and the rudiments of Christian dogma were foreigners. Some were so-called missionary bishops, who had no see and no permanent diocese, but wandered from land to land. They had been consecrated solely to convert the heathen, establish churches, and perhaps to ordain priests.[3] The names of a few of the bishops who worked in Iceland in the eleventh century were recorded by Ari in the 'Book of the Icelanders',[4] and Ari's list is supplemented by a later text, the *Hungrvaka*,[5] which gives details about the lives and work of some of them. The sources of the *Hungrvaka* and its historicity will be discussed in a later chapter. On the whole, its author seems to be a careful and critical historian.

The first missionary bishop who visited Iceland after the Conversion, according to Ari's list, was Bjarnharðr. He was nicknamed 'Book-wise', and Ari says that he stayed five years. The *Hungrvaka* adds that Bjarnharðr (Bjarnvarðr) was believed to be an Englishman, and was said to have been an attendant of S. Ólafr, at whose instigation he went to Iceland. These suggestions, made so tenta-

---

[1] See *Eyrbyggja Saga*, loc. cit.    [2] Bede, *Historia Ecclesiastica*, i. 30.
[3] Cf. the description which Theodoricus gives of an early bishop in Norway: ... *ad hoc ipsum ordinatus fuerat, ut gentibus prædicaret verbum Dei* (ed. G. Storm in *Monumenta Historica Norvegiæ*, Oslo, 1880, p. 15).
[4] Ch. viii.    [5] *Hungrvaka*, chs. ii–iii.

tively in the *Hungrvaka*, have led scholars to identify Bjarnharðr the Book-wise with Bernhard, whom Adam of Bremen[1] names among the clergymen and bishops who sailed with S. Ólafr from England to Norway in 1015. It has also been surmised that Bjarnharðr was a member of a delegation which S. Ólafr sent to Iceland about the year 1016.[2] If so, Bjarnharðr's five years in Iceland must have fallen about 1016–21.

Another of the missionary bishops was Rúðólfr (Hróðólfr). Ari and the *Hungrvaka* agree that he stayed in Iceland for nineteen years, and it is said in several sources that he lived at Bœr in Borgarfjǫrðr. According to a version of the *Landnámabók* (Book of Settlements),[3] Rúðólfr left three monks at Bœr when he departed from Iceland, but it would be an exaggeration to say, as is said in one later source,[4] that Rúðólfr had founded a monastery. According to a tradition quoted in the *Hungrvaka*, this man's real name was Úlfr, but people called him Rúðólfr because he came from Rúða in England, by which the author perhaps means Rouen in Normandy. Because of his association with England, Rúðólfr of the Icelandic sources has been identified with Rudolf of Norway, who visited Archbishop Libentius of Hamburg between 1029 and 1032.[5] If this is correct, his nineteen years in Iceland probably fell between 1029 and 1051. Rúðólfr has also been equated with a certain Roðulf, who is named in an English source and described as *quidam de Norvegia gente episcopus*. This man was appointed Abbot of Abingdon by Edward the Confessor about the year 1050.[6]

Another interesting missionary was Jauhan (Jón), whom Ari describes as an Irishman, saying that he stayed only a few years. The *Hungrvaka* adds that some people think that Jauhan went to Wendland after he left Iceland. There he was seized and beaten, his arms and legs were cut off, and finally his head, and God received his soul. Adam of Bremen[7] speaks several times of Johannes

---

[1] *Gesta Hammaburgensis Ecclesiae Pontificum*, ed. B. Schmeidler, 1917, ii. 57.
[2] Cf. K. Maurer, op. cit. i. 595.
[3] *Landnámabók*, ed. Finnur Jónsson, 1900, *Hauksbók*, ch. 21.
[4] Ibid. Jón Sigurðsson, 1843, i. 332.    [5] Cf. K. Maurer, op. cit. i. 597.
[6] On Rudolf see Ch. Plummer, *Two Saxon Chronicles*, ii, 1899, p. 234 and references; K. Maurer, op. cit. i. 597–83, and ii. 561 f., 582.
[7] Adam of Bremen, op. cit. iii. 21 and 51.

Scotus, Bishop of Mecklenburg, who was also seized by the Slavs, and his martyrdom, dated 10 November 1066, is described in words strikingly similar to those in which the martyrdom of Jauhan is described in the *Hungrvaka*. If the two are to be identified, the years which Jauhan spent in Iceland probably fell shortly before the middle of the eleventh century.

I have spoken of missionary bishops whom medieval historians associate with the British Isles. In the eleventh century Iceland was—nominally at any rate—a part of the province of Bremen, and German missionaries also came to strengthen the Icelanders in the faith. A second Bishop Bjarnharðr (Bjarnvarðr) appears on Ari's list of foreign missionaries, and it is said that he stayed in Iceland for nineteen years. In the *Hungrvaka* this bishop has the nickname *inn saxlenzki* (the German). Bjarnharðr has not been identified in continental sources but, according to the *Hungrvaka*, he had been an attendant of King Magnús the Good (1035–47) in Norway. He stayed in Iceland throughout the reign of Haraldr Harðráði (1045(8)–1066), because he and that king could not agree. Bjarnharðr lived in Vatnsdalr in the north of Iceland, and he was renowned for his benedictions of 'churches and bells, bridges and wells' and of other pious and useful objects.

Besides these orthodox missionaries, several impostors and heretics preached in Iceland. In the *Hungrvaka* mention is made of bishops who came from foreign lands without the leave of Archbishop Aðalbert of Bremen (1043–72) and, because of the laxity of their doctrines, gained the support of wicked men. Ari also named three 'Armenian' (*ermskir*) bishops who visited Iceland. Whatever their nationality, these men were probably adherents of heresies prevalent in eastern Europe in those days. In the early Christian laws of Iceland provision is made for the treatment of strange bishops who used Armenian or Greek instead of Latin.[1] These indications of contact between eastern Europe and Iceland in the eleventh century are interesting, but the evidence is not strong enough to justify conclusions about the influence of eastern Europeans upon the civilization of the Icelanders.

[1] See *Grágás*, i, ed. Vilhjálmur Finsen, 1852, p. 22.

Some of the missionaries must have played a part in developing Icelandic civilization, especially those of them who remained for many years, like Rúðólfr of Bœr and his monks. These men must have learned to speak Icelandic, and preached to the people in it. They probably told them something about the philosophy and theology then fashionable in Europe, although a people whose literary tastes were so concrete as those of the Icelanders could have little interest in eleventh-century dialectic. They would be more ready to listen to tales from the scriptures and legends about the saints. Many of the best homilies in Icelandic consist of narratives of this kind. It is possible that some of them were told in Icelandic for the first time by foreign missionaries of the eleventh century. If so, these men contributed something to the narrative art in which the Icelanders were later to excel.

The nickname 'Book-wise', applied to the first Bishop Bjarnharðr, suggests that he spent much time reading and expounding Latin texts. Undoubtedly missionaries brought books and showed some people how to use them. Probably they also taught them to copy books, which implies that they taught a little Latin, and introduced the Roman script.

Hitherto the Icelanders had known no script but the runes. Although runes could quite well be used for writing books on parchment, there is nothing to suggest that they ever were.[1] As already stated (Chapter I, § 4), the chief purpose of the runes was monumental and magical, and they were probably known to few in Iceland. The tenuous evidence suggests that Icelanders began to use the Roman script about the middle of the eleventh century, or perhaps a little earlier.

The oldest Icelandic manuscripts which survive are assigned to the middle of the twelfth century,[2] but these were not the first manuscripts to be written in Iceland, for they are the work of experienced scribes who had learnt letter-forming and vernacular spelling from a long and well-established tradition. The characters

[1] For another view see B. M. Ólsen, *Runerne i den oldislandske literatur*, 1883.
[2] Cf. M. Hægstad in *Reallexikon der germanischen Altertumskunde*, iii, 1915–16, p. 338.

used in these manuscripts are based mainly on the Caroline minuscule as it was used in England for writing Latin. Specialists have shown that some of the characters in the oldest Icelandic manuscripts closely resemble those used by English scribes who wrote Latin during the first half of the eleventh century. The similarity between the *y* of the oldest Icelandic manuscripts and that of the English manuscripts of Latin texts written in the eleventh century is particularly striking.[1]

It is well known that, until the twelfth century, English scribes commonly used the distinctive Insular script for writing in the vernacular, and reserved the Caroline for Latin. Norwegian scribes, at any rate those of eastern and northern Norway, followed their English teachers in this distinction. The Icelanders, on the other hand, adopted no script but the Caroline, which they used for writing Icelandic and Latin alike. But since the Caroline script had no sign to express the sound of *th* (hard and soft), which the Icelandic language shared with English, the Icelanders borrowed the letter þ from the English Insular script, calling it by its English name *þorn*, and not *þurs*, as the corresponding symbol in the Norse runic alphabet was called. H. Spehr[2] has shown that the þ used in the oldest Icelandic manuscripts closely resembles a kind of þ which was current in England about the middle of the eleventh century. This suggests that, about that date, if not before, Icelanders were beginning to write, not only in Latin, but also in Icelandic, and that it was English clerics who taught them, and helped them to devise a system of spelling for their own language. This would not be surprising, for vernacular literature was far more highly developed in the British Isles than in any continental country in the eleventh century. It should be added that a number of Icelandic words used to designate books, writing, parchment, appear to be influenced by English usage, e.g. *bókfell* (vellum, cf. Old English *bocfell*), *rita* (to write, cf. O.E. *writan*), *stafróf* (alphabet, cf. O.E. *stæfræw*). On the other hand, the Icelandic

---

[1] Cf. H. Spehr, *Der Ursprung der isländischen Schrift*, 1929, pp. 49 ff.; A. Holtsmark, *En islandsk scholasticus fra det 12 århundre*, 1936, pp. 40 ff.

[2] Op. cit., pp. 8 ff.

*skrifa* (to write) and *lesa* (to read) are probably influenced by German usage.

These suggestions need not imply that the Icelanders began to write history or other ambitious literature in their own language as early as the middle of the eleventh century. It is more likely that they confined themselves at first to translations of Scripture, such as the *Credo* and the *Pater Noster*, which every Christian had to know. They might also have written some diplomatic documents and laws, especially those which related to churches and religious practices.

During the first three decades of Christianity the foreign clergymen were probably the only teachers in Iceland, and it was through them that Icelanders first came to know of the learning and literature of the south. But the importance of these foreigners should not be over-emphasized, for the early Icelandic Church was remarkable for its national character. Its leaders and its most eminent teachers were not, as in Norway, international citizens of the universal Church, but native Icelanders. They were drawn from powerful Icelandic families, who traced their ancestry to chieftains who had settled in Iceland in the ninth century, and even farther back to princes of Norway and kings of Sweden. Tradition was dear to such men, for their claims to distinction were based upon it, and this was one of the reasons why the traditional culture of the Icelanders survived the Conversion and developed under the stimulus of southern learning.

The first of the native teachers whose name is remembered was Ísleifr. He was a son of Gizurr the White, one of the earliest converts and foremost advocates of Christianity. In his pagan days Gizurr had been no less warlike than other chieftains and had led the assault on Gunnarr of Hlíðarendi about the year 992.[1] He was a distant cousin of King Ólafr Tryggvason, and his family could trace their descent from the half-mythical Ragnarr Loðbrók. Gizurr's son, Ísleifr, was born about 1005 and, at an early age, his father brought him to the convent of Herford in Westphalia,[2]

---

[1] *Brennu-Njálssaga*, ed. Finnur Jónsson, 1908, chs. lxxv–lxxvii.
[2] See *Hungrvaka*, ch. ii; cf. F. Paasche, *Kristendom og Kvad*, 1914, p. 59.

THE FIRST CENTURY OF CHRISTIANITY

where he was entrusted to the care of the Abbess Godesti. Ísleifr returned to Iceland shortly before the year 1030, and was then a priest. He settled down in the south of Iceland at Skálaholt, the farm which he had inherited from his father Gizurr. Gizurr had built a church at Skálaholt and was himself buried there.

Shortly after the middle of the century, the people of Iceland, who realized the great worth of Ísleifr, invited him to be their bishop. He set forth on the long journey to Rome, where his election was approved by the Pope, who sent him with letters to Archbishop Aðalbert of Bremen for consecration. Ísleifr was consecrated bishop on Whit Sunday, 1056, and shortly afterwards sailed for Iceland and returned to Skálaholt.

Ísleifr's visit to Bremen was not forgotten. Adam of Bremen, who wrote his *Gesta Hammaburgensis Ecclesiae Pontificum* about 1072, recorded his consecration, and spoke of Ísleifr as a most saintly man.[1] In this same passage Adam throws light on social and political conditions in Iceland in his day. He attributed almost unlimited authority to the bishop, whom the people obeyed as a king. If we can judge from the Icelandic sources, these words would be better applied to Ísleifr's son and successor, Gizurr, than to Ísleifr himself, for Ísleifr suffered deeply from the moral laxity and disobedience of the Icelandic people.[2] Nevertheless, it is plain that Adam understood how closely the temporal and spiritual authority in Iceland were linked. Their unity was one of the causes of the cultural wealth and vitality of the Icelanders in the early Middle Ages.

When Ísleifr returned to Iceland, there were still foreign clerks and bishops preaching and teaching there, but the chieftains could see that Ísleifr was a better man than they, and now they sent their sons to Ísleifr to be educated.[3] This shows how eager the chieftains were for European and clerical education and, more important still, it shows that they preferred to receive this education from a clerk who knew and appreciated their own traditions.

Icelandic and European civilization blended happily under

[1] Op. cit. iv. 36, cf. iii. 77.     [2] See *Hungrvaka*, ch. ii.
[3] See Ari, op. cit., ch. ix; *Hungrvaka*, ch. ii; *Kristni Saga*, ch. xiv.

Ísleifr's guidance. The importance of his work, and of the school which he founded at Skálaholt, have often been overlooked by modern students, but the nineteenth-century scholar Jón Sigurðsson[1] seemed to attribute the intellectual superiority of the Icelanders over neighbouring nations, and hence their great medieval literature, chiefly to the work of Ísleifr and his pupils. Perhaps Jón Sigurðsson claimed too much for Ísleifr, but his importance can best be judged when his pupils and their contributions to civilization are considered. One of Ísleifr's pupils was Kollr (Kolr) Þorkelsson, of whom little is known except that he was a cousin of Ísleifr, and was made Bishop of Vík (Oslo) in Norway,[2] a tradition supported by the Norwegian sources. The appointment of an Icelandic bishop to a see in Norway at this early date is a tribute to the learning of the young Icelandic Church. It is worth noting that no Norwegian occupied an episcopal see in Iceland until 1238,[3] and the reasons why Norwegians were appointed after that date were political and not cultural. Jón Ǫgmundarson was another of Ísleifr's pupils. In 1106 he was made first Bishop of Hólar, the diocese of northern Iceland. Jón never forgot his master and, following his example, he founded a school at Hólar. The work which Ísleifr had begun in the south of Iceland was carried on in the north by Jón.

Among Ísleifr's pupils his son Teitr (died 1110) should also be counted. Teitr founded the school of Haukadalr, only a few miles from Skálaholt. Teitr was not only a priest, and learned in the clerical arts; he is also remembered as an authority on the history of Iceland, on the settlement, the pagan laws, and the Conversion. Ari was one of Teitr's pupils, and a share in Ari's learning must be ascribed to him, and consequently to Ísleifr. It is to the credit of Ísleifr, no less than to that of his successor, Gizurr, that it could be said of most chieftains living in Iceland in the first years of the twelfth century that they were educated men and ordained priests.[4] But great as was Ísleifr's influence, the traditions of learning which

---

[1] *Um skóla á Íslandi* in *Ný Félagsrit*, ii, 1842, pp. 84–85.
[2] See Maurer, op. cit. ii. 561 n., 568, 573, 576.
[3] See Bishop Jón Helgason, *Islands Kirke*, 1925, pp. 152 ff.
[4] See *Kristni Saga*, ch. xvii.

he established would not be sufficient to account for the classical literature of Iceland, for the great Kings' sagas and Icelanders' sagas of the thirteenth century.

The most famous of Ísleifr's sons was Gizurr, who was elected bishop after his father's death (1081), and completed his work. Like his father, Gizurr went to school at Herford in Westphalia, but he is depicted in the sources as a man of very different stamp. He is remembered rather for social and political reforms than for his work as a teacher. In the *Hungrvaka*,[1] Gizurr is described as a man of large stature and noble bearing, with bright, wide eyes. He was endowed with great physical strength, and skilled in every manly accomplishment. Although educated and ordained at an early age, Gizurr had not intended to pursue a clerical career. During his father's lifetime he had lived as a merchant, sailing from land to land and consorting with princes and noblemen wherever he came. His travels brought him to Rome, and to the court of Haraldr Harðráði, in whose judgement he was worth three men, for he was at once fit to be a viking chief, a king, and a bishop.[2]

No figure in the history of Iceland was admired so generally as Gizurr, and it could truly be said of him that he was both king and bishop, for everyone strove to do his will.[3] The years when he was bishop were the most peaceful in the history of Iceland, for the ruling families laid aside their hereditary feuds, and collaborated with the bishop in reforming laws and securing the organization of the Church. Modern scholars attribute the peace and welfare which characterized this period chiefly to economic and other external causes,[4] but Ari and the medieval historians[5] write as if they were due to the dominating character of the bishop himself. This illustrates a typical difference between modern and medieval interpretations of history.

The chief of Gizurr's achievements was to place the Church on a secure footing. Hitherto there had been no see, for Skálaholt was

[1] Ch. v.
[2] See *Flateyjarbók*, ed. G. Vigfússon and C. R. Unger, iii, 1868, p. 379.
[3] *Hungrvaka*, loc. cit.
[4] See Sigurður Nordal, *Íslenzk menning*, i, 1942, pp. 288 ff.
[5] Ari, op. cit., ch. x; *Hungrvaka*, loc. cit.; *Kristni Saga*, chs. xv–xvi.

the hereditary property of Gizurr and his family. Gizurr built a new church, and dedicated it to S. Peter, replacing the church built by his grandfather early in the century.[1] Besides this, he made over the whole of the estate of Skálaholt to the Church as an episcopal see, stipulating that the residence of the bishop should never be moved. In fact, Skálaholt remained the see until the end of the eighteenth century, and for nearly seven centuries it was a centre of learning and civilization.

When Ísleifr was bishop he had complained bitterly of the poverty and financial straits of the Church, for it had no assured source of income. Tithes were not, at that time, levied in any Scandinavian country, but with the help of other able men, Gizurr drew up a law, under which they were introduced in Iceland in the year 1096. They were to be levied from nearly all self-supporting farmers, and provision was made not only for the bishop and the see, but also for the guardians of the smaller churches and for the maintenance of the poor.[2]

Gizurr died in 1118, and the last reform with which he may be credited was the decision, taken by the *Alþingi* in the year 1117, to inscribe the civil laws on parchment. Hitherto these laws had been remembered by heart and recited by the Law-speaker at the *Alþingi*. In the winter of 1117–18 the first sections of the civil code were written down, and they included the clauses relating to manslaughter and many others. Some modifications were made when these clauses were written but, for the most part, the traditional laws of Iceland remained unaltered.[3]

The revision and writing of the civil law were entrusted to Hafliði, a powerful *goði* of the northern districts, who was assisted by the Law-speaker Bergþórr and a number of other learned men. The book or scroll which they made was called 'Hafliði's Scroll' (*Hafliða Skrá*), and it was read out at the *Alþingi* by clerks in the summer of 1118.

Although no civil laws had been written before this time, some of the ecclesiastical clauses may already have existed on parchment.

---

[1] *Hungrvaka*, loc. cit.     [2] Ari, op. cit., ch. x; *Hungrvaka*, ch. vi.
[3] Ari, op. cit., loc. cit.

Til kirkiu ligr i raukiaholæ heimaland meþollö landſ ny·tiom
þar fylgia ky·r tottogu griþungr tueuetr·xȝx·a·ochundraþ·
þar ligr til fim hluter·grimſor altar enþrir huer ſa undan·nema
þat eſ munnu tdia·þat eſ hlaupa alr·oeþrir bluer arennar fy·r
            garþr
norþan miþberg·en fiorgongr en huer fr fra·þat fylger oc
fiorþongr haorgſ hyliar ſiþan eſ ſettungr eſ af teken oc oſtéma
at rauþa uatſoſe·þar fylgia heſtar þrir enge uerre an·uiii aurar
þar huer fr    oc til ſelfon ikioz meþoueþe þeirte eſ þar fylger at
helfninge    ocafretr alhrutaſtiar þar heþe·oc toc þan eſ han a tſȝra
dal·oc geitland meþ ſooge·Soogr tſandale niþr fra ſelakkagile umb
ſcala toſſt·gengr mark fy·r neþan or ſtemö þei eſ heita klofningar
þeir ſtanda uiþ ſundalſo·okþ·r up aſ ialſbrun·þar fulger oc ſoog·
þuerar lip at uiþa til ſelſ·  tſcurþr i ſtempozſſtaþa land·Galdſ
ſaþe niþr fort·  her liggia til hundrop ſcx alna aura
ibokö ocimeſſoſotö oc i kirkio ſkruþe·ſyir  ur an kluokor
þeir ero uerþar·Magö oc hallſcipr gefa til kirkio roþo kroſſ oc lic
neſke þau eſ ſtanda uſer altara·ocbuneng a plenario·þat eſ kirkio
fe umb ſram oſ þat eſaþr eſ talt·kirkio fe folgia tuer meter
uax·oc tottogo·þau liggia lond til kirkio öteiþa bolſtaþr·
or raukia land·oc hogende·her fulgia ey kirkiofe ſiau·
oc tuau kugilde buſiar meþ·þui fe ſkal aumaz haſſ land
omage huer  unſſere·oc ſkal ſa haſ til taka eſi raukia
holte bur·þeſſe kirkio fe eſ ero ibokö ocimeſſoſotö oc i uaſkio
ſkruþe piroþ til iextogo hnndra þa uaþmala   þendr Snor
ra þeir Giton oc þorþr·ocketill her munndar ſ·oc þogue pſtr
Skrin þat eſ ſtendr a altara meþ helgö domo geſa þeir Claghſee
Suorte at helfninge huait þeirra·ocſ þetta kirkio fe umb ſi
am oſ þat eſaþr eſ talet i kirkia aey uþſa klukur þer er þau
Snore z halluoge leoia til ſtaðar ſone imoyiar·ii·ſt·ii·arna naraur
en iþ ſaulmaar naror en·vi·peorl naver z þar med meſo þar en
beiſto ſindra ſar·n·ſepe·þeſſa reka atkia i rephia holtte·þnder þelli þé
þroþin·ıg hualreka oh halþur uidrekı ıſland ha  lxv·ynd iöa þelli þridi
oungx hualreka      i logt iagoha·ſe yn    nir·þt þelli kiþiunɡ
hvart tueggia iagoða a  Amunaðar neſi þ    nþunɡi hualreka·
Gld hambi þroþonɡ ıþualreka·þiragſt  uiþ þroþong iþual reka

The laws of tithe were probably inscribed when they were drawn up in 1096, and it is likely that certain diplomatic documents had been written in Icelandic before 'Haflíði's Scroll'. These would include inventories of churches and deeds of gift. At least one document of this kind, preserved in a later transcript, must be assigned to Gizurr's time, for he is there named as bishop.[1]

Among the most interesting of early diplomatic documents is a record of the privileges granted by S. Ólafr to Icelanders in Norway, and of the duties which he imposed upon them. This survives only in manuscripts of the late Middle Ages, but its authenticity can hardly be questioned. It recalls a treaty concluded between the Icelanders and S. Ólafr, to which Bishop Ísleifr had been a witness, although probably an indirect one. To begin with, it must have been made verbally, and its precise date cannot be decided, but the existing text was written according to the sworn testimony of Bishop Gizurr, his son Teitr, and of Markús (Law-speaker 1084–1107) and of several others. These chieftains testified that Bishop Ísleifr had sworn that S. Ólafr had given these privileges to their countrymen. The wording of the text suggests that the record was first written in Norway, although transcribed in Iceland. Since Gizurr was in Norway in the year 1083, after consecration as bishop, it may well have been written in that year, although some would assign it to a rather later date.[2]

Some years after the death of Bishop Gizurr, laws governing religious observances were encoded and written under the direction of Bishop Þorlákr the Elder of Skálaholt (1118–33) and of Bishop Ketill of Hólar (1122–45), who were advised by Sæmundr the Wise and many other clerks.[3] These early Christian laws are preserved in later manuscripts, although not exactly in their original form.

Not only were laws and charters written in Gizurr's time, but historical research began. The first scholastic historian was Sæmundr Sigfússon, who was born in 1056 according to the Icelandic Annals.[4] Few facts are recorded about Sæmundr's life, but

[1] See *Diplomatarium Islandicum*, i, 1857–76, p. 169, cf. p. 172.
[2] Ibid. i. 65 ff.; B. M. Ólsen, op. cit., pp. 129 ff.
[3] *Hungrvaka*, ch. xi; *Grágás*, i, ed. Vilhjálmur Finsen, 1852, p. 36.
[4] *Islandske Annaler*, ed. G. Storm, 1888, p. 108.

that he studied in France in his youth, most probably in the school of Nôtre Dame in Paris.[1] The date of his return to Iceland is given variously as 1076, 1077, and 1078, and he was subsequently ordained priest.[2]

Sæmundr's family seat was Oddi, some twenty or thirty miles south-east of Skálaholt, and it had belonged to his ancestors since Iceland was settled. His father, Sigfúss, is described as a priest, but little is known of him, and it was evidently Sæmundr who raised the family and the estate of Oddi to the pre-eminence which they enjoyed throughout the twelfth century.[3] It is told in the 'Saga of S. Þorlákr' that Sæmundr built a church at Oddi, and that it was dedicated to S. Nicholas, bishop.[4] Sæmundr took an active part in social affairs, for he was one of those who helped Bishop Gizurr to draw up the laws of tithe in 1096, and he helped the Bishops Ketill and Þorlákr to encode the laws of Christian observance. Sæmundr died in 1133.

Medieval writers frequently give Sæmundr the nickname *fróði* (wise), which is applied especially to men versed in the native and Scandinavian traditions. His reputation for learning grew so great that scholars of the seventeenth and eighteenth centuries believed that he had collected the lays of the *Edda* and ascribed to him works in which he can have had no part. Within a century of his death, credulous people began to think of Sæmundr as a sorcerer, and in the later folk-stories he appears as the most skilled of magicians.[5]

Sæmundr's chief contribution to Icelandic civilization was as an historian. Although he probably wrote little, he exercised an influence on the later historians. The first author to allude to his learning was Ari, and Sæmundr was one of those to whom Ari submitted the first version of his 'Book of the Icelanders' for criticism.[6] Ari also quotes Sæmundr as his authority for the date of the death of Ólafr Tryggvason.[7] In the latter instance we cannot be sure

[1] Storm, op. cit., p. 471; cf. Halldór Hermannsson, *Sæmund Sigfússon and the Oddaverjar*, 1932, pp. 5 ff.; A. Budinszky, *Die Universität Paris*, 1876, p. 224.
[2] Ari, op. cit., ch. ix.
[3] See Halldór Hermannsson, op. cit., pp. 5 ff.; and Einar Ól. Sveinsson, *Sagnaritun Oddaverja*, 1937.    [4] *Biskupa Sögur*, i, 1858, p. 320.
[5] See Halldór Hermannsson, op. cit., pp. 6 ff. and 45 ff.
[6] Ari, op. cit., Prologue.    [7] Ibid. ch. vii.

whether Ari is quoting the spoken word of Sæmundr or a written work. If he is quoting a written work, this can be no other than the 'History of the Kings of Norway', which we have good reason to ascribe to Sæmundr, although it no longer survives.

The strongest evidence that Sæmundr wrote a book about the kings of Norway is found in the 'Saga of Ólafr Tryggvason', written about 1190 by Oddr Snorrason, monk of Þingeyrar. Oddr wrote his saga in Latin, but it was translated into the vernacular language, probably early in the thirteenth century, and survives only in translation. One manuscript of the Norse version of this saga contains the following sentences:

This meeting is mentioned by Sæmundr, who was renowned for his wisdom, and this is what he said: 'In the second year of his rule Ólafr Tryggvason assembled many people and held a meeting at Staðr on Dragseið, and he did not desist from preaching the true faith to the people until they submitted to baptism. King Ólafr greatly put down plunder and theft and manslaughter, and he gave the people good laws and a good religion.' Thus did Sæmundr write about King Ólafr in his book.[1]

It has been shown that Oddr did not write these sentences in the Latin text of his book. Nevertheless, they were inserted into the Norse version at an early stage in its textual history,[2] and it is plain that the interpolator knew a book which he ascribed to Sæmundr. The reason why the interpolator inserted these two sentences has also been discerned. It was because he recognized that in this chapter, or rather in the preceding one, Oddr had quoted the first of the two sentences and had expanded the other without mention of Sæmundr. This shows that Oddr also knew Sæmundr's book. In an earlier passage, Oddr had quoted Sæmundr as an authority for the length of Earl Hákon's reign.[3]

The two interpolated sentences appear to be taken directly from Sæmundr's book, and they help to show what kind of a book it was. It was short and concise, but allowed greater scope for the author's personal judgement than an annalistic catalogue would do.

---

[1] Saga Ólafs Tryggvasonar (Oddr Snorrason), ed. Finnur Jónsson, 1932, p. 114; on Oddr see Ch. VII below.
[2] Cf. Bjarni Aðalbjarnarson, Om de norske kongers sagaer, 1937, pp. 33 ff.
[3] Saga Ólafs Tryggvasonar, p. 90.

Further light is thrown on the scope and form of Sæmundr's book by the poem *Nóregs Konunga Tal* (Succession of the Kings of Norway).[1] This was composed about the year 1190 in honour of Jón Loptsson (died 1197), a grandson of Sæmundr and owner of the family seat, Oddi. It had lately been made known that Þóra, the mother of Jón, was an illegitimate daughter of King Magnús Bareleg (died 1103), and the poem consists of eighty-three strophes in the metre *Kviðuháttr*, in which the history of the kings of Norway is summarized, and Jón's descent from them is demonstrated. The *Nóregs Konunga Tal* is devoid of embellishments and, indeed, of artistic merit, and the poet is content to enumerate the chief events associated with each king, often adding the manner of his death, the place where he was buried and the length of his reign. In strophe 40, after he had eulogized Magnús the Good, who died in 1047, the poet looked back and said:

Now I have told of ten rulers, each of whom was of Haraldr's House. I have related their lives, just as Sæmundr the Wise did.

A poet so closely associated with Jón Loptsson, and consequently with Oddi, must have had access to Sæmundr's history. The pause which the poet makes in his narrative in strophe 40 has led scholars to suppose that Sæmundr's history ended with the death of Magnús the Good in 1047.[2] It might also be suspected from the evidence of the *Nóregs Konunga Tal* that Sæmundr began his series of kings with Hálfdan the Black, father of Haraldr Finehair, but it cannot be said how much of Sæmundr's history was repeated in the *Nóregs Konunga Tal*, or how much the poet left out. The emphasis which the poet lays on the length of each king's reign suggests that Sæmundr's book was concerned largely with chronology, and this accords well with the little known of it from other sources. As I have already said, Ari and Oddr both allude to Sæmundr as an authority on problems of this kind.

Several other references to Sæmundr are found in later literature. One of the most interesting is in Sturla's version of the *Land-*

[1] See *Skjald*. B.I. 575 ff.
[2] Cf. Halldór Hermannsson, op. cit., p. 34; Bjarni Aðalbjarnarson, op. cit., p. 31.

*námabók* (Book of Settlements),[1] where Sæmundr is named as the
authority for the story of the discovery of Iceland by Naddoðr. This
passage was probably added by Sturla to an older version of the
*Landnámabók*,[2] and seems to show that Sturla, who died in 1284,
knew Sæmundr's book, and that it did not deal with the history of
the kings of Norway alone, but also contained a note on the discovery of Iceland during the reign of Haraldr Finehair.

It is recorded in certain versions of the Annals of Iceland that
the winter of 1047, the year when Magnús the Good died, was so
severe that wolves ran over the ice between Norway and Denmark,
and Sæmundr is quoted as the authority for this statement.[3] In a
version of the 'Saga of the Jómsvíkings', Sæmundr is named as the
authority for the tradition that the Jómsvíkings' fleet consisted of
sixty ships, all of tremendous size.[4] Since this allusion to Sæmundr
appears only in one version of the saga, and that a late one, little
importance can be attached to it. It is said in the *Kristni Saga*[5] that,
according to Sæmundr, so many people died in the year following
Bishop Gizurr's death (1118), that they cannot have numbered
fewer than those who attended the *Alþingi*. It is not known when
this last statement was first written, but it is not likely that it was
part of Sæmundr's book, for that book probably ended with the
year 1047. It may be derived from an oral statement of Sæmundr.

A number of instances in which Sæmundr's book appears to
have influenced later historians have been mentioned, but it must
be admitted, considering the great fame which Sæmundr enjoyed,
that the influence of his book was slight. Snorri does not mention
him at all, although he was brought up at Oddi by Jón Loptsson,
the grandson of Sæmundr. It is generally agreed that Sæmundr
wrote his book not in Icelandic, but in Latin, for Snorri in his Prologue to the *Ólafs Saga* and the *Heimskringla* says that Ari was the
first to write works of learning in the vernacular. It need hardly be
said that Icelandic historians of the thirteenth century showed a
marked preference for the vernacular. That is why the works of

---

[1] See *Landnámabók*, ed. Finnur Jónsson, 1900, p. 130.
[2] Cf. Jón Jóhannesson, *Gerðir Landnámabókar*, pp. 73–74.
[3] See *Islandske Annaler*, p. 108.
[4] See Bjarni Aðalbjarnarson, op. cit., p. 33.                    [5] Ch. xviii.

Oddr Snorrason and of Gunnlaugr Leifsson survive only in Icelandic, although they were first written in Latin. I have already suggested that Sæmundr's book was concerned largely with chronology, and this probably implies that he assembled traditions preserved orally in Iceland and arranged them in chronological sequence. The poet of the *Nóregs Konunga Tal* evidently based his account of the kings who ruled before Magnús on Sæmundr's book, and his chronological system down to 1047 must represent that of Sæmundr. It is interesting to see how widely this system differs from those followed by other medieval historians, such as Theodoricus, the authors of the *Historia Norvegiae* and the *Ágrip*, Snorri and probably Ari. For instance, it is said in the *Nóregs Konunga Tal* that Haraldr Greycloak ruled for nine years, whereas he ruled for fourteen years according to the *Historia Norvegiae*, and for fifteen according to Snorri.

The only history which agrees closely with the *Nóregs Konunga Tal* on points of chronology is the *Fagrskinna*.[1] Moreover, when the author of this book comes to Magnús the Good, he pauses and reflects, just as the author of the *Nóregs Konunga Tal* did in strophe 40. It would be hard to believe that an historian so learned as the author of the *Fagrskinna* would base his chronology on a poem of such recent date and so little significance as the *Nóregs Konunga Tal*. It is, therefore, probable that he and the poet followed a common source, and that this source was Sæmundr's book.

Sæmundr is occasionally quoted in Icelandic literature as the authority for assertions not immediately related to the history of Norway or of Iceland. In a short history of the world, preserved in a manuscript of the fourteenth century,[2] he is quoted as the source of the following description of Adam:

He was sixty (feet?) tall, according to the account of Sæmundr; in bodily form he was made after the likeness of God himself, having 248 bones and 360 veins.

This passage may suggest that Sæmundr's history began with the creation of the world and of the first man, just as Florence of

---

[1] Cf. G. Indrebø, *Fagrskinna*, 1917, pp. 43 ff.
[2] See *Diplomatarium Islandicum*, i. 503.

Worcester's English chronicle did. This suggestion might be supported by the following sentence, found in a chronological-astronomical tract, in which material of great antiquity is preserved:

At the beginning of the world, said Sæmundr the priest, the sun, newly fashioned, rose up due east, and a full moon rose in the evening.[1]

This last passage may also be associated with the tradition that Sæmundr studied astronomy while he was abroad, and became so skilled in it that he surpassed the famous master who taught him.[2] The sciences astronomy and chronology were scarcely distinguished in the Middle Ages, for the one was based upon the other. During the period when Sæmundr was studying, these subjects were pursued with great ardour in Europe, and especially in France. The established system of dating and chronology was being attacked by such men as Gerland (*circa* 1080), Marianus Scotus, and Roger of Hereford.[3] It is not unlikely that Sæmundr turned his attention to this controversy while he was abroad.

[1] *Alfræði íslenzk*, ii, ed. N. Beckman and Kr. Kålund, 1914–16, p. 91.
[2] See *Biskupa Sögur*, i. 156–7, 227–9.
[3] Cf. C. H. Haskins, *Studies in the History of Medieval Science*, 1927, pp. 82 ff.

# IV

## ARI AND HIS INFLUENCE

SNORRI STURLUSON says, in the Prologue to the 'Saga of S. Ólafr' and the *Heimskringla*, that the first Icelander who wrote works of learning in his own language was the priest Ari Þorgilsson. Modern scholars commonly call Ari the father of Icelandic history, for he was the first author of narrative prose in Icelandic, and remained one of the strongest influences on the literature throughout the Middle Ages.

Little is known about Ari's life, although his family tree and kinship with the leading chiefs of his day are recorded in detail. He was born in 1067 or 1068, and spent the first seven years of his life at Helgafell on the Breiðafjǫrðr. Helgafell is among the most famous houses in the history both of pagan and of Christian Iceland. The Holy Hill, from which it takes its name, had been sacred to the pagan Icelanders. Neither man nor beast might look at it unwashed, and some believed that they would go to live in it after death.

At the beginning of the eleventh century the owner of Helgafell was Snorri goði, whose character is described in many sagas, and especially in the *Eyrbyggja Saga*, the *Laxdæla*, and the *Heiðarvíga Saga*. He was foremost among his contemporaries in wisdom and cunning, if not in valour, and was the friend and counsellor of Guðrún, heroine of the *Laxdæla Saga*. It was because of this friendship that the estate of Helgafell passed into Ari's family. Guðrún persuaded Snorri to exchange houses with her about the year 1008. Her fourth and last husband was Þorkell Eyjólfsson. Þorkell and Guðrún were the great-grandparents of Ari.

Ari's interest in antiquity, and especially in the history of pre-Christian Iceland, might have awakened already in his first years at Helgafell. His career is known chiefly from his own work, or else from work which is derived from his. His father, Þorgils, was drowned in the Breiðafjǫrðr while still a young man. It seems that, on the death of his father, Ari was taken in charge by his grandfather, Gellir. In his old age, Gellir made a pilgrimage to Rome, but he died at Roskilde on his way back in 1073. After Gellir's death the estate of Helgafell passed to his son Þorkell, the uncle of Ari. Ari, now seven years old, was sent to live with Hallr Þórarinsson, at Haukadalr, in the south of Iceland.

Ari remained at Haukadalr for fourteen years, and it is there that the chief influences on his mind and work should be sought. Hallr, the owner of Haukadalr, was nearly eighty years old by the time Ari came to live with him. His character may be pieced together from Ari's words, and from some remarks which Snorri makes in the Prologue already cited. Hallr was not 'learned'; he could not read or write, but he was very wise, and gifted with a remarkable memory. He could remember the day when he was baptized at the age of three by the German missionary Þangbrandr (998). As a young man Hallr had entered the service of King Ólafr the Saint (died 1030), and had travelled extensively abroad. Snorri alludes to him as an authority on S. Ólafr's reign, and according to Ari's testimony he was renowned for good deeds no less than for wisdom. He died in 1089 at the age of ninety-four. Ari probably learnt more from Hallr than from any other about the history of ancient Iceland and Norway. He was one of the main channels through which tradition flowed from ancient to medieval Iceland.

Another man who exercised influence on Ari during early years was Teitr (died 1110), son of Bishop Ísleifr and brother of Bishop Gizurr. Teitr had also been brought up by Hallr, and he lived at Haukadalr in adult years, where he used to instruct young clerks. Ari was one of his pupils. Little is known about Teitr's own education or early life but, as already noted, his father, Ísleifr, and his brother, Gizurr, were both educated at Herford, in Westphalia. Teitr was himself a priest, and it must largely have been a European education which Ari acquired from him, although he remembers him also as an authority on the history of Iceland.

Ari mentions many other wise people from whom he derived his immense knowledge of history. They included his uncle,

Þorkell, from whom he learnt about Greenland and Wineland, and Þuríðr, the daughter of Snorri goði, who died in 1112 at the age of eighty-eight. The Law-speaker and poet Markús Skeggjason (died 1107) was also one of Ari's informants, and gave him a complete list of Law-speakers from the time when the *Alþingi* was founded, about the year 930, to his own time. It was perhaps a part of Markús's duty as Law-speaker to know this list by heart, just as he had to know the laws. By giving the names of those from whom he learnt his history, Ari helps his reader to estimate its value, and shows how traditions could be preserved among an illiterate, though civilized, people for a period of 200 years or more.

Practically nothing is known about Ari's later life. As the grandson of Gellir he could have inherited a *goðorð* with magisterial privileges and duties, but there is nothing to suggest that he took an active part in public affairs. He was ordained priest, presumably by Bishop Gizurr, and his name is included in the *Kristni Saga* in a short list of ordained noblemen who lived in Gizurr's time. Ari had a son called Þorgils, named in a list of nobly born clerics drawn up in 1143, probably by Ari himself.[1] The date of Ari's death is given in the Annals as 1148.

The only surviving work which may certainly be ascribed to Ari is the *Libellus Islandorum*, often called *Íslendingabók*, and known in English as the 'Book of the Icelanders'.[2] This is a slim volume covering about ten pages of printed text. Its great age gives it inestimable value as a source of history, and it is no less precious as a literary monument, for it is the oldest example of narrative prose in a Scandinavian language.

The *Libellus* is not preserved in an early manuscript, but only in two transcripts made by a certain Jón Erlendsson in the seventeenth century. These transcripts were copied directly from a codex of the twelfth century. A modern scholar, Björn Sigfússon,[3] has shown

[1] Printed in *Diplomatarium Islandicum*, i, 1857-76, pp. 180-94.
[2] The best edition of the 'Book of the Icelanders' is undoubtedly that of Halldór Hermannsson, 1930. There are many others, of which a list is given by Halldór Hermannsson, *Islandica*, i, 1908, pp. 56 ff. and xxiv, 1935, pp. 49 ff.
[3] *Um Íslendingabók*, 1944, ch. ii.

that the seventeenth-century scribe followed his original carefully and accurately. This scholar's arguments also suggest that the lost codex represented Ari's work faithfully, although it was not his autograph. Therefore, despite adverse fortune, the text of the *Libellus* remains whole and, for the most part, uncorrupt.

The *Libellus* was probably planned as a summary of the history of Iceland, but Ari selected his material so arbitrarily and treated it so disproportionately, that some modern readers have regarded it merely as a collection of notes about the history of Iceland.[1] Ari tells us the name of the first settler, Ingólfr, but says nothing about the discovery of the island and the first exploratory visits of Flóki and others. He writes a few words about the foundation of the *Alþingi*, but his account of it crumbles into details which seem irrelevant. In the sixth chapter Ari interrupts his history of Iceland, and inserts some sentences about the discovery and settlement of Greenland.

It is not until the later chapters of the *Libellus* that Ari shows that he is a gifted narrator, although untrained. In chapter vii he describes the Conversion of the Icelanders to Christianity. He tells how King Ólafr Tryggvason sent the overbearing German priest, Þangbrandr, to convert the Icelanders, and how Þangbrandr slew the Icelandic poets who satirized him.

The scene at the *Alþingi* in the year 1000, when the pagans and Christians quarrelled, is well described. Ari tells how the rival parties outlawed each other, and came to the point of battle. Their tempers were finally assuaged by the wise Law-speaker Þorgeirr, whom both parties trusted to decide the issue. Þorgeirr lay in his tent for a day and a night, his head covered with a cloak. Thus isolated from the rabble he sought a decision acceptable to both parties. He resolved that all should be baptized and be Christians in name, but made concessions to the pagans, who had the right to observe their established practices, so long as they did so in private.[2] Ari tells this story with admirable objectivity. Although he was a

---

[1] See A. Heusler, *Arkiv för nordisk filologi*, xxiii, 1907, pp. 320–37; cf. H. Schneider, *Zeitschrift für deutsches Altertum*, lxvi, 1929, pp. 69–92.
[2] See above, Ch. II.

Christian and a cleric, he rarely showed partiality towards the Christian party.

It is plain that Ari regarded the Conversion as the most important event in the history of Iceland, and thought that it deserved to be treated in greater detail than the rest. Moreover, he knew more about the Christian than about the pagan period of Icelandic history. It is partly for this reason that he treats later events with greater precision than earlier ones.

Valuable as it is, the *Libellus* does not account for the great fame which Ari enjoyed among the scholars and saga-writers of the later Middle Ages. Snorri says of him: 'I think his history altogether remarkable.' Ari's name crops up in the histories of Oddr and of Gunnlaugr, in the *Laxdœla* and in the *Eyrbyggja Saga*, and in numerous works of the late twelfth and thirteenth centuries. He is always quoted as an outstanding authority, both on the history of the kings of Norway and on that of the Icelanders.

It is partly because they find the *Libellus* insufficient to account for Ari's reputation that most modern scholars believe that he wrote other and more important works than the *Libellus*. But these scholars do not agree what these works were, nor at what period of his life Ari wrote them.

Ari himself says something about his other work in his Prologue to the *Libellus*. In this Prologue he tells much about his career as an author, but it is difficult to understand, and has been the subject of much learned argument. Some measure of agreement has now been reached, and most, though by no means all, would agree with the rendering which I give below:

I made the *Íslendingabók* (Book of the Icelanders) first for our bishops Þorlákr and Ketill, and I showed it both to them and to the priest Sæmundr; and accordingly as they were satisfied with it as it was, or else wished to add to it, I wrote this book on the same subject (*or* in the same way), excluding the genealogical list and the histories of the kings, and I added that which later became better known to me, and is now told more fully in this book than it was in that. . . .

Ari says here that he wrote the *Íslendingabók* first for the bishops Þorlákr and Ketill. *Íslendingabók* (Book of the Icelanders) is, therefore, strictly the name of a book written earlier than the existing one. This book is lost. The text of the existing book is introduced with the words: *incipit Libellus Islandorum*. This, in itself, need not imply that the first book was bigger than the second, or that the second book was called *Libellus* because it was an abridged edition of the first. Nevertheless, the distinction between *Liber* for the first book and *Libellus* for the second is convenient and, in some ways, enlightening.

The *Libellus* dealt with the same subject as the *Liber*. But Ari had included a genealogical list and some histories of kings in the *Liber*, which he did not repeat in the *Libellus*. But some subjects were treated more fully in the *Libellus* than they had been in the *Liber*. Therefore the revision consisted of additions as well as of omissions.

Ari also shows in his Prologue that he wrote the first book while Þorlákr (the Elder) was Bishop of Skálaholt and Ketill Bishop of Hólar, i.e. between 1122, when Ketill was made Bishop, and 1133, when Þorlákr died. It may also be inferred from the Prologue that Ari undertook to revise the *Liber* and to make the *Libellus* before 1133. There is strong internal evidence in the text of the *Libellus* which supports the conclusion that both books were written between 1122 and 1133. Ari was fifty-five years old in 1122.

Snorri Sturluson, in his Prologue to the *Ólafs Saga* and the *Heimskringla*,[1] throws further light on the lost *Liber*. In this passage Snorri describes a book by Ari which he had used as a source for his history. The book which Snorri describes cannot be the *Libellus*, for it contained material not to be found there. But yet the arrangement of the book to which Snorri alludes, and its contents, resembled those of the *Libellus* so closely that it can only be another and in some ways a fuller version of the *Libellus*. At the beginning of the book of which Snorri speaks, Ari wrote mostly about the settlement of Iceland, and about the early laws. He dealt next with the Law-speakers, saying how long each of them had held office. To this Ari added many stories illustrating the lives

---

[1] *Saga Ólafs Konungs hins helga*, ed. O. A. Johnsen and Jón Helgason, i, 1941, pp. 1–5; *Heimskringla*, ed. Bjarni Aðalbjarnarson, i, 1941, pp. 5–7.

of kings in Norway, Denmark, and England, and he told of great events in the history of Iceland.

Although many details in Snorri's Prologue are obscure, it is plain that he is describing a version of the *Íslendingabók* in which the lives of the kings were present. This book can be no other than the lost *Liber Islandorum*.

To judge by Snorri's description, the *Liber* was rather larger than the *Libellus*, but in composition the two were much alike; they were, to use Ari's phrase, *of et sama far*. I have already suggested that Ari introduced some material into the *Libellus* which was not in the *Liber*, but from Snorri's description we learn chiefly about passages which were in the *Liber* but were omitted from the *Libellus*.

In the *Liber* Ari had written considerably more about his oral informants, and about those who instructed him in history, than he did in the *Libellus*. Ari had learnt about the kings of Norway chiefly from Oddr Kolsson, who was probably born early in the eleventh century. Oddr in his turn had learnt from Þorgeirr Afráðskollr, who was so old that he was in Niðarnes in Norway when Hákon the Great was killed in the year 995. Ari's chief informant about S. Ólafr's reign was Hallr of Haukadalr, who was mentioned above. It is evident from Snorri's Prologue that Ari had written much more about Hallr in the *Liber* than he did in the *Libellus*. He also wrote more about several other informants, about Teitr and about Þuríðr, the daughter of Snorri goði.

Snorri does not allude to the Genealogical List (*Ættartala*) which Ari implies that he had written in the *Liber*, but excluded from the *Libellus*. But since Snorri was introducing his work about the kings of Norway, and especially about S. Ólafr, when he wrote this Prologue, Ari's list of Icelandic genealogies would not have concerned him deeply.

In this Prologue, Snorri speaks of Ari's 'book' in the singular (*sinnar bókar*), and seems to refer only to the *Liber*. But this does not necessarily imply that Ari did not write other books besides the *Liber* and the *Libellus*, nor even that Snorri did not know them.

The question whether Ari wrote other books besides the *Liber* and the *Libellus* has long been debated, and so much in the history of Icelandic literature depends on the answer given to it that it must be considered, at least briefly.

The scholars who discussed this question most thoroughly were the Icelander B. M. Ólsen and the German K. Maurer, whose chief works on the subject were published between 1870 and 1900.[1] In fact, Ólsen and Maurer agreed on most major points, although this has not always been recognized by those who have claimed to follow the one or the other.

Icelandic authors of the twelfth and thirteenth centuries often show the influence of Ari. They not infrequently cite him as the authority for their statements about history, using such expressions as: 'This is what Ari the Wise says', or 'this is found in the history of Ari the Wise'. These references appear both in sagas about kings of Norway and in those about heroes of Iceland.

In some instances it is plain that the authors are merely quoting the existing *Libellus*. In nearly every case the manuscripts of the *Libellus* preserve the text in an older form than do the works of later authors who made abstracts from it. Therefore, instances of this kind need not be discussed here.

But the allusions to Ari are so frequent that it is evident that authors, both of Kings' sagas and of sagas and histories of Icelanders, owe a great part of their learning to him. Not all of this learning can be traced to the *Libellus*, and it remains to be seen whether it was contained in the *Liber*.

When the authors of Kings' sagas cite Ari as their authority, they do so mainly, although not exclusively, on points of chronology. Thus, it was Ari who first recorded the age of Ólafr Tryggvason when he came to Norway. The length of S. Ólaf's reign and

[1] The earlier views on Ari's work were conveniently summarized by K. Maurer, *Germania*, xv, 1870, pp. 302 ff. Later views are summarized by Halldór Hermannsson, 'The Book of the Icelanders', Introductory Essay, pp. 25 ff. Important papers by Maurer were published in *Germania*, xxxvi, 1891, pp. 61 ff., and in his *Über die Ausdrücke: altnordische, altnorwegische und altisländische Sprache*, 1867, pp. 57 ff. Important papers by B. M. Ólsen include those in *Aarbøger for nordisk Oldkyndighed og Historie*, 1885, pp. 341–71, and 1893, pp. 207–352, and in *Tímarit hins íslenzka bókmenntafélags*, x, 1889, pp. 214–40. See further Halldór Hermannsson, *Islandica*, i, 1908, p. 60.

his age when he died are also known on the authority of Ari. The monk Gunnlaugr (died 1218), who wrote a life of Ólafr Tryggvason, said that he had gathered his material largely from the 'books' of Ari.[1]

The authors of sagas of Icelanders and of works on Icelandic history also refer frequently to Ari. They regard him as an authority especially on genealogy, although they also quote him as the authority for several isolated events in the history of the Icelanders. It is said in the *Njáls Saga* (ch. cxiv) that, according to Ari, the settler of the Breiðafjǫrðr, Þórólfr, was son of Þorgils Whale-side. In the *Eyrbyggja Saga* (ch. vii) it is said that this same Þórólfr married in later life, and that his wife was called Unnr. The *Eyrbyggja Saga* adds that some say that Unnr was a daughter of Þorsteinn the Red, but that Ari does not count her among his children. The *Laxdœla Saga* (ch. iv) credits Ari with the story of Þorsteinn the Red's death on Caithness, and the same saga (ch. lxxviii) cites Ari as the authority for the date of Snorri goði's death. Similarly, according to a version of the *Landnámabók*[2] (Book of Settlements), it was Ari who recorded how many ships sailed from Iceland to Greenland in the year 984.

Besides those passages in which Ari is named as an authority there are a number of others which appear to be derived from works by Ari, although he himself is not named. In such passages, reference is sometimes made to one of those older men whom Ari mentions among his teachers and informants. Thus, in the *Landnámabók*, mention is made of a mythical land, called the Land of White Men (*Hvítra manna land*) or alternatively Ireland the Great (*Íraland hit mikla*). This land was said to lie in the Atlantic Ocean, three days west of Ireland. Ari Másson, great-great-grandfather of Ari the Wise, had been driven by the sea to this Land of White Men, and could not get away. The authority for this story was said to be Þorkell, uncle of Ari the Wise.[3] Ari several times quoted Þorkell among his authorities in the *Libellus*. If Þorkell told

---

[1] See *Saga Ólafs Tryggvasonar* (Oddr Snorrason), ed. Finnur Jónsson, 1932, pp. 88–89; *Heimskringla*, ii, ed. Bjarni Aðalbjarnarson, 1945, pp. 326 and 410; *Flateyjarbók*, ed. G. Vigfússon and C. R. Unger, i, 1860, p. 511.

[2] Ed. Finnur Jónsson, 1900, p. 35.          [3] Ibid., pp. 41 and 165.

the story of White Men's Land, it was probably Ari who first wrote it.

Similarly, it is told in the *Landnámabók*[1] how a certain Ketilbjǫrn Ketilsson settled in a district of southern Iceland. This story is also told in the *Sturlunga Saga*[2] in nearly the same words, but in this text Ari's tutor, Teitr, is cited as the authority for it. It will be helpful to quote a part of this passage as it is written in the *Sturlunga Saga*:

Ketilbjǫrn Ketilsson, a famous Norseman, came to Iceland after the coastal districts had mostly been populated. His mother was called Æsa, daughter of Grjótgarðr, and she was the sister of Hákon, Earl of Hlaðir. Ketilbjǫrn married Helga, daughter of Þórðr Skeggi, son of Hrappr, and Ketilbjǫrn stayed with Þórðr below Bláskógaheiðr during his first winter in Iceland. And in the following spring he went up the moor to look for land. This is what Teitr said. And in the place where they sheltered for the night they built a shed, and so they called that place 'Shed Slope'. They had not gone far from there before they came upon a frozen river, and they cut a hole in the ice and dropped their axe through it, and because of this they called the river Axe River. This river was afterwards directed into the Almannagjá, and now it flows through Þingvǫllr. They went on to the place which is now called Salmon Hill. There they left behind some salmon which they were carrying, and that is why they called it Salmon Hill. Ketilbjǫrn established his farm below Mosfell, and took possession of the surrounding land, as far as he wished.

The reference to Teitr shows that the author of this part of the *Sturlunga Saga* (i.e. the *Haukdœla Þáttr*) did not derive the passage from any of the existing versions of the *Landnámabók*, for Teitr is not quoted in any of them. It is altogether improbable that the compilers of the *Landnámabók* borrowed the passage from the *Sturlunga Saga*. It is in a style typical of the *Landnámabók* and bears little resemblance to the rest of the *Sturlunga Saga*. Whatever the immediate source, the ultimate source can hardly be other than a work of Ari. The thoughtless way in which the compiler of the *Sturlunga* writes: 'this is what Teitr said', without explaining who Teitr was, suggests that he is following his source closely, even

[1] Ibid., pp. 120–1 and 228.
[2] Ed. Jón Jóhannesson and others, i, 1946, p. 57.

slavishly. Although Teitr is not quoted in the existing versions of the *Landnámabók*, their texts differ only trivially from that of the *Sturlunga*.[1] This suggests that they also follow their source closely. It cannot yet be said whether the immediate source for the *Sturlunga Saga* and the *Landnámabók* was a work by Ari, or whether it was a later one, derived from a work by Ari.

If the *Liber* contained all the material which we have to assign to Ari, we must picture it as an imposing volume, quite unlike the *Libellus*. It would consist, perhaps, of a hundred pages of printed text. It must have included numerous details about the histories of Scandinavian and English kings. Its author must have described some of the settlements of Iceland in much detail, stating precisely where the settlers lived, and what were the limits of their territory. The ancestors and descendants of the settlers would also be named in many cases. The story of Ketilbjǫrn quoted above might be taken as a specimen of the section of the *Liber* in which the settlement of Iceland was described. In addition, the *Liber* must have contained a notice about the Land of White Men, and an account of Greenland and of Wineland which was much more detailed than that in the *Libellus*. K. Maurer was among those who believed that the *Liber* was a book of this kind. He expounded this view more thoroughly and defended it more ably than any later scholar has done. Its implications should be considered in the light both of Ari's allusions to the *Liber* in his Prologue to the *Libellus*, and in the light of Snorri's description of the *Liber* in his Prologue to the *Ólafs Saga* and the *Heimskringla*.

Ari says that, when he wrote the *Libellus*, he excluded some *Konunga ævi*, which he had written in the *Liber*. Snorri, describing the *Liber*, shows that, while it was much like the *Libellus* in form, it differed from it in recording many events in the lives of kings in Norway, Denmark, and England.

The precise meaning of Ari's expression *Konunga ævi* is hard to determine. In itself, it might mean nothing more than chronological notes, giving sequences and dates of kings' reigns. The expression *ævi allra lǫgsǫgumanna*, as Ari uses it in the *Libellus* (ch.

---

[1] Cf. Björn Sigfússon, op. cit., pp. 65 ff.

x), means a list of Law-speakers with chronological notes. Alternatively, the term *konunga ævi* might be applied to a book, or part of one, which included details about the lives of kings besides the purely chronological ones. If we are satisfied that Snorri was describing the *Liber* in his Prologue, it seems that Ari must have used the term *konunga ævi* in this latter sense.

It is thus possible to conclude that all Ari's work about the lives of foreign kings was contained in the lost *Liber*. A specimen of the *konunga ævi* of the *Liber* is perhaps preserved in the following passage, which is appended to the manuscripts of the *Libellus*, but is not part of its text:

Hálfdan White-bone, King of the Upplanders, son of Ólafr Woodcutter, King of the Swedes, was the father of Eysteinn 'fret', father of Hálfdan the generous but niggardly of food, father of Guðrøðr the Huntsman King, father of Hálfdan the Black, father of Haraldr Fine-Hair, who was the first of this tribe to be king of all Norway.[1]

It is, of course, likely that Ari treated some of the kings in greater detail than those mentioned in this passage, for otherwise his book would not have been so valuable as Snorri says that it was.

A. Gjessing,[2] B. M. Ólsen and some other scholars believed that Ari wrote a separate book of Kings' Lives. References to Ari found in the existing Kings' sagas were mainly to be traced to that book. This theory has been revived in a rather different form by J. Schreiner,[3] but few have accepted his arguments. In fact, it is quite possible that Ari wrote a separate work on the kings, and perhaps even probable, but there is nothing which compels us to believe it. It is consistent with the facts known to believe that Ari's work on the kings was all included in the *Liber Islandorum*.

The *Konunga ævi* may have formed a separate section of the *Liber*. But it seems more likely that these notices of kings were strewn through the book, and related chronologically to the history of the Icelanders. Remnants of the *Konunga ævi* can perhaps be found in the *Libellus*, e.g. in chapter vii of that book, where Ari

[1] Edition quoted, p. 57.
[2] *Undersögelser om Kongesagaens Fremvæxt*, i–ii, 1873–6.
[3] *Tradisjon og saga om Olav den Hellige*, 1926. Schreiner's view is criticized by Bjarni Aðalbjarnarson, *Om de norske Kongers Sagaer*, 1937, pp. 177 ff.

gives a number of details about the career of Ólafr Tryggvason, and especially about his part in the conversion of the Icelanders. If this passage is a remnant of the *Konunga ævi*, we might expect that it was fuller in the *Liber* than it is in the *Libellus*. There are some indications that this was the case. The same story of King Ólafr's efforts to convert the Icelanders is told by the monk Oddr Snorrason, in his saga of Ólafr Tryggvason, which was probably written late in the twelfth century. Oddr's story is fuller than that of the *Libellus*, and he records certain incidents and several names which are not in the *Libellus*. In the only manuscript of Oddr's *Ólafs Saga* written in Iceland, the source for this story is named as *Íslendingabók*.[1] It seems that this must have been the lost *Liber* rather than the existing *Libellus*.

I have already mentioned several other passages in later literature, which must be derived from Ari, but cannot be included under the designation *Konunga ævi*. It should first be considered whether they could be traced to any part of the lost *Liber*.

Ari says in his Prologue that, besides the *Konunga ævi*, he wrote an *ættartala* in the *Liber*, but left it out of the *Libellus*. There is nothing to suggest that Ari excluded from the *Libellus* any material which he had written in the *Liber* other than that covered by the terms *ættartala* and *Konunga ævi*. In subsequent sentences of his Prologue, Ari speaks only of matter not in the *Liber*, which he had added to the *Libellus*.

If we accept Maurer's conclusion that Ari wrote nothing but the *Liber* and the *Libellus*, we have also to conclude that everything which later authors derived from Ari must have been included in the *ættartala*, unless it was a part of the *Konunga ævi* or of the existing *Libellus*.

If this be so, the *ættartala* must have been the largest and most important section of the *Liber*. Nearly everything that Ari wrote about the history of the Icelanders was contained in it, except for the little which still survives in the *Libellus*, and we must suppose that the lost *Liber* was dominated by this *ættartala*. It contained not only names and dates, but also many details about the lives of the

[1] Ed. Finnur Jónsson, p. 127.

settlers and about their descendants. The story of Ketilbjǫrn, already quoted, might be regarded as a specimen of it. In this case, the *ættartala* might be regarded as an early version of the *Land-námabók*, even though smaller than the existing versions of that book. Maurer, in fact believed that the *ættartala* of the *Liber* was the basis of the existing *Landnámabók*.

Many objections could be raised against this conclusion. The first is to be found in the meaning of the term *ættartala*. Formally it means 'genealogical list' (cf. *tala* 'counting, number', *telja* 'to count'). The term is used in an appendix to the *Libellus* and, in that passage, it means 'genealogical list' and no more. It is questionable whether a story like that of Ketilbjǫrn could be covered by such a term as *ættartala*. To say the least, it would be a strain on this term. It is even more improbable that passages like those about Greenland, Wineland, and the Land of White Men could be part of the *ættartala*.

A second objection to Maurer's conclusion may be found in Ari's Prologue to the *Libellus*. Ari says that both the *Liber* and the *Libellus* were written *of et sama far*. This may mean 'in the same way', or it may mean 'about the same subject', but neither of these meanings would be suitable if the *Liber* and the *Libellus* were as dissimilar as Maurer's theory implies.

A third objection against Maurer's conclusion may be seen in Snorri's Prologue, which was mentioned above. Snorri, describing the *Liber*, has much to say about the histories of the kings contained in it, making it clear that they formed an important part of the lost book. But Snorri says nothing at all about the *ættartala*, which was evidently a part of it. According to Maurer's theory, the *ættartala* was the largest and most influential section of the whole *Liber*, and Snorri could hardly fail to mention it in his description, even though he was interested primarily in the kings of Norway.

It was said that the word *ættartala* (*áttartala*) was used in an appendix to the manuscripts of the *Libellus*. It is there applied to a collection of genealogical lists showing the descent of five Icelandic bishops. Internal evidence suggests that this *ættartala* was not written later than 1133, and it is probably Ari's work. In this case it is most probably an excerpt from the *ættartala* of the lost *Liber*. One section of it is concerned with the descendants of Ketilbjǫrn, who is familiar from quotations already made. This section may be rendered:

The settler Ketilbjǫrn, who established his house in the south, at Upper Mosfell, was the father of Teitr, father of Gizurr the White, father of Ísleifr, who was the first Bishop of Skálaholt and was father of Bishop Gizurr.[1]

This passage may perhaps be regarded as a specimen of the *ættartala* of the *Liber*.

If the arguments outlined above are admitted, it can hardly be doubted that Ari wrote a work or works other than the *Liber* and *Libellus*. There is also external evidence which supports this conclusion. As I have already said, the monk Gunnlaugr claimed that his history was based largely on the 'books' of Ari. The author of the 'Grammatical Treatise', a work on spelling and grammar, probably written about 1170, alludes once to the various branches of literature which, up to his time, had been written in Icelandic. These branches of literature include: 'those works of learning, which Ari Þorgilsson had put into his books, with his keen wisdom'.[2] The use of the plural 'books' (*bœkr*) would be surprising if the author were referring only to the *Liber* and the *Libellus*, most especially if these were merely two editions of one book, as Ari's Prologue and Snorri's Prologue both seem to show that they were. The great age of the 'Grammatical Treatise' enhances the value of its evidence. Snorri also speaks once of Ari's 'books', which may suggest that he knew a book or books by Ari other than the *Liber* and the *Libellus*.[3]

When later authors speak of Ari's 'books' they may refer to the *Liber* (or *Libellus*) and to a separate work on the kings of Norway which, as was said, Ari may have written. It is at least equally possible that they refer to another book by Ari.

Ever since the seventeenth century, when modern methods were first applied to the study of Icelandic literature, some scholars have

---

[1] Edition quoted, p. 58.
[2] *Islands grammatiske Litteratur*, i–ii, ed. V. Dahlerup and Finnur Jónsson, 1886, p. 2.        [3] *Heimskringla*, ii, p. 326.

believed that Ari was the author of the *Landnámabók* (Book of Settlements). The reasons for this belief have not always been clear. It was not until the latter decades of the nineteenth century that B. M. Ólsen[1] expounded this theory in a scientific and logical manner, while engaged in controversy with Maurer. Ólsen was discursive and sometimes erratic in his judgements, and this may explain why his work had, at first, less influence than it deserved.

No one who has seriously studied this question has doubted that Ari's work was a very important influence on the *Landnámabók*, or even that the compilers of the *Landnámabók* incorporated much material which was first written by Ari. Maurer accepted this view, and he supposed that the material which the compilers of the *Landnámabók* derived from Ari was mostly contained in the *ættartala* of the *Liber*. He would perhaps have said that the *ættartala* was a short *Landnámabók*. I have already explained why I consider this improbable.

The *Landnámabók* exists today in five versions, dating variously from the thirteenth to the seventeenth centuries. The mutual relationship of these five versions is still largely obscure, and it hardly began to be clarified until the publication of Jón Jóhannesson's *Gerðir Landnámabókar* in 1941. This is one of the most important studies of Icelandic textual history published during the present century. We learn from it that the five extant versions of the *Landnámabók* are all derived from a lost version which was made by the Prior Styrmir the Wise, who died in 1245, about a century later than Ari died. This version is called *Styrmisbók*.

Comparison between the existing versions of the *Landnámabók* gives us a picture of the *Styrmisbók* although, for the present, this is rather a hazy one. It was probably written in the third decade of the thirteenth century. It proceeded clockwise round the map of Iceland, describing the original settlements in some detail, recording the names of the settlers and of many of their descendants. It would be hard to believe that Styrmir compiled this book

---

[1] See works quoted in note on p. 95 above, also paper in *Aarbøger for nordisk Oldkyndighed og Historie*, 1920, pp. 283–300, and others listed by Halldór Hermannsson, *Islandica*, i. 73–74 and xxiv. 56.

exclusively from oral stories about the settlement. Most of these must either have been dead or hopelessly corrupt by the time he wrote. He must have relied largely on earlier writings.

One of the later redactions of the *Landnámabók* is contained in the vast compilation *Hauksbók*, made by a certain Haukr Erlendsson, who died in 1334. In a postscript to his redaction of the *Landnámabók*, Haukr gives some ideas, not only of his own, but also of Styrmir's sources. Haukr writes:

Now the account of the settlements of Iceland is completed, according to what wise men have written, first the priest Ari Þorgilsson the wise, and Kolskeggr the wise (*vitri*). But I, Haukr Erlendsson, wrote this book, following the book which was written by Herra Sturla the Lawman (*lǫgmaðr*), a most learned man, and also that other book, written by Styrmir the Wise. . . .[1]

Haukr here tells us that Ari and Kolskeggr both wrote about the settlement of Iceland. He does not assert that either or both of them wrote the *Landnámabók*. Nevertheless, there is some further evidence which suggests that, between them, Ari and Kolskeggr did write such a book.

The author of the *Laxdœla Saga*, writing about the middle of the thirteenth century, derived a lot of genealogies and notices about early Icelandic history from a book which closely resembled the *Landnámabók*, although this cannot have been one of the extant redactions of that book. It was shorter, poorer, and certainly older than the existing versions, as was demonstrated by B. M. Ólsen.[2] Jón Jóhannesson[3] has since shown that the *Landnámabók*, which the author of the *Laxdœla Saga* followed, was not the same as *Styrmisbók*. The only authority for ancient history named by the author of the *Laxdœla Saga* was Ari. But the reference to Ari is made in such a way that it cannot be said with certainty whether Ari is the chief authority for the ancient history contained in the *Laxdœla*, or only a subsidiary one. If he regarded Ari as his chief authority, and this is the more probable interpretation of the text, it can be said that the author of the *Laxdœla* possessed an early

[1] Edition quoted, p. 124.  [2] *Aarbøger*, 1908, pp. 151 ff.
[3] Op. cit., esp. pp. 213 ff.

redaction of the *Landnámabók*, and that he thought it was Ari's work.

B. M. Ólsen, in his detailed study of the *Laxdœla Saga*, and Jón Jóhannesson, in his work on the *Landnámabók*, have brought to light many details about the version of the *Landnámabók* which the author of the *Laxdœla Saga* used. It is not certain that it covered all districts of Iceland, although it probably did, for areas as far apart as Vestur-Skaptafellssýsla and Vestfirðir were mentioned in it.

Evidence which supports the suggestion that Ari was an author of the first version of the *Landnámabók* may also be gathered from other sagas about Icelanders, e.g. from the *Eyrbyggja Saga* and the *Njáls Saga*, but none of this evidence carries so much weight as that derived from the *Laxdœla Saga*.

A theory which has been gaining ground in recent years is that Ari did not compile a *Landnámabók* or even part of one. Instead of this, some scholars believe, Ari wrote numerous short notices (*schedulae*), which he left unattached and unordered. Most of the learning which later authors derived from Ari was preserved in these formless notes.[1]

This theory contributes much to the understanding of the problem. Like many other medieval writers, the author of the first *Landnámabók* must have begun his work on *schedulae* or slips. No one could attempt to compile such a work without using this method. But it is scarcely credible that the compiler of the first version of the *Landnámabók* based his history and modelled his style on the unordered slips of an earlier author, whose work had been left unpublished, and had no apparent purpose. This is not to deny that *schedulae*, which Ari had not used for his major works, might have survived, and eventually have been used by later writers. But this would be the exception rather than the rule.

In conclusion it may be said that it is certain that Ari wrote fairly extensive work about the settlement of Iceland. It is not certain

---

[1] See Halldór Hermannsson, 'The Book of the Icelanders', pp. 41 ff., and the same scholar's paper in *Skírnir*, cxxii, 1948, esp. pp. 20 ff.; see also Einar Ól. Sveinsson, *Laxdœla Saga*, 1934, Introduction, pp. xxxvi ff.

that he compiled this work in the form which the *Landnámabók* has now, but the evidence, such as it is, suggests that he did so.

It was suggested above that the story about Ketilbjǫrn in the *Sturlunga Saga* had not been greatly altered since Ari wrote it. The form in which this story is preserved in the *Sturlunga Saga* does not differ appreciably from that of the *Landnámabók*. The story of Ketilbjǫrn, as told in the *Landnámabók* is, in form and in choice of material, much like many other stories in the *Landnámabók*. This implies that Ari provided not only material for later redactors of the *Landnámabók*, but also that he gave them the style and form for their work. Nevertheless, the later redactions of the *Landnámabók* were much fuller and more detailed than the earlier ones. That of Haukr, e.g., contains many incidents of which Ari could never have heard.

If it is believed that Ari wrote the first version of the *Landnámabók*, it has yet to be considered at what period of his life he wrote it. He wrote the *Liber* and the *Libellus* between the years 1122 and 1133, when he was between fifty-five and sixty-five years old. Those who believe that Ari wrote a *Landnámabók* are generally satisfied that he cannot have undertaken it until after he had written the *Libellus*.[1] The reasons which have been given for this conclusion carry little weight. There is some evidence which supports an opposite conclusion.

Earlier in this chapter mention was made of some of those wise men and women from whom Ari learned his history of Iceland. All of them were much older than Ari, and were the associates of his early years. Ari's tutor, Teitr, died in 1110, and his uncle Þorkell can hardly have lived later than that date. This implies that Ari made his researches into the history of Iceland while still a young man. If he was to be the author of a *Landnámabók*, it is plain that these researches must have been systematic and purposeful. He must have worked with *schedulae*, and not merely from memory.

Ari's early researches bore fruit in the *Liber* and *Libellus* and, it seems, in the *Landnámabók* as well. It is unlikely that he preserved

[1] See Jón Jóhannesson, op. cit., p. 221.

the notes made in his youth in disorder, and had no intention of making a book of them until he was past middle life. It is more probable that he began to compile the *Landnámabók* about the beginning of the twelfth century, or even before. It must have taken many years to complete it. The *Liber* and *Libellus* were offshoots of the same roots from which the *Landnámabók* grew, and they might have been written at any time while the *Landnámabók* was in progress, or after it was complete.

This relative chronology of Ari's literary career is supported by the postscript of Haukr, quoted above, and by the text of the *Landnámabók* itself. In the postscript, Haukr couples a certain Kolskeggr together with Ari among those who first wrote about the settlement of Iceland. Little is known about Kolskeggr, but the position assigned to him in genealogical lists suggests that he must have died, at latest, about 1130.

In the text of the *Landnámabók* Kolskeggr is named as the authority for a series of chapters covering a large area of east and south-east Iceland, from Húsavík in Múlasýsla to Jǫkulsá á Sólheimasandi. Certain stylistic peculiarities have been noticed in these chapters. They tend to be more summary and less detailed than most of those in the rest of the book. They are introduced with the words: 'from this point Kolskeggr has told about the settlements' (Nú hefir Kolskeggr fyrir sagt heðan frá um landnám, v. l. Heðan frá hefir Kolskeggr Ásbjarnarson fyrir sagt um landnám). The expression *fyrir sagt* could imply that Kolskeggr was the oral source, and had told Ari about the settlement of the eastern and south-eastern districts. It could alternatively mean that Kolskeggr was the author of these chapters. In either case the simplest interpretation of this passage, combined with the statement in Haukr's postscript, is that Kolskeggr collaborated with Ari in composing the first *Landnámabók*.

If Ari composed the first *Landnámabók* he must have had many assistants and collaborators besides Kolskeggr. It may be supposed that he gathered his information at public assemblies, and consulted men who knew the local history of each district. It would otherwise be impossible to construct a *Landnámabók*.

If it is admitted that Ari wrote the first draft of the *Landnámabók*, the fate of this book in the latter decades of the twelfth century is still obscure, and it is not known in what state it reached Styrmir the Wise. Nor can it be said what additions and alterations were made by Styrmir. The best guide to this last question is probably the *Laxdœla Saga*, but this does not give a clear picture of the version of the *Landnámabók* on which Styrmir worked.

Such questions as these are of utmost importance for the study of Icelandic literature. The *Landnámabók* was a source from which the authors of sagas drew a great part of their material about the early history of Iceland, and even about the history of other lands. If this material was first written early in the twelfth century by authors so careful as Ari, it must contain a large proportion of historical truth. If, on the other hand, the *Landnámabók* was first put together from oral sources in the thirteenth century, its value as history must be slight.

# V

# THE SCHOOL OF HÓLAR AND EARLY RELIGIOUS PROSE

THE preceding chapters have been concerned chiefly with literature in the south of Iceland. The sources show that the people of the south were the first to adopt the learned culture of Europe. The three chief centres of learning were Skálaholt, Haukadalr, and Oddi, grouped closely together in the south of the island. The best-known teachers and scholars of the eleventh century, Ísleifr, Teitr, Sæmundr, and Ari, were all associated with these three houses. Because of their contacts with Europe these men were able to combine foreign learning with the traditional culture of their own people. Foreign learning and foreign letters helped them to preserve ancient memories and to express traditional thoughts.

Nothing is said in the sources about schools or organized teaching in northern Iceland during the first century of the Christian period, although by the end of the twelfth century the northerners had come to surpass the people of the south in literary productivity and in imaginative qualities.

It is related in the *Íslendingabók* (ch. x) that in 1106, after Gizurr Ísleifsson had been bishop for twenty-four years, Jón Ǫgmundarson was consecrated Bishop of Hólar in northern Iceland. The people of the north had complained that Skálaholt was too far away from the northern districts, and there can, indeed, have been little intercourse between the inhabitants of these districts and the see of Skálaholt. In response to the request of the northerners, Bishop Gizurr relinquished a third of his diocese with all its revenues, and a new diocese was established. The choice of the new bishop fell on Jón Ǫgmundarson, a man of fifty-four years, who remained bishop of the northern diocese until his death in 1121.

Jón was of south Icelandic family, and he was born and brought up at Breiðabólstaðr in Fljótshlíð. The chief record of his life is the

*Jóns Saga Helga* (Life of S. Jón), written during the first years of
the thirteenth century by Gunnlaugr Leifsson (died 1218), monk of
the Benedictine monastery of Þingeyrar.¹ The *Jóns Saga* was designed as a hagiographic biography of the northern bishop, whom
Gunnlaugr revered as a saint. Nevertheless there can be little doubt
that Gunnlaugr was well versed in the traditions about Jón, and
the saga probably gives a fair account of Jón's life and work, if
Gunnlaugr's conventional rhetoric and his extravagant tales of
Jón's piety and miracles are discounted.

Jón was one of the pupils of Bishop Ísleifr at Skálaholt and
throughout his life he maintained his devotion to his former
teacher. He said himself that he could never hear praise of a good
man without thinking of Ísleifr.² As a young man Jón had travelled
extensively in Europe. He had been in Rome and in Denmark, and
it was he who discovered Sæmundr immersed in the study of
astrology (*astronomia*) in a foreign land.³ He was involved in several
adventures abroad. On one occasion, while in Trondheim, he inter-
vened on behalf of an Icelandic poet who had avenged his father
by killing one of the courtiers of King Magnús Bareleg (died 1103).
After all other means had failed, Jón saved the poet's life by cutting
him down from the gallows and restoring him.⁴

After Jón had been elected bishop by Gizurr and other chieftains,
he went first to Lund in Denmark (Scania) for consecration. A new
archbishopric had been established there in 1104 and, like other
Scandinavian countries, Iceland was made subject to it, and was
released from the archbishops of Bremen and Hamburg.⁵ When he
discovered that Jón had been married twice, Archbishop Qzurr
declined to consecrate him until he had obtained the dispensation
of the Pope. This compelled Jón to make the journey from Lund
to Rome and back. But the Pope, Paschal II, was so struck with
Jón's chieftainly bearing and with his frank admission of his

---

¹ The *Jóns Saga* has been published in a shorter and a longer version in
*Biskupa Sögur*, i, 1858, pp. 152–212 and 215–60. It was first written in Latin,
but the text in Latin is lost. The longer version is the closer to the original,
despite the editor's assertion to the contrary. References in this book apply to
the longer version unless otherwise stated.

² *Biskupa Sögur*, i. 219 ff.          ³ Ibid., pp. 227 ff.          ⁴ Ibid., pp. 221 ff.
⁵ See Bishop Jón Helgason, *Islands Kirke*, 1925, pp. 69 ff.

impediments that he weighed the pros and cons of granting the
dispensation on the 'wise scales of his perception' and found that
the pros outweighed the cons.

In the summer of 1106 Jón returned to Iceland, and took up
residence at the see of Hólar. One of his first acts as bishop was to
build a cathedral church, and the records give some idea of what
it was like. This was not the first, but the third church to be built
at Hólar. The first had been built by a certain Oxi Hjaltason about
the middle of the eleventh century.[1] Oxi's church had been among
the finest in Iceland in its time, and had had a leaden roof, but it
was burnt down, and another was built in its place. This second
church was demolished by Bishop Jón, and he replaced it with a
memorable structure, which remained standing for many years.[2]
It was not built of turf, as many Icelandic churches must have been,
but of timber which Jón had obtained in Norway. The builder was
Þóroddr Gamlason, who is perhaps to be identified with Þóroddr
the Rune-Master (*Rúnameistari*).[3] Þóroddr was thought to be one
of the most skilful craftsmen in Iceland, and received large sums
for his work. The fact that the church was built of timber, and so
elaborately worked, suggests that it was a stave or mast church,
such as those preserved in Norway to this day. There are, indeed,
many indications that church architecture of this kind was favoured
in Iceland as well as in Norway.[4]

Jón had many interests. One of them was in music, and several
stories are told of his singing and harp-playing.[5] His chief work
was in founding the school of Hólar, for this was to be as great an
influence in the north of Iceland as the school of Skálaholt in the
south. Among the teachers whom Jón employed was Gísli Finsson,
from Gautland (Sweden), who was headmaster and taught Latin.
Another teacher was called Ríkini, and he is described as a French-
man. He taught singing and verse-making, and was himself a skilful exponent of both.[6]

---

[1] Cf. Brynleifur Tobiasson, *Heim að Hólum*, 1943, pp. 16–17.
[2] *Biskupa Sögur*, i. 235.
[3] On Þóroddr see Björn M. Ólsen, *Runerne i den oldislandske Literatur*, 1883,
pp. 44 ff.      [4] Cf. K. Vrátný, *Arkiv för nordisk filologi*, xxxii, 1916, p. 33.
[5] *Biskupa Sögur*, i. 220–2.                    [6] Ibid., pp. 235 f. and 239 f.

Many of the chieftains of northern Iceland sent their sons to the school of Hólar, whether to learn 'Latin or singing or both', and Gunnlaugr gives a detailed if rather flowery description of life and work at that school in the time of Bishop Jón. He writes:

> Great industry was to be seen in every building at the See; some were reading holy scripture, some were writing, some were singing, some were learning, some were teaching. . . . When the signal for service was given, all of them would hurry from their cells to the church, like the busy bee bringing with them to the bee-hive of Holy Church the sweet honey which they had gathered in the delightful wine-cellar of holy scripture.[1]

Among the pupils of the school of Hólar were Klœngr Þorsteinsson, who was afterwards Bishop of Skálaholt (1152–76), Bjǫrn Gilsson, who was afterwards Bishop of Hólar (1147–62), Vilmundr Þórólfsson (died 1148), first abbot of the monastery of Þingeyrar, and Hreinn Styrmisson, who was fourth abbot of that monastery (died 1171). Among other students of the school, Bjarni Bergþórsson should be mentioned. He is probably to be identified with the astronomer and mathematician Bjarni 'the number-wise' (*enn tǫlvísi*), whose tract on astronomy still survives.[2] Another of the students, whom Gunnlaugr mentions, was a 'chaste virgin' called Ingunn. She was no less proficient in letters than her male companions, and she used to teach Latin, allowing the students to read their compositions to her while she played draughts, or embroidered stories from the lives of the saints.

It is not recorded that Bishop Jón was himself an author, but it is plain that he took a great interest in literature, and that he had positive although rather exclusive taste. He regarded it as his first duty to raise the standard of morals in his diocese. When he came to Hólar, Christianity was young, and many pagan superstitions and practices lingered. He severely condemned 'witchcraft and the black arts, incantations and magic, and all kinds of sorcery which deceived the eye . . . he strictly forbade all kinds of superstition,

[1] *Biskupa Sögur*, i. 240.
[2] See *Alfræði íslenzk*, ii, ed. N. Beckman and Kr. Kålund, 1914–16, esp. Introduction, pp. xxiii ff.

such as men of old had drawn from the phases of the moon or the
length of days . . . he forbade men to assign days of the week
to pagan sages, as by talking of "Týr's Day", "Óðinn's Day",
"Þórr's Day".[1]

Indeed, Bishop Jón attempted to abolish several customs which
antiquarians might rather he had preserved. It used to be the custom in those days for men to chant alluring and obscene verses to
women, and for women to reply with love-ditties. This practice
was condemned by the bishop, but he did not succeed in abolishing
it altogether.[2]

Not only did Jón condemn the traditional practices which he
associated with paganism and loose living. He was just as un-
compromising in his condemnation of the less reputable kinds of
classical letters, which were beginning to be known in Iceland. He
once found Klœngr Þorsteinsson deep in the study of Ovid's *Ars
Amatoria*. He forbade him to read books of this kind, saying that
human nature was sufficiently prone to concupiscence without
such incitements.[3]

Although Jón was too serious to tolerate love songs and other
frivolous poetry, there are indications that he played an important
part in fostering and developing the literature of his period. The
*Jóns Saga* shows that he was much interested in homilies and in
pious tales, and there can be no doubt that he introduced some of
these into Iceland.

It is recorded that the Gautish teacher, Gísli Finsson, whom Jón
employed at Hólar, used to preach on feast-days. When he did so,
he did not speak *ex tempore*, nor did he rely on his memory, for he
was both young and humble, and he knew that the congregation
would take his words more deeply to heart if they could see that he
was reading from a book, which lay before him on the lectern.[4]
This story implies that a book of homilies was kept at Hólar in the
time of Bishop Jón. This book can only have been written in the
vernacular, for Gísli could not have preached in Latin to the hun-
dreds who flocked to the cathedral on feast-days. The vernacular

[1] *Biskupa Sögur*, i. 237.
[2] Ibid., loc. cit.
[3] Ibid., p. 238.
[4] Ibid., p. 236.

need not necessarily mean Icelandic for, at that date, it would be possible to read from a book in Norwegian, or even in Swedish, in such a way that an Icelandic audience would understand.

There are no records of homilies written in Swedish in the early Middle Ages. But it is probable that the Norwegians, because of their contacts with England, began to write homilies in their own language early in the twelfth century, if not already in the eleventh century.[1] Most probably the Icelanders who, like the Norwegians, were subject to the influence of English clerks, also began early to write homilies and other pious literature in the vernacular.

Such arguments suggest that Gísli's book of homilies was written either in Icelandic or in Norwegian. Since Gísli had come from a foreign land, he might well have brought the book with him. It is suggested by one passage of the *Jóns Saga* that books of pious literature were sometimes carried from Norway to Iceland. It is told there that Bishop Jón once dreamed that he was praying before a great crucifix, and the figure of Christ bowed down and whispered some words in his ear. None of the bishop's friends could read the dream, but on the next day some men who had lately arrived from Norway came to visit the bishop, and they brought him a little book, which contained a story not known in Iceland before. In this story it was told how some Jews had derided the image of Christ on the crucifix. They struck the image and spat upon it, blaspheming and cursing, just as their ancestors had done to Christ himself. But when the Jews pierced the side of the image with a spear, blood and water gushed forth, and many sick people were healed by it. Then the Jews realized the wickedness of their crime and repented.[2]

This is the well-known story *Flagellatio Crucis*. A complete version of it in Icelandic is preserved in two manuscripts, which are assigned to the latter half of the fourteenth century.[3] It cannot be affirmed that this version of the *Flagellatio* goes back to a translation made in the days of Bishop Jón, although this is not impossible.

[1] Cf. G. Indrebø, *Gamal norsk homiliebok*, 1931, Introduction, esp. pp. 39 ff.; D. A. Seip in *Maal og Minne*, 1943, 97 ff., 1945, 8 ff., 21 ff., and 30 ff.

[2] *Biskupa Sögur*, i. 246–7.

[3] Published in *Heilagra Manna Sögur*, i, ed. C. R. Unger, 1877, pp. 308–11.

Klœngr Þorsteinsson was mentioned among the students of the school at Hólar. Klœngr was born about 1105,[1] and was entrusted to the care of Bishop Jón at the age of twelve. He remained at Hólar as a teacher under the bishops Ketill Þorsteinsson (1122–45) and Bjǫrn Gilsson (1147–62), and was himself Bishop of Skálaholt from 1152 until his death in 1176. It is said in the *Jóns Saga* that, when Klœngr was teaching at Hólar, he had many diligent pupils, and many remarkable books, still preserved when the saga was written, were produced under his guidance.[2] Although it is not said in the sources what kind of books Klœngr and his pupils wrote, it is not unlikely that they contained homilies and other instructive prose, such as flourished in the religious houses of Iceland during the twelfth century.

The religious prose written in Iceland in the twelfth century might be divided into several classes. Although most of it is either based upon or else strongly influenced by foreign models, it allows some scope for the expression of native thought and taste, and deserves closer attention than modern scholars have given it.

Most of the early Icelandic homilies are preserved in the so-called Stockholm Homily Book, now kept in the Royal Library of Stockholm.[3] It is generally agreed that this book was written about 1200 or a little earlier, and it is thus one of the oldest existing Icelandic manuscripts of any size or scope. It contains more than fifty homilies, designed for different feasts of the year. Many of these can be shown, from linguistic and textual evidence, to be much older than the book itself.

Eleven of the homilies in the Stockholm Book are also preserved in the Norwegian Homily Book.[4] This book was probably written in Selja or in Bergen a little later than the Stockholm Book. It is written in three (or perhaps four) hands and, throughout, the

---

[1] Cf. Jón Helgason, op. cit., p. 101.    [2] *Biskupa Sögur*, i. 240–1.
[3] *Homiliu-Bók*, ed. T. Wisén, 1872; an edition in facsimile has been published in the series *Corpus Codicum Islandicorum*, viii, 1935, with an Introduction by F. Paasche.
[4] Three editions of the Norwegian Homily Book have been published: *Gammel norsk homiliebog*, ed. C. R. Unger, 1864; *Codex A.M. 619 Quarto*, ed. G. T. Flom (Illinois Studies in Language and Literature, 1929); references in this chapter apply to the edition of G. Indrebø, *Gamal norsk homiliebok*, 1931.

scribes were copying older originals. These older originals were written in various dialects of Norwegian, partly in East Norwegian, partly in the dialect of Rogaland, and partly in that of Trondheim.

Only a few of the sources for the early Icelandic homilies have yet been brought to light,[1] but detailed study would disclose a greater number, and this would help to show what kinds of foreign literature were studied in Iceland and Norway during the twelfth century. It would also help to show how far the northern preachers were independent of their foreign masters, and how closely they followed their models. Needless to say, the chief sources are works by, or ascribed to, the famous apologists of the Middle Ages, e.g. Jerome, Alkuin, Bede, Paulus Diaconus, Gregory. But besides these, the northern homilists used the scriptures, and especially the apocryphal gospels, which were much studied in Iceland during the twelfth and thirteenth centuries.

Following the fashion of their age, the northern homilists delighted in symbolism. Pious objects, such as the Cross, or events in the life of Christ and his mother, are explained by means of symbols.

One of the most interesting of all the Icelandic or Norwegian homilies bears the title *Kirkjudagsmál* or *In dedicatione templi*, and it is designed to be read on the day of dedication of a church. This homily is preserved, not only in the Norwegian and Stockholm Homily Books,[2] but the greater part of it is also found in the manuscript No. 237, a folio of the Arnamagnean collection in Copenhagen.[3] No. 237 was written in Iceland, and it is perhaps the oldest surviving manuscript in Icelandic. It is generally supposed to have been written about 1150,[4] although such dating has rather limited value, since there are so few manuscripts of the period with which this one can be compared.

G. Indrebø[5] has studied the relationship between the three texts

---

[1] See K. Vrátný, *Arkiv för nordisk filologi*, xxix. 174 ff., and xxxii. 31 ff., and xxxiii. 141 ff.

[2] *Norsk Homiliebok*, ed. Indrebø, pp. 95 ff.; *Homiliu-Bók*, ed. Wisén, pp. 98 ff.

[3] Published in *Leifar fornra kristinna fræða íslenzkra*, ed. Þorvaldr Bjarnarson, 1878, pp. 162 ff. See also my paper in *Medieval Studies*, xi, 1949, pp. 206-18.

[4] On this manuscript see H. Spehr, *Der Ursprung der isländischen Schrift*, 1929, pp. vi and 167; facsimiles in *Reallexikon der germanischen Altertumskunde*, ed. J. Hoops, iii, 1915–16, pl. 24.       [5] Op. cit., Introduction, pp. 51 ff.

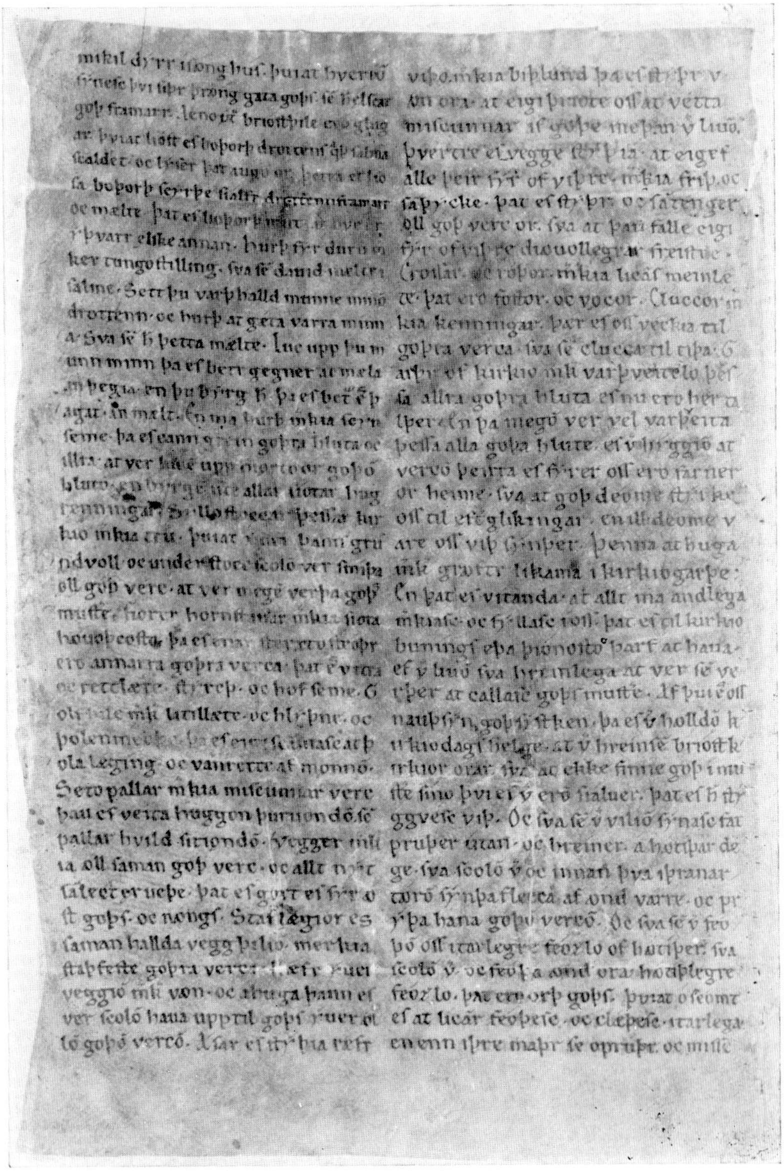

*In dedicatione templi.* Manuscript of mid-twelfth century

of this Dedication homily, and has shown that No. 237 agrees with Norwegian Book more closely than with the Stockholm Book. On the whole, Indrebø is unquestionably right in his conclusion that No. 237 and the Norwegian Book preserve the text of the Dedication homily in a form closer to the original than that of the Stockholm Book, although in rare instances the Stockholm Book contains readings which appear to be older than those of the other two.[1] Indrebø has also attempted to show that, although its manuscript is much younger, the text of the Dedication homily preserved in the Norwegian Book is closer to the original than that of No. 237. This conclusion is not supported by strong evidence and it should be pointed out that, in at least one instance, the text of No. 237 is plainly older than that of the Norwegian Book.[2] It was partly because he considered the text of the Norwegian Book older than that of No. 237, that Indrebø decided that the Dedication homily was first written in Norway rather than in Iceland.

However that may be, it is plain that the scribe who wrote No. 237 was copying from an older manuscript, and it is reasonably safe to say that the Dedication homily was composed not later than the middle of the twelfth century, whether in Norway or in Iceland. The homilist mentions the chief parts of a church and, in every case, he explains their significance in symbols. It is interesting to notice that the church which the homilist is describing is not a stone church of European type, but a church of timber, with its maze of beams and rafters and posts.

A few of these symbols may be quoted. The four main pillars (*hornstafir*) symbolize the four gospels, the altar symbolizes Christ, the altar cloths symbolize either the saints in Heaven or else good deeds. The two main walls (south and north) symbolize the two peoples, Jews and heathen nations, who make up the Christian community. The front wall, which joins these two main walls, symbolizes the Lord, who joins the two peoples in one faith. Most parts of the church are symbolized in two ways. They may represent Christ, his saints in heaven, or members of the Church

---

[1] See my paper in *Medieval Studies*, xi, 1949, p. 214.
[2] Ibid., p. 213.

militant on earth. Alternatively the parts of the church may be explained allegorically as parts of the body, mind or soul of a man, for every Christian is the temple of the Holy Ghost. Thus, the altar symbolizes love, the floor humility, and the roof hope.

Although this Dedication homily has been adapted to give symbols to the parts of a timber church, it contains little, if any, original thought. It has been said that it is based upon chapters 129–45 of the *Gemma Animae* of Honorius Augustodunensis.[1] Indeed, many passages of the Dedication homily resemble these chapters of the *Gemma*, but it has perhaps been overlooked that this part of the *Gemma* hardly contains an original thought nor even an original sentence. Honorius was copying earlier writers, just as later writers copied him. A long series of writers from Hrabanus Maurus in the ninth century to Durandus in the thirteenth century used the same terms and often the same sentences to symbolize the parts of a church.[2] In many ways the Dedication homily corresponds more closely with the *de Universo* of Hrabanus[3] than with the *Gemma*. Hrabanus wrote:

Parietes enim templi dei, fideles sunt ex utroque populo, hoc est Iudaico et gentile, ex quibus Christus aedificavit ecclesiam suam:[4]

and again:

Angulus autem sive angularis in scripturis intelligitur Christus, eo quod duos parietes conjungat in unum, credentes videlicet ex Iudaeis et gentilibus.[5]

These sentiments hardly differ from those expressed in the Norse homily:

Tveir kirkjuveggir merkja tvinnan lýð kominn til einnar Kristni, annan af gyðingum en annan af heiðnum þjóðum,[6]

and:

Brjóstþili, er samtengir báða veggi . . . merkir dróttin várn, er samtengir tvinnan lýð í einni trú.[7]

---

[1] Published in Migne, *Patrologia Latina*, clxxii, cols. 586–92.
[2] Cf. J. Sauer, *Symbolik des Kirchengebäudes*, 1902.
[3] Published in Migne, *Patrologia*, cxi, cols. 400 ff.
[4] Hrabanus, op. cit., loc. cit., col. 401.    [5] Hrabanus, op. cit., loc. cit.
[6] *Norsk homiliebok*, p. 96.    [7] Op. cit., loc. cit.

From such passages as these it can be seen that the Norse Dedication homily is not based upon the *Gemma Animae*, but is parallel to it. In several instances it appears to be more archaic than the *Gemma*. Its source was perhaps an older work than the *Gemma*.

Two homilies in the Stockholm Book bear the title *á allra heilagra messu* (On the Feast of All Saints).[1] The first of these is also found in the Norwegian Book,[2] and the two texts of it differ little. The source is a homily attributed to Bede,[3] which the northern homilist follows closely and soberly. The second homily designed for the feast of All Saints is found only in the Stockholm Book. It is based ultimately on the same pseudo-Bedean model, and includes certain passages of it which have been omitted from the first homily of All Saints. At the same time, the second homily of All Saints is much expanded; it is a more ambitious work than its pseudo-Bedean model, and more personal. When he speaks of the diverse classes of angels, the homilist departs from his theme, and introduces the story of Job, saying that he thinks that this exemplary tale will give strength to those who suffer ill health or loss of friends or property. After this the homilist tells how Antichrist will come towards the end of the world, and he will say that that which is true is false, and that which is false is true. Antichrist will cause Enoc and Elias to be put to death, and shortly afterwards he will himself be killed by lightning. People will crowd around his tomb, expecting Antichrist to rise on the third day, as he had told them he would, but instead they will find his body seething with maggots and with all filthiness.

In a later passage the author of this homily turns his thoughts to moral qualities. He contrasts the virtues attendant on simplicity with the vices which accompany duplicity. This passage is alliterative and rhythmical, and sometimes approaches the verseform *fornyrðislag*, with 'props' and 'pillars' and lines of two beats. Among the attributes of duplicity are:

> Lygi ok lausung
> ok lestir margir,

---

[1] Pp. 39 and 151.    [2] Pp. 143 ff.
[3] Ed. Migne, *Patrologia Latina*, xciv, cols. 452 ff.

skopun ok skjalsemi
ok skeitun optliga,
gjálp ok gáleysi,
gleði ófallin,
gildingr ok geðleysi,
grand er þat andar.

The homily *Nativitas Sanctae Mariae* is also preserved in the Stockholm Book alone.[1] It is less original than many of the others but it is interesting from another point of view. G. Neckel[2] has shown that it is a compilation of two apocryphal gospels, the Gospel of the Birth of Mary and the Gospel of Pseudo-Matthew.[3] Neckel believed that the immediate source of the Icelandic homily was a work in Latin, in which these two gospels had been combined.[4] This may be true, but it is hardly less likely that it was the Icelandic homilist who combined the two gospels. Such conflation of diverse foreign sources could be paralleled in the history of Icelandic literature, and even in that of Icelandic Mariology.[5]

The homily *Assumptio Sanctae Mariae*, found both in the Stockholm and Norwegian Books,[6] is hardly less interesting. The homilist develops the conventional symbol of the Virgin as the glass pierced by the rays of the sun. This homily also contains a number of general reflections about Mary's sanctity and chastity and an allusion to the disputed question whether her body rose from the dead or not.

K. Vrátný[7] has shown that, in some passages, the homily on the Assumption closely resembles the *Maríu Saga* (Saga of the Virgin Mary).[8] Vrátný's explanation of the relationship between the homily and the saga was that the homilist had used the saga as a

[1] P. 127.
[2] *Beiträge zur Geschichte der deutschen Sprache und Literatur*, xxxviii, 1913, pp. 481 ff.
[3] Ed. C. de Tischendorf, *Evangelia Apocrypha*, ed. 2, 1876, pp. 113 and 51 ff.; cf. *Liber de infantia Mariae et Christi Salvatoris*, ed. O. Schade, 1869, and M. R. James, *The Apocryphal New Testament*, 1926, pp. 70 and 79 ff.
[4] A conflated text was published by M. R. James, *Latin Infancy Gospels*, 1927. This conflation is quite unlike the Icelandic homily.
[5] See my paper in *Medieval Studies*, ix, 1947, pp. 131–40.
[6] Ed. Wisén, pp. 4 ff., ed. Indrebø, pp. 129 ff.
[7] *Arkiv för nordisk filologi*, xxxii. 42.
[8] *Maríu Saga*, ed. C. R. Unger, 1871, pp. 1–62 and 332–401.

source, and had freely copied passages from it. Indrebø[1] accepted Vrátný's conclusion on this point, but it has led to difficulties. The homily, since it is found both in the Norwegian and Stockholm books, must have been written a good many years before the end of the twelfth century. The *Maríu Saga* is preserved in a number of manuscripts, the oldest of which date from the first quarter of the fourteenth century. According to tradition it was the work of a certain Kygri-Bjǫrn Hjaltason (died 1237 or 1238). If this tradition is correct, the *Maríu Saga* can hardly have been written before the beginning of the thirteenth century. These difficulties can, however, be overcome.

It is true that the passages which the homily shares with the *Maríu Saga* cannot have been copied by the compiler of the *Maríu Saga* from the homily in its present form. For these passages are much fuller in the *Maríu Saga* than they are in the homily, which gives no more than a shortened text of them. But the passages can hardly have been abstracted by the compiler of the homily from the *Maríu Saga* for, in some instances,[2] they consist of no more than a sentence or a few lines, which are found in the *Maríu Saga* embedded in passages of which no trace can be found in the homily. In such instances, the foreign sources for the passages of the *Maríu Saga* are generally easy to trace, except for those of the lines in question, for which the source is often less obvious. The simplest explanation is that the homily and the *Maríu Saga* have both been influenced by a lost homily written in Icelandic or Norwegian. The main source for this lost homily was none other than the famous letter on the Assumption, popularly ascribed to S. Jerome, and said to be addressed to the holy women Paula and Eustochium.[3] It should be added that this letter was also the basis of Ælfric's English homily on the Assumption.[4]

There is no reason to reject the tradition that Kygri-Bjǫrn was the author of the *Maríu Saga*. Since this saga is a remarkable work,

---

[1] *Gamal norsk homiliebok*, Introduction, p. 62, footnote 2.

[2] *Maríu Saga*, p. 2, lines 12–13; p. 1, line 20 to p. 2, line 2. For further details see my paper on the *Maríu Saga* quoted above.

[3] See *Eusebii Hieronymi opera omnia*, ed. J. P. Migne, xi. 122 ff.

[4] Published in the *Homilies of Ælfric*, ed. B. Thorpe, i, 1844, pp. 436 ff.

and unique of its kind, it may be helpful to consider it and its reputed author a little more closely. Kygri-Bjǫrn was a well-known and influential clerk in northern Iceland in the first decades of the thirteenth century. It is described in the *Guðmundar Saga* (Saga of Bishop Guðmundr the Good)[1] how, in 1202, Kolbeinn Tumason appointed Kygri-Bjǫrn secretary at the see of Hólar. This appointment was contrary to the will of Bishop Guðmundr, who had just been elected Bishop. He and Kygri-Bjǫrn were not on friendly terms, and relations between them grew more bitter as time passed on, or as the biased author of the *Guðmundar Saga* says:

> Bjǫrn took a dislike to Guðmundr, bearing him a grudge because he felt that Guðmundr had slighted him. This was an augury of Bjǫrn's conduct later, for the greater and more manifold grew the diabolical and unremittant hatred, which the enemy of all mankind had implanted in his heart; it only became the worse the longer it dwelt in him.

This estimate of Bjǫrn's character was probably confined to Bishop Guðmundr and his followers. Guðmundr's belief in his divine mission was fanatical, and neither he nor his followers could tolerate opposition. It is said, in another text,[2] that Bjǫrn was always a friend of Guðmundr's enemies, first of Kolbeinn Tumason and later of Sturla Sighvatsson. Indeed, the restrained and cautious views expressed in the *Maríu Saga* would be more easily compatible with Guðmundr's enemies than with his friends. It was suspected that, on visits which he made to Trondheim and Rome (about 1213–14), Bjǫrn had prejudiced the dignitaries of the Church against Guðmundr.[3] This was perhaps one of the reasons why Bishop Guðmundr was advised by the Pope to resign and twice suspended from office.

In 1236, when Guðmundr was seventy-five years old, Bjǫrn was elected to succeed him as bishop. In that year Bjǫrn went abroad, apparently to Rome to have his election confirmed,[4] but he died on his

---

[1] *Biskupa Sögur*, i. 475–6; cf. *Life of Gudmund the Good*, translated by G. Turville-Petre and E. S. Olszewska, 1942, p. 50.
[2] Abbot Arngrímr's Saga of Guðmundr, ed. in *Biskupa Sögur*, ii, 1878, p. 92.
[3] *Biskupa Sögur*, ii. 92.
[4] *Sturlunga Saga*, ed. Jón Jóhannesson and others, i, 1946, pp. 396–7; *Biskupa Sögur*, ii. 147–8.

way home in 1237 or 1238. His death might be interpreted either as the fulfilment of a prophecy or as the result of a curse laid by Guðmundr.[1]

The ascription of the *Maríu Saga* to Kygri-Bjǫrn is based upon a statement found in an appendix to Abbot Arngrímr's life of Guðmundr, which was written about the middle of the fourteenth century. It is said there:

Kygri-Bjǫrn was an outstanding clerk, as may easily be appreciated by the fact that he composed (*samsett*) the *Maríu Saga*.[2]

The sources of the *Maríu Saga* were many and of diverse kinds, and this shows that the author had read widely in European letters. His method of 'putting the saga together' (*samsetja*) was much the same as that of Snorri and of many other Icelandic historians. But, while Snorri worked from native sources, the author of the *Maríu Saga* worked mainly from foreign ones. Like Snorri's Saga of S. Ólafr, the *Maríu Saga* is a mosaic. It is, like the *Ólafs Saga*, a well-proportioned and balanced whole, and so skilfully put together that it is often difficult to see when the author departs from one source and follows another. The chief source for the first twelve chapters of the *Maríu Saga* is the *Gospel of the Birth of Mary*, which the author followed closely in most passages, supplementing it occasionally with others, such as the *Gospel of Pseudo-Matthew*[3] and the *Trinubium Annae*.[4] It was told in the *Trinubium* how S. Anne, the mother of the Virgin, was married three times, first to Ioachim, the father of Mary the Virgin, and secondly to Cleophas, the brother of Joseph and father of Mary Cleophas. A version of this story in English is found in MS. Vespasian D, xiv, of the early twelfth century, and a text of it in Latin is found in MS. Ashmole 1280, of comparable date.[5] Full versions of the same story in Icelandic are preserved in a manuscript of the fifteenth century[6] and, in somewhat corrupt form, in one of the fourteenth-century manuscripts of the *Maríu Saga*.[7]

[1] *Biskupa Sögur*, ii, loc. cit. and pp. 185–6.          [2] Ibid. ii. 186.
[3] e.g. *Maríu Saga*, pp. 14, lines 28–30 appear to be from *Pseudo-Matthew*.
[4] P. 16, lines 26 ff.
[5] On the *Trinubium Annae* see M. Förster, *Englische Studien*, liv. 58 ff.
[6] See *Alfræði íslenzk*, i, ed. Kr. Kålund, 1908, p. 56.
[7] *Maríu Saga*, p. 17, footnote 2.

The *Gospel of the Birth of Mary* ends with the birth of Christ, after which the compiler of the *Maríu Saga* uses a greater variety of sources. In chapter xiv he tells how the shepherds came to adore the new-born Christ, following S. Luke (II). The visit of the magi is told in chapter xvi according to S. Matthew (II), but in greater detail. The magi are described here, as in most medieval books, as kings from the east, and they are said to be astrologers, who could read the movements of the heavenly bodies. The flight into Egypt (chapter xviii) is told partly as in the *Gospel of Pseudo-Matthew*. It is related in the *Maríu Saga*, as in that text, that the idols fell from their pedestals when Christ and his mother arrived in Egypt.

Among the strongest influences on the *Maríu Saga* were Books XVI and XVII of the *Antiquities of the Jews* of Josephus. The author used them to supplement the canonical and apocryphal gospels, and he was thus able to give a fairly detailed account of the politics and intrigue in Palestine during the time of Christ. It is not known in what form the work of Josephus reached the author of the *Maríu Saga*, but it is known that this work, or a derivative of it, was also used by Brandr Jónsson (died 1264) for his *Gyðinga Saga* (History of the Jews). Josephus's *Antiquities* and *War of the Jews* are works of detailed history of the kind which might be expected to interest the Icelanders. Josephus's stories of ruthless ambition, cruelty, and deceit bear a close resemblance to parts of the Icelandic *Sturlunga Saga*.

Besides these historical and pseudo-historical sources, the author of the *Maríu Saga* frequently used works of the Fathers and commentators, some of whom he names, e.g. Augustine, Jerome, Gregory. Sometimes he interrupts his story and explains it in symbols. In this way he explains the fifteen steps of the temple, up which Mary ran at the age of three (chs. iv–v). In a later chapter (xxvi) he describes the last judgement, as it will be held above the Valley of Josaphat, in a way which recalls the *Lucidarius* attributed to Honorius Augustodunensis.[1]

The compiler of the *Maríu Saga* has put his own stamp on the work throughout. Not only has he selected his material according

[1] See below, pp. 137 ff.

to his own taste, but he has also expressed his own views. He was doubtful about the Assumption of Mary's body (ch. xxvii), and condemned the belief in the Immaculate Conception, saying that Mary was begotten with the old sin, but was purified in the womb (ch. iii). While explaining the meaning of the *Magnificat* (ch. xi), he pauses to reprove those Icelanders who are so careless about their Latin that they translate *magnificat anima mea dominum* with *miklar dróttinn ǫnd mína* (The Lord doth magnify my soul).

The learned works so far discussed were probably intended chiefly to be instructive and edifying. The author of the *Maríu Saga* uses the story of Mary, and describes the different moments in her life largely to demonstrate their philosophical significance, and to express views on certain theological problems. But both the *Maríu Saga* and the homilies contain a large proportion of straight-forward narrative, and it is these passages which probably interest modern readers most, and they were of greatest consequence for the development of Icelandic literature. The story of John the Baptist and Salome has sometimes been quoted as one of the finest specimens of narrative in the early homilies.[1]

The religious or quasi-religious literature of Europe, on which religious writers of Iceland modelled their work, also included many texts in which theology had given way to legend and romance; doctrine had become subject to story. In literature of this kind tales were told of Christ, the Apostles, and later saints less because they were edifying than because they were adventurous and entertaining. It might be expected that the Icelanders would be quick to adopt literature of this kind as their own. Many of the legendary stories resembled the stepmother tales (*stjúpmœðra sǫgur*) and the traditional tales of men of old (*fornaldar sǫgur*, better *lygi sǫgur*), such as the Icelanders cultivated orally both in prose and in verse, although they did not write them in these early times.

But, despite obvious similarities, there are marked differences between the Christian legends of Europe and the traditional tales of Iceland. A great part of the legendary literature had been written first by pious men in Africa and the Near East. If these legends are

[1] Ed. Wisén, p. 13, lines 25 ff.; cf. Vrátný, *Arkiv för nordisk filologi*, xxxii. 46·

compared with the heroic tales of Iceland, differences between east and west, some would say differences between Christianity and northern paganism, come to light. The leading figures in the legendary literature were self-effacing ascetics, e.g. S. Blasius, S. Alexis, S. Placid. They were quite unlike the proud and vengeful heroes whom the northmen admired most.

Mention has already been made of certain apocryphal histories of Christ and his contemporaries. These books were of diverse origin, but many of them were written during the first four centuries of the Christian era, and were designed to propagate the doctrines of the Gnostics, Manichaeans, and other early heretics.[1] But heretical or not, these books swept over Catholic Europe in the early Middle Ages, and they were accepted rather for the stories told in them than for the doctrines which their authors had intended to propagate. In their western forms they were often expurgated so thoroughly by Catholic redactors that they contained few traces of heresy, and little remained but the story.[2]

Books of this kind were known in Iceland in the twelfth century, probably as early as the middle of that century. They gained immense popularity. This is shown by their numberless manuscripts, as well as by the entries in the catalogues of libraries of monasteries and bishoprics in Iceland.[3] One of the most important of them is ascribed to Nicodemus, the disciple of Christ. In the second part of it the story of Christ's descent into Hell is related. It is the most fascinating and mysterious of apocryphal writings. According to legend, Nicodemus compiled it from a record left by Karinus and Leucius, who were themselves in Hell, and were restored to life when Christ harrowed it after the Crucifixion.

Four texts of the Descent into Hell have been published in Ice-

[1] A useful account of New Testament Apocrypha is given by M. R. James, *The Apocryphal New Testament*, 1926.

[2] It may be noted that the heretical doctrine, which the stories were designed to propagate, can sometimes be perceived in their western texts, despite expurgation. E.g. in the *Thomas Saga Postola* (*Postola Sögur*, ed. C. R. Unger, 1874, pp. 712 ff.), the Apostle's advice to the newly married couple accords better with Gnostic or Manichaean doctrine than with that of the Catholics.

[3] A number of catalogues and inventories have been printed in *Diplomatarium Islandicum*, 1857 (in progress).

landic,[1] and it has the title *Niðrstigningar Saga*. Two of these texts
(Unger's I and II) are found in manuscripts ascribed to the first
half of the thirteenth century, whose archaic word and letter forms
show that they were copied from older originals.[2] The manuscripts
of the other two (Unger's III and IV) date from the fourteenth and
fifteenth centuries. The differences between the four texts of the
*Niðrstigningar Saga* are occasionally interesting, but not great, and
it is plain that they are all to be traced to the same original translation, which must have been made in the twelfth century.

On the whole, the Icelandic version of the Descent into Hell
agrees with the Latin text designated by Tischendorf[3] and M. R.
James[4] as *A*, and this was the text followed by most translators in
western Europe.[5] A noticeable difference between the Icelandic
version and the Latin original is that, in the Icelandic, Hell is not
personified as it is in the Latin, but is replaced by a host of devils.[6]
Hell appears as a person only in the latest Icelandic text (IV), and
this is probably due to the revision of a learned scribe.

The Icelandic version of the Descent into Hell is not a slavish
translation of the Latin original. The translator begins with an
editorial note, saying that, although this book has not been given
the same prominence as other sacred writings, it contains nothing
dubious. Moreover, the Icelandic version of the tale contains a
number of interesting additions and embellishments not found in
the standard Latin text. These are partly derived from *Revelation*
(XIX) and partly from the *Book of Job* (XLI). Besides this the
descriptions of the monsters of Hell have been enriched and made
more vivid. The following description of the expulsion of Satan
from Hell will serve as an example:

Then the inhabitants of Hell said unto Satan: 'begone from our

[1] In *Heilagra Manna Sögur*, ed. C. R. Unger, 1877, ii. 1–20. Unger's second
text (ii) is also printed diplomatically in *A.M. 623, 4to*, ed. Finnur Jónsson, 1927,
pp. 1–9.          [2] Cf. Finnur Jónsson, *A.M. 623*, 1927, Introduction.
[3] *Evangelia Apocrypha*, ed. Tischendorf, ed. 2, pp. 389 ff.
[4] *Apocryphal New Testament*, pp. 118 ff.
[5] e.g. by the author of the translation into Old English, *The Gospel of Nicodemus*, ed. S. J. Crawford, 1927; and by the author of the translation into Irish,
published by G. Dottin, *Manuel d'Irlandais Moyen*, ii, 1913, pp. 12 ff.
[6] This is also a feature of *Blickling Homily*, No. vii (ed. R. Morris, *The Blickling Homilies of the Tenth Century*, 1874–80).

dwellings if thou canst, and fight doughtily against the King of Glory, for we should not care to have dealings with him'. Then they drove their chieftain from Hell. And when Satan came out he saw a great host of angels come to Hell; he did not go to meet them, but passed them by. Then he changed himself into the likeness of a dragon, and made himself so large that he thought he could encompass the whole world. And now he saw what was happening in Jerusalem, that Jesus Christ was on the point of death, and Satan hurried towards him, thinking to tear the soul from him. And when he came to the place, intending to swallow Jesus and carry him off, the hook of Godhead caught him, and the sign of the Cross fell down upon him, and thus he was taken like a fish on a hook, or a mouse under a trap (literally 'a wooden cat', *trékǫttr*), or like a fox in a snare, as had been foretold.[1]

The translator has often improved upon the Latin original in his descriptions of the dwellers of Hell by drawing on the vocabulary of Norse mythology and by using expressions which even in his time must have been archaic and poetical. Thus Satan is the *Miðgarðs ormr* (the World Serpent of Norse mythology); he is the *jǫfurr helvítis* (Prince of Hell), *dauða skilfingr* (Lord of Death). The lesser devils are called *ríkisþursar*, *ríkistrǫll* (mighty giants, mighty trolls).

Many apocryphal books current in the Middle Ages were concerned with the fortunes of the Apostles after Christ had ascended into Heaven. Several Apostles had taught in strange and savage lands, where they came into conflict with magicians, idols, and monsters of various shapes. Among the best known of these apocryphal Acts were those of Andrew. These were revised and made orthodox by Gregory of Tours (died 594), and were subsequently included in the great collection of apocryphal Acts and Passions which survives as the *Apostolic History of Abdias*.[2] It is believed that the *Apostolic History* was compiled in its present form in France towards the end of the sixth century. It was ascribed to Abdias, who was said to have been a contemporary of the Apostles and first Bishop of Babylon. It was supposed that Abdias had

[1] *Heilagra Manna Sögur*, ii. 4–5.
[2] Printed in *Codex Apocryphus Novi Testamenti*, ed. J. A. Fabricius, 1719, 1743, ii. 402 ff. See R. A. Lipsius, *Die apokryphen Apostelgeschichten*, 1883–90, i. 117 ff.; cf. M. R. James, op. cit., pp. 462 ff.

written in Hebrew, and his work had been translated into Greek, and from Greek into Latin by the celebrated scholar Africanus. Some sections of the *Apostolic History* were also ascribed to Craton, another contemporary of the Apostles, and some to Marcellus, who was at one time a follower of Simon the Magician, from whom he was converted by S. Peter.

The apocryphal Acts were among the first foreign literature to win favour among the Icelanders, and their popularity persisted until the seventeenth century, or even later. Throughout the Middle Ages fresh redactions and copies were frequently made. It was the custom to read them in churches on the feasts of the Apostles whose lives were related in them.[1] The whole corpus has been published by C. R. Unger under the title *Postola Sögur* (1874). This volume was not the least of Unger's services to Old Icelandic literature. It is not to detract from it to say that much work needs still to be done on the *Postola Sögur*. The relationship of the different Icelandic texts to each other needs to be investigated and, in many cases, the relationship of the Icelandic versions to their Latin originals is obscure.

In a number of cases the *Postola Sögur* can be shown to be faithful and accurate translations of apocryphal Acts in late Catholic forms, such as those attributed to Abdias. Some of the Icelandic versions, on the other hand, appear to be somewhat expanded, and are occasionally combined with Canonical Acts and with other sources. The Latin originals are often difficult to trace, partly because of the inaccessibility, and because of the poor state in which they are preserved and edited.

The translators who made the older Icelandic versions of the *Postola Sögur* have striven for linguistic purity, while adhering closely to their originals. Proper names, such as those of classical gods, or even of places, are sometimes replaced by others which would have more vivid associations for people brought up in the northern tradition. Thus, in the *Clemens Saga*, Þórr, Óðinn, and Freyja replace Jove, Hercules, and Venus.[2] Both Achaia and

---

[1] This is sometimes shown in the texts themselves, e.g. *Postola Sögur*, p. 743.
[2] *Postola Sögur*, pp. 146–7.

Scythia are sometimes translated as *Svíþjóð hin mikla* (Sweden the Great); the Proconsul appears as the *Jarl*, and the centurion as the *hundraðshǫfðingi*.

The oldest collection of Icelandic *Postola Sögur* is preserved in a manuscript written about 1220 (No. 645, 4to).[1] This manuscript contains *Clemens Saga*, *Petri Saga*, *Jacobs Saga*, *Bartholomeus Saga*, *Matheus Saga*, and a part of *Andreas Saga*.

The sources for the first two are difficult to decide, but the texts of the *Jacobs Saga*, *Bartholomeus Saga* and *Matheus Saga* closely resemble the corresponding texts of the *Apostolic History of Abdias*, as printed by Fabricius. The *Matheus Saga* is an interesting tale in itself, and its Icelandic version has rather an interesting textual history. In it, the martyrdom of S. Matthew in Ethiopia is described against a background of dragons, sorcerers, and black men. A fragment of this saga is also found in a manuscript of much earlier date than No. 645, viz. in No. 655, 4to, IX, which is believed to have been written about 1150, or little later.[2] This fragment was apparently acquired by Árni Magnússon in Iceland early in the eighteenth century, but it was written in Norway, probably in the neighbourhood of Trondheim, as is shown both by the forms of its words and of its letters. The text of the *Matheus Saga* preserved in this Norwegian manuscript differs greatly from that of No. 645 or of later Icelandic manuscripts. Indeed, the differences are so great that it might be thought that the Icelandic and Norwegian versions of the *Matheus Saga* were made independently from the same source. But yet, some passages in the two versions resemble each other so closely that this conclusion can hardly be maintained, e.g.:

*Norwegian No. 655*: En ef þer ætleð mec guði glickian, hværsu miclu hældr sculu þer trua a þan guð, er ec em hans þræll. Oc ec ræista up í hans nafne þenna konongs sun af dauða, en þer aller er skilia megoð retta scynsemi, ða takeð abraut fra augliti minu gull þetta ok silfr yðat, eða gereð mynstere guði með þvi fe.

*Icelandic No. 645*: En ef ér ætlið mik glíkjan goði, þá mun ek segja

[1] Cf. A. Holtsmark, *En islandsk scholasticus*, 1936, p. 113; H. Spehr, *Der Ursprung der isländischen Schrift*, 1929, pp. viii and 174.

[2] See M. Hægstad, *Reallexikon der germanischen Altertumskunde*, ed. J. Hoops, 1911–19, s.v. *Nordische Schrift*, p. 336, and pl. 24; D. A. Seip, *Norsk Språk-historie*, 1931, pp. 90 ff.

yðr, hversu miklu heldr ér skuluð trúa á þann goð, es ek em þræll hans, ok reista ek í hans nafni konungs son af dauða. En ér allir, er rétta skynsemi meguð skilja, takið braut heðan gull þetta ok silfr ok gersemar, ok farið ok gerið musteri goði.

If the Norwegian version were closer to the Latin text than the Icelandic version is, it might be safe to conclude that the Icelandic was based upon the Norwegian. But the Icelandic version generally represents the Latin more closely than does the Norwegian, which appears to be greatly abbreviated. The most probable explanation of the relationship between the two is that the compiler of the Icelandic version made use of the Norwegian, but referred anew to the Latin text. Within certain limits, therefore, the Icelandic version could be called a new translation.

Pious legends and tales of popular European saints, which cannot strictly be called apocryphal, also found their way to Iceland early, and won widespread and lasting popularity. It has already been described how, according to the *Jóns Saga*, the story *Flagellatio Crucis* was brought from Norway to Hólar when Jón was bishop there. The author of the saga does not say whether the text of the saga which Jón received was in Latin or in the vernacular. But, in several instances, it looks as if vernacular versions of pious legends were made first in Norway, and were afterwards revised and re-edited in Iceland.

The story of S. Placid (*Plácítús Saga*) has a textual history rather like that of the *Matheus Saga*. A fragment of it is found in the same Norwegian manuscript (655, 4to, IX), which preserves a part of the *Matheus Saga*, and it is believed to have been written about 1150. A version of the *Plácítús Saga* is also found in certain Icelandic manuscripts of later date.[1] But the differences between the Norwegian and Icelandic texts of the *Plácítús Saga* are so great that they are best regarded as independent translations from the Latin. Another Icelandic manuscript contains a third and much shorter version of the *Plácítús Saga*.

Whatever may be the relationship between the different versions of the *Plácítús Saga*, the story of S. Placid was known in Iceland

---

[1] See *Heilagra Manna Sögur*, i, p. xx.

in the twelfth century, for it was the theme of the *Plácítús Drápa*, an Icelandic poem found in a manuscript written hardly later than 1200.[1] Some scholars believe that this poem was composed as early as the middle of the twelfth century. The story contained several motives which would recommend it to a western audience. Placid began his career in the time of Trajan, as a good pagan, living with a pagan wife no less virtuous than himself. One day out hunting, he was separated from his companions, and pursued a solitary hart, until it stood at bay beside a rock. The hart turned out to be no other than Christ himself, and he carried the mark of the Cross between his horns. Thus it was that the hunter became the hunted. The motive of the lone quarry, which leads its pursuers to mysterious places, is known in the popular literature of Iceland,[2] as well as in that of other western nations, especially in that of the Welsh and Irish. In the rest of the story Placid is subjected to trials like those of Job, and he bears them no less patiently. His servants die and his cattle are stolen. He is separated from his wife and his sons. Later in the story he is reunited with his family, and appears as a victorious general in the army of Trajan. Finally he and his wife and sons, refusing to offer sacrifice to the heathen gods, were brutally executed by the Emperor Hadrian, the successor of Trajan.

A part of the story of S. Blasius is also found in the same Norwegian manuscript, 655, 4to, IX, and the complete text of it is preserved in the Icelandic manuscript 623, 4to, written during the first half of the thirteenth century, as well as in later manuscripts.[3] If the Norwegian text of the *Blasius Saga* is compared with that of the Icelandic manuscript, it will be seen that both of them depend on the same translation from the Latin. The differences between the two texts are very noticeable, but they are, in reality, superficial. The Norwegian version of the *Blasius Saga* is considerably closer to the Latin than the Icelandic version is. The *Blasius Saga* is a colourful and spirited tale. Its hero, Blasius (or Blase), lived in the time of Constantine the Great, and was Bishop of Sebastia.

---

[1] Cf. F. Paasche, *Kristendom og Kvad*, 1914, pp. 85 ff.
[2] See e.g. *Íslenzkar Þjóðsögur og Ævintýri*, ed. Jón Árnason, ii, 1864, p. 360.
[3] See *Heilagra Manna Sögur*, i. 256–71.

Persecuted by the apostate King Licinius, he fled to the hills. Deprived of the company of men, he became the friend of animals, like the Irish S. Coemgen, and many other hermits. Blasius was seized by a heathen chief called Agricolaus, and after many refined tortures, which he bore with Job's patience, he was put to death. S. Blasius worked many miracles during his lifetime. A boy was brought to him choking with a fish-bone in his throat, and Blasius saved his life. Henceforth, those who have fish-bones stuck in their throats are advised to invoke the aid of S. Blasius. A wolf made off with a widow's pig, her only means of subsistence. Because of the intercession of S. Blasius, the wolf brought the pig back unharmed. Because of the strength of his faith, S. Blasius was able to walk before his persecutors on a lake. When they tried to do the same as he, invoking the aid of their own gods, they sank to the bottom like lead.

The cult of S. Blasius was widespread in Iceland throughout the Middle Ages. This is shown by the churches dedicated to him in various parts of the island, and by the images representing him, of which there are records in several diplomatic documents.[1]

Some of the saints' lives consist of little more than miracles. One of the most popular of the saints in Iceland, if church dedications and personal names are any guide, was Nicholas, Bishop of Myra. His story consists of little other than miracles and it is preserved both in Icelandic and in Norwegian manuscripts of comparatively early date.[2] There is also a more elaborate life of S. Nicholas, written early in the fourteenth century by Bergr Sokkason, monk of Þingeyrar and Abbot of Þverá (died 1345). The story of S. Martin, Bishop of Tours, also consists chiefly of miracles, and it must have been known in Iceland in early times. It is related in the Saga of Bishop Jón[3] that one of S. Martin's bones was kept at Hólar in the time of Bishop Jón. The bone split miraculously in two, and a part of it was taken to another church. The Saga of S. Martin is preserved in an Icelandic manuscript of the first half of the thirteenth century, as well as in several later ones.[4]

[1] Cf. *Diplomatarium Islandicum*, i, p. 170 and footnote 2, p. 594; ii, p. 63; iii, pp. 340, 343, &c.
[2] See C. R. Unger in *Heilagra Manna Sögur*, i, pp. xv–xx.
[3] *Biskupa Sögur*, i. 169, 242.     [4] See C. R. Unger, op. cit., i, pp. xiv–xv.

K

Readers in these days may find little interest in miracle tales, but they exercised a powerful influence on many Icelanders towards the end of the twelfth century. Several hundred miracles were attributed to the native Icelandic saints, Jón of Hólar and Þorlákr the Younger, Bishop of Skálaholt (died 1193). The miracles of Þorlákr were assembled in the so-called Miracle Book (*Jarteiknabók*).[1] The miracles of Jón were collected by Gunnlaugr, and mostly placed at the end of his saga of that saint. It was chiefly as a result of supernatural happenings that Þorlákr was declared a saint by the *Alþingi* in 1199, and Jón in the following year. It was, moreover, in this period that Guðmundr the Good, afterwards Bishop of Hólar (1203-37), used to travel through Iceland with a bodyguard of unruly vagrants, and he performed miracles from one end of the country to the other.[2] Many of the miracles of these native saints resembled those of the more famous foreigners, and were probably modelled on them. The Icelandic saints calm the storms and rescue men at sea; they cure illnesses in men and beasts, and they help to find lost property.

It was suggested, earlier in this chapter, that at the beginning of the twelfth century, homilies and other religious prose were studied with especial ardour in the bishop's school at Hólar. It can hardly be doubted that some of the early homilies and saints' lives were compiled and translated there. The students of the school at Hólar included many distinguished men, who afterwards worked in religious houses in various parts of Iceland. These men must have continued to write and to study religious prose in their new homes, and have trained others to do the same. Klœngr Þorsteinsson, a student at Hólar in the days of Bishop Jón, was made Bishop of Skálaholt about the middle of the twelfth century.[3] A large proportion of the literature discussed in this chapter should probably be claimed for Skálaholt. In one version of the Saga of S. Peter, the Icelandic compiler mentions the see of Skálaholt, and remembers that S. Peter was its patron.[4]

---

[1] *Biskupa Sögur*, i. 333–56; published in facsimile in *Corpus Codicum Islandicorum*, xii.        [2] See *Guðmundar Saga góða* in *Biskupa Sögur*, i. 407 ff.
[3] On Klœngr see Brynleifur Tobiasson, *Heim að Hólum*, 1943, pp. 110 ff., 151 ff. &c.        [4] *Postola Sögur*, p. 215.

The pupils trained at Hólar also numbered several abbots, and the inmates of Icelandic monasteries must have done much to develop the homilies and legendary literature. At least five monasteries were founded during the twelfth century.[1] The oldest and foremost of them was Þingeyrar, a Benedictine house near the shores of the Húnaflói. This monastery was founded in 1133, and throughout the twelfth century its monks maintained close relations with Hólar. There were good reasons for this. It is recorded in the Saga of Bishop Jón that Jón had himself intended to found a monastery at Þingeyrar, and had marked the site of the church, although the monastery was not founded until after his death. The first Abbot of Þingeyrar, Vilmundr Þórólfsson (died 1148), was a pupil of Jón, and so was the fourth abbot, Hreinn Styrmisson (died 1171). Gunlaugr Leifsson (died 1218), author of the Saga of Jón, was a monk of Þingeyrar, and he compiled many other works, some of which will be mentioned in a later chapter. Among the works attributed to Gunnlaugr was a life of S. Ambrose. It is related in Abbot Arngrímr's life of Guðmundr the Good[2] how Gunnlaugr brought his new story of S. Ambrose into the church at Hólar, intending to read it aloud without leave of the bishop. Bishop Guðmundr forbade him, under pain of interdict, to introduce such innovations into his church, saying that Pope Gregory's life of S. Ambrose was more suitable for reading in church. A saga of S. Ambrose survives in Iceland, and its chief source is Paulinus's *Vita S. Ambrosii*,[3] but it cannot be said whether this was the one which Gunnlaugr wrote.

A few words should be said about the translations of standard works on theology. Among those known in Iceland in the twelfth century were the *Dialogues* of Gregory the Great. This book was popular in many lands,[4] and extensive fragments of an Icelandic version of it are preserved in MS. 677, 4to, which is believed to date from the beginning of the thirteenth century. Several other

---

[1] See Janus Jónsson, *Um klaustrin á Íslandi* in *Tímarit hins íslenzka bókmenntafélags*, 1887, pp. 174 ff.
[2] *Biskupa Sögur*, ii. 77.    [3] *Heilagra Manna Sögur*, i. 28 ff.
[4] An especially interesting translation is the one into Old English made by Bishop Werferth of Worcester at the request of King Alfred. See *Bibliothek der angelsächsischen Prosa*, v, ed. H. Hecht, 1900.

early fragments of it have been found, both in Iceland and in Nor-way.[1] The *Dialogues* consist chiefly of stories told by S. Gregory to his disciple Peter, and each story illustrates a moral precept. For the Icelanders, at any rate, the story was more important than the precept, and it is interesting to see how motives from Gregory's *Dialogues* gradually found their way into the traditional literatures of Iceland and Norway. This was noticed already by Þorvaldr Bjarnarson.[2]

Among the most interesting stories contained in the *Dialogues* are those about Totila, King of the Goths, in Italy (died 552). According to one of them, Totila had heard about the prophetic gifts of S. Benedict, and he wished to test them. He dressed one of his servants in his own clothes, and sent him with a retinue to the hermit. The saint quickly saw through the disguise, and told the servant to lay aside the clothes which were not his. Shortly after-wards Totila himself came to visit the hermit. Not daring to draw near, Totila cast himself on the ground, and lay there until Bene-dict took him by the hand and raised him up. The saint rebuked Totila for his cruelty, and foretold many things which afterwards came to pass, including Totila's death ten years later.

Stories both of S. Ólafr and of Ólafr Tryggvason were modelled on this passage in the *Dialogues*, and they became current in the sagas of these two Norse kings. The Norse story which resembles that of Totila most closely is probably the one about S. Ólafr, told in the 'Legendary Saga'.[3] S. Ólafr sent one of his servants dressed as himself to try the prophetic powers of a hermit in England. A similar tale is told of Ólafr Tryggvason in the *Historia Norvegiae*, *Ágrip*, *Heimskringla*, &c.

Þorvaldur Bjarnarson[4] remarked on similarities between Gregory's tales of Mellitus and Valerianus,[5] and the dream of Flosi in the *Njáls Saga*.[6] Einar Ól. Sveinsson has since shown be-

---

[1] See *Heilagra Manna Sögur*, i, Introduction, p. x; cf. *Leifar fornra kristinna fræða íslenzkra*, ed. Þorvaldur Bjarnarson, 1878, Introduction, pp. xiii ff.

[2] Op. cit., p. xv.

[3] *Ólafs Saga hins helga*, ed. R. Keyser and C. R. Unger, 1849, ch. 19; cf. *Ólafs Saga hins helga*, ed. O. A. Johnsen, 1922, ch. 18.        [4] Op. cit., p. xv.

[5] *Leifar*, pp. 136–7; cf. *Heilagra Manna Sögur*, i. 242–3.

[6] *Brennu-Njálssaga*, ed. Finnur Jónsson, 1908, ch. cxxxiii.

yond doubt that the story of Flosi's dream was modelled largely on Gregory's story of the monk Anastasius.[1] One night Anastasius heard a voice calling his name from a high cliff, and afterwards the names of seven other brethren were called. After this the voice paused, and then called the name of an eighth monk. All the monks died in the order in which their names had been called, and there was a pause of a few days before the last one died. It is not necessary to emphasize the similarity between this story and that of Flosi's dream. Þorvaldur Bjarnarson suggested that several other tales in Icelandic literature had been coloured by the *Dialogues*. In some instances it looks as though the *Dialogues* had influenced folk-tales before these folk-tales were included in books. An example of this might be seen in the story, told by the monk Oddr, of how Ólafr Tryggvason's courtiers spent a night in a cave in Naumudalr, and overheard the conversation of the wicked trolls, who had tried to tempt the king.[2] This is rather like Gregory's story of the Jew who spent a night in a heathen temple, and heard the demons describing how they had quickened lust in the heart of Bishop Andreas.[3]

Another interesting translation is that of the *Lucidarius* (or *Elucidarius*). This is a handbook of theology, and was perhaps the only one of its kind to be translated into Icelandic in the twelfth century. The *Lucidarius* is commonly ascribed to Honorius Augustodunensis, who is also believed to be the author of the *Imago Mundi* and of the *Gemma Animae*, and of several other works. Little is known about the life of Honorius, but there are reasons to suppose that he died about the middle of the twelfth century, and that he was an enclosed monk of the Irish foundation of Regensburg.[4] Honorius probably wrote the *Lucidarius* about the beginning of the twelfth century. It was designed as a summary of theological knowledge and was, of course, based chiefly on older works. It cannot be called a pleasing book. The author, whenever he

---

[1] *Á Njálsbúð*, 1943, pp. 8 ff.
[2] *Saga Ólafs Tryggvasonar* (Oddr Snorrason), ed. Finnur Jónsson, 1932, pp. 174 ff.  [3] *Heilagra Manna Sögur*, i. 222–3.
[4] On the person and work of Honorius see J. Sauer, *Symbolik des Kirchengebäudes*, 1902, pp. 12–22; Eva M. Sandford in *Speculum*, xxiii, 1948, pp. 397 ff.

comes to light, shows himself vain and self-assured. He writes in
the form of dialogue, and is never in doubt what answers he shall
give to his pupil's puzzling questions. This was probably one of the
reasons for the popularity of the book. Honorius writes, he tells us,
lest he should be condemned for concealing the wisdom given him
by God. He hides his own name, and writes anonymously lest he
should rouse envy in others. He gives rich descriptions of the
creation, of the Garden of Eden, of Christ, Heaven and Hell. The
greater part of humanity, it seems, is destined for Hell. There is
little hope for the knights or for the merchants, and little for the
craftsmen, because they often deceive their customers. The minstrels will all be damned, for they are the servants of Satan. But
many workmen will be saved, and so will idiots and baptized children under three. Some children of five will also be saved, but not
all. One of the greatest pleasures of the blessed in Heaven will be
to watch the writhings of the damned in Hell. This will be hardly
less delightful for them than it is for us to watch a fish darting in
a pool.

The *Lucidarius* is little read today, but in the Middle Ages it was
among the most popular of all handbooks of theology. It deserves
to be read, if only because of its place in cultural history, and because it shows what kind of doctrines were handed out to many in
the Middle Ages. This may help us to understand the unrestrained
fanaticism of Ólafr Tryggvason or of Guðmundr the Good, or of
other Christian teachers in Norway and other lands.

Versions of the *Lucidarius* are preserved in most of the languages
of Europe,[1] and the oldest of them is probably an English one
dating from the early years of the twelfth century, of which a small
part survives.[2] Some of the later versions were much altered and
expanded. The more conservative versions also show marked
differences, and could be divided into various classes. These
vernacular versions would be of great value to any scholar who
might undertake a critical edition of the Latin original.

[1] On the vernacular versions of the *Lucidarius* see K. Schorbach, *Das Volks-
buch Lucidarius*, 1894.
[2] See M. Förster in *Miscellany to J. Furnivall*, 1901, pp. 86 ff.

The oldest manuscript of the *Lucidarius* in Icelandic is No. 674 A, 4to, which now consists of thirty-three leaves in octavo, and covers about one-third of the whole text.[1] It is generally supposed that this manuscript was written about 1200, although some scholars would ascribe it to an earlier date. It contains numerous archaic word-forms, which may suggest that the translation was made before the end of the twelfth century.[2] A larger part of the *Lucidarius* is found in the *Hauksbók*, which was written for Haukr Erlendsson early in the fourteenth century.[3] These two manuscripts must be traced to the same original translation, and the differences between them are due largely to corruption in the text of the *Hauksbók*. There are, in addition, a number of smaller and later fragments of the *Lucidarius* in Icelandic.[4]

Two versions of the *Lucidarius* are preserved in Swedish,[5] and the Icelandic text bears a certain resemblance to the younger of them, made late in the fifteenth century. It is also interesting to notice that the Icelandic version compares more closely with the Welsh one, probably made in the thirteenth century, than it does with the Vulgate text printed by Migne.[6] This implies that, on some points, the text of the Icelandic *Lucidarius* resembles that of the Bodleian MS. Laud. 237, which Sir J. Morris-Jones and Sir J. Rhŷs consulted when they prepared their edition of the Welsh *Lucidarius*.[7]

Whatever judgement may be passed upon the *Lucidarius* as a theological work, none will deny that the Icelandic translation is masterly, and it contrasts sharply with the clumsiness of the Swedish versions. It has great linguistic interest, for it shows how

[1] Published in facsimile in *Arnamagnæanske Haandskrifter i fotolitografiske Aftryk*, No. 2, 1869. See also Konráð Gíslason, *Um frum-parta íslenzkrar túngu*, 1846, pp. lxxxvii ff., and the same author's paper in *Annaler for nordisk Oldkyndighed og Historie*, 1858, pp. 51 ff.; H. Spehr, op. cit., pp. viii and 174; A. Holtsmark, op. cit., p. 115.

[2] Cf. the Introduction to the edition in facsimile already quoted.

[3] *Hauksbók*, ed. Finnur Jónsson, 1892–4, pp. 470–99.

[4] See *Katalog over den Arnamagnæanske Håndskriftsamling*, ii, 1894, 658.

[5] Ed. R. Geete in *Svenska kyrkobruk under medeltiden*, 1900.

[6] *Patrologia Latina*, clxxii, cols. 1105 ff.

[7] *The Elucidarium and other Tracts in Welsh*, 1894; cf. *Selections from the Hengwrt MSS.*, ed. R. Williams and G. H. Jones, ii, 1892.

the Icelandic language could be used to express foreign thoughts, and how native words could be found or devised to represent abstract philosophical conceptions, which must have been strange to the Icelanders of the twelfth century. Like most Icelandic translators of his age, the translator of the *Lucidarius* disliked loanwords, and he had sufficient aesthetic sense to resist standardized clichés. A few of his renderings of Latin philosophical terms may be quoted:

*skilningar himinn* (intellectual heaven), *hugrenningar skrímsl* (imagines phantasmatum), *fyrirætlan* (praedestinatio), *hǫfuðskepnur* (elementa), *andlegr hórdómr* (spiritualis fornicatio), *í áblæstri sínum* (inspirando).

It was suggested above that, in several instances, the vernacular versions of religious texts were made first in Norway, and were later revised and rewritten in Iceland. The influence of the Norwegians in Iceland probably increased after the middle of the twelfth century. In the earliest Christian period, the Churches of Norway and Iceland were wholly independent of each other, and until 1104 they had both been subject to the archbishops of Bremen and Hamburg. From 1104, when the province of Lund was established, until 1152, both Iceland and Norway belonged to that province. But in 1152 Iceland was made a part of the province of Trondheim, which Nicholas Breakspear created in that year.[1] Despite the resistance of certain powerful Icelandic chiefs, the ecclesiastical administration of Iceland fell more and more under the influence of the Norwegians as the twelfth century drew to its close. This had far-reaching consequences for Iceland, both political and cultural. One of the results was a widening cleavage between the laity and clergy of Iceland, and a sharpening distinction between the lay and the learned literatures. In earlier times the protagonists of the traditional and 'learned' cultures had been the same men. Hereditary chieftains studied European letters and took orders, and they led the people in temporal as in spiritual matters. Sæmundr, Ari, and Jón Loptsson (died 1197) might be cited as examples. But after the province of Trondheim was established the influence of Universal Church movement began to be felt

[1] See A. O. Johnsen, *Nicolaus Brekespears legasjon til norden*, 1945.

in Iceland as elsewhere. The ecclesiastical dignitaries in Norway made it their purpose to weaken the power of the temporal chiefs over the Icelandic Church. In 1190 Archbishop Eiríkr forbade the ruling chiefs of Iceland (*goðar*) to take orders.[1]

We may suppose that learned books were brought to Iceland from Norway in greater numbers after the arch-see of Trondheim was established. In such cases the vernacular versions might have been made in various parts of Norway, but especially, we should suppose, in the neighbourhood of Trondheim. This is a suggestion rather than a conclusion. It has something in common with the suggestions recently made by D. A. Seip,[2] although it is not based on the same arguments. Seip has minutely examined the orthography, script, and vocabulary used in certain manuscripts of learned literature written in Iceland about 1200, or little later. On the evidence which he finds, Seip concludes that the originals, from which these Icelandic manuscripts were copied, were written in Norway, and especially in eastern Norway. Seip's arguments appear to be too slender to carry the great weight attached to them, at least to those less familiar with the problems of dialect and orthography than Seip himself. Not the least of the difficulties is the scarcity of manuscripts written in Norway, and especially in eastern Norway, which are old enough to be compared with these early Icelandic ones.

The influence of the religious houses of Norway may have been great. But it should be emphasized that a much larger proportion of learned literature survives in Icelandic than in Norwegian manuscripts. It was in Iceland rather than in Norway that literature of this class was cultivated and developed. It was also in Iceland that its influence was strongest and most lasting.

In this chapter only a small proportion of the religious prose which could be assigned to the twelfth and early thirteenth centuries has been mentioned. Such literature has often been neglected in popular studies of Icelandic literature, and even in authoritative works. This is easy to understand, and it is excusable. The saints'

---

[1] See *Diplomatarium Islandicum*, i, 1857–76, pp. 289 ff.
[2] See *Maal og Minne*, 1943, pp. 97 ff.; 1945, pp. 8 ff., 21 ff., 30 ff.

lives and the homilies are not among the best or most interesting of Icelandic literature. Only occasionally do they express the thoughts or the artistic taste of the Icelandic people, and they tell little about the traditions and antiquities of the north. But they were more important for the Icelanders of the twelfth century than they are for us. They were the first written biographies which the Icelanders came to know. The Icelanders learned from them how biographies and wonder-tales could be written in books. Thus, they helped the Icelanders to develop a literary style in their own language, and gave them the means to express their own thoughts through the medium of letters. In a word, the learned literature did not teach the Icelanders what to think or what to say, but it taught them how to say it. It is unlikely that the sagas of kings and of Icelanders, or even the sagas of ancient heroes, would have developed as they did unless several generations of Icelanders had first been trained in hagiographic narrative.

# VI

## THE POETRY OF THE
## EARLY CHRISTIAN PERIOD

ST. ÓLAFR died fighting at Stiklastaðir in the summer of 1030. After his body had lain in the grave for a year and five days, it rose to the surface. When the shroud was lifted, the king's countenance was pink and white as when he was alive, and he looked as if he had lately fallen asleep. Álfífa, the English mother of King Sveinn, who was present when the relics were translated, scoffed at the uncorrupt state of Ólafr's body, but the other spectators were now convinced of his sanctity, even those who had fought against him at Stiklastaðir. The cult of S. Ólafr spread rapidly. Miracles were worked, not only in Niðaróss, but throughout Norway and even in distant lands, where those in distress called upon the saint to intercede for them.

The Icelandic scalds were among the first to sing the praises of the new saint, both those who had been his friends and those who had lived among his enemies. One of the first to praise Ólafr as a saint was Þórarinn Loftunga (Praise Tongue). Þórarinn was known already as the poet of Knútr the Great, and eight strophes of a poem, Tøgdrápa, in which he praised that king, are preserved.[1] The content of the Tøgdrápa is of little interest. It owes its name to its remarkable metrical form, the Tøglag (see p. 34 above). After the translation of S. Ólafr, Þórarinn addressed a poem to Sveinn, the son of Knútr, who was then ruler of Norway, in name at least. It is called Glælognskviða (Calm-sea Lay?),[2] and Þórarinn shows again that he preferred the rarer metrical forms. In this poem he used the Kviðuháttr, an ancient metre which had long passed out

---

[1] See Den norsk-islandske Skjaldedigtning (Skjald.), ed. Finnur Jónsson, B. i, 1912, p. 298. References made to scaldic poems in this chapter apply to this edition unless otherwise stated, but the interpretations and emendations given by Finnur Jónsson have not always been followed. The reader may also consult the diplomatic texts of Finnur Jónsson (Skjald. A. i), and the revised texts of E. A. Kock (Den norsk-isländka skaldediktningen, i, 1946), who prints the poems in the same order as Finnur Jónsson.   [2] Skjald. B. i, p. 300.

of fashion (see p. 34 above). As a poem the *Glælognskviða* is more valuable than the *Tøgdrápa*, and it has the added value of an historical document. It was evidently composed about 1032, within a year or two of the saint's death, and Þórarinn shows that the cult of Ólafr was now established among his former enemies as among his friends. Þórarinn advised Sveinn to call upon S. Ólafr that he might be secure in the Kingdom of Norway, for Ólafr could win peace and prosperity for all from God himself. The saint was already famous for his miracles. The bells over his shrine would ring without human agency, and the candles would flare up on the altar; the blind and the deaf would creep before his shrine and depart healed. New subjects for poetry were introduced with the *Glælognskviða*.

Sigvatr, the favourite poet of S. Ólafr, was not present when the king laid down his life. He had exchanged the sword for the staff and scrip and had gone as a pilgrim to Rome. He first heard of the king's death when he was on his way home. Sigvatr left several strophes in which he mourned his master's death. In one of them he told how he came upon a man weeping for his dead wife.[1] He could spare little sympathy for the widower, for the loss of his own king was the harder to bear. When he came back to Norway, Sigvatr contrasted the land which he saw under the tyranny of Sveinn Knútsson with that which he remembered under Ólafr. The leaning cliffs had seemed to laugh when Ólafr ruled, but now the slopes of Norway were sad.[2]

Sigvatr refused to join the court of Sveinn, although pressed to do so. When Magnús Ólafsson returned to Norway in 1035, Sigvatr became his most loyal friend and adviser. In the *Bersøglisvísur* (Plain-speaking Verses),[3] Sigvatr rebuked the young king for his harsh and injudicious rule, and urged him to mend his ways. These verses probably saved the king's throne and life. He became a generous monarch, and went down to history as Magnús the Good. The style of the *Berøglisvísur* is simple, and they are easy to understand. Few kennings are used and the syntax is straight-

---

[1] *Skjald*. B. i. 251, No. 22.    [2] Ibid., p. 252, No. 26.
[3] Ibid., p. 234.

forward. As poetry they are perhaps the least valuable of Sigvatr's work, and they show how court poetry, when shorn of figurative diction and other poetic devices, may be little better than dead wood.

Sigvatr's last big poem was a Memorial Lay (*Erfidrápa*) for S. Ólafr,[1] and he composed it shortly before his own death, probably about the year 1043. The lay itself has an interesting history. Once when the poet landed on the holy island of Selja, off the west coast of Norway, a farmer nearby was lying dangerously ill, nursed by his wife. S. Ólafr appeared to the woman in a dream, and told her that he was displeased with Sigvatr because, in the *Memorial Lay* on which he was then working, he was using a refrain (*stál*, *stef*) from the story of Sigurðr the Dragon-slayer. Ólafr would rather he used a refrain from a sacred story, the *Uppreistarsaga*.[2] The name *Uppreistarsaga* is used in another text for the story of *Genesis*, and this may be the meaning here. Alternatively, it might mean the raising of Christ from the Jordan after baptism. The following lines ascribed to Sigvatr by Snorri Sturluson[3] may belong to the refrain of the *Memorial Lay*:

> Of old the Lord of Jordan
> Angels four sent earthward,
> the holy river washed the
> hair of the prince of peoples.

The *Memorial Lay* contains much that is best in Sigvatr's poetry. It cannot be said how much of it has been lost, but the surviving strophes have great value as sources of history. The poet seems to pass quickly over the early years of Ólafr's reign, and concentrates on his return from Russia and his last campaign in Norway. The scene at Stiklastaðir, when the king was killed, is described as nowhere else. The enemies of the saint dare not look into his eyes, piercing as spears and keen as the eyes of a serpent. Even more striking was the moment when the sun grew cold and

[1] *Skjald.* B. i. 239.
[2] See *Flateyjarbók*, ed. G. Vigfússon and C. R. Unger, ii, 1862, p. 394, and other sources.
[3] *Skjald.* B, i. 245, No. 28; cf. *Edda Snorra Sturlusonar*, ed. Guðni Jónsson, 1935, p. 206; see also F. Paasche, *Kristendom og Kvad*, 1914, p. 20.

its light failed to guide the warriors groping in battle. Sigvatr speaks also of miracles worked at the shrine of the saint and of the celebration of his feast.

The *Memorial Lay* differs from the earlier poetry of Sigvatr chiefly in the use of kennings, which he now uses more liberally, and constructs more elaborately than he did in his earlier work. In old age he seems to return to the traditional style of the scalds of the tenth century.[1] Gold is now the 'fire of the pool' and the generous princes are those who hurl it; battle now sates the hunger of the she-wolf's husband.

Sigvatr was not a great artist. He was admired in his own age, as he is today, for his human qualities, which are plainly expressed in his poetry. He combined loyalty with magnanimity. He could admire the king's enemies, even those who caused his death. He was the chief representative of the simplified style of scaldic poetry, but he exercised no great influence on those who came after him, and this may suggest that his poetry was not highly valued.

Steinn Herdísarson was the spiritual descendant of Sigvatr, and poems which he made in praise of Haraldr Harðráði (died 1066) and of Ólafr Kyrri (died 1093) are preserved.[2] In the first of these, Steinn described the battle of Niz (1062), in which Haraldr had defeated Sveinn Úlfsson, King of the Danes. Steinn is magnanimous as Sigvatr, and praises the defeated Sveinn no less than Haraldr. Two bolder warriors never greeted each other with spears. Steinn's lay on Ólafr Kyrri (1066–93) is more valuable, for it is one of the few sources of the history of that king. It is a conventional *drápa*, but the poet shows some technical originality in using the 'broken' or 'inlaid' refrain (*klofastef*). The refrain consists only of three lines, in which the poet says that the noble-hearted Ólafr knows that he is the greatest born under the sun, but these three lines are cleverly distributed between three different strophes. The *drápa* opens with a prayer to God, and the story told in it begins with the fatal expedition of Haraldr Harðráði to England in 1066.

---

[1] Cf. J. de Vries, *Altnordische Literaturgeschichte*, i, 1941, p. 255.
[2] *Skjald.* B. i. 376 ff.

Although several poets of the early and middle eleventh century worked in the simplified style of Sigvatr, there were others who clung to the older traditions. Among these was Refr Gestsson. He came of a family of Snæfellsnes in western Iceland, and his mother was Steinunn, a poetess of some note.[1] She was remembered for her attempts to convert the missionary, Þangbrandr, to heathendom, as well as for some verses which she made in derision of him when his ship was wrecked off the coast of Iceland. Only a few fragments of the poetry of Refr are known now but, as Finnur Jónsson[2] pointed out, they show outstanding talent and skill. It is said that Refr made poetry about S. Ólafr, but this is lost. Refr tells us in one passage that he was brought up by an older poet, Gizurr Gullbrárskáld, who died on the side of Ólafr at Stiklastaðir. Some fragments of a lay which Refr made in memory of Gizurr are preserved, and in them he describes how his foster-father had led him to the hallowed cup of the Raven-god (Óðinn), the sacred mead of poetry. In some other fragments Refr describes a voyage on a stormy sea. The sea-goddess tries to drag the bear of twined ropes (ship) into the jaws of her husband; but the horse of the sea-mountains (ship), splashed with spray, tears his red-painted chest out of the mouth of Rán (the sea-goddess). Such descriptions of nature are rarely found in early Icelandic poetry, and these fragments may be compared with the strophe in which Egill Skalla-Grímsson described the sea in a storm (see p. 42 above). The poetry of Refr is characterized by wealth of kennings, many of which contain allusion to pagan myth and legend. It would be rash to conclude, with Paasche,[3] that, for Refr, such allusions were meaningless form. Not all of those who followed S. Ólafr were Christians, and Refr's mother, Steinunn, had been a courageous defender of the old religion.

Arnórr Þórðarson was among the most remarkable poets of the eleventh century. He was the son of Þórðr Kolbeinsson, himself a poet, whose work is preserved in the *Bjarnar Saga Hítdœlakappa*. Arnórr was born in western Iceland about the year 1011. In his

---

[1] On Steinunn see *Kristnisaga*, ed. B. Kahle, 1905, ch. ix.
[2] *ONOI*, i. 598–600.       [3] Op. cit., p. 37.

early childhood, his peaceful disposition earned the scorn of his neighbours in Iceland, and he spent his best years abroad. He is listed among the poets of Knútr the Great,[1] but none of the verses which Arnórr made for Knútr are known now. He spent some years in Orkney and in northern Scotland, and he was the friend of the rival Jarls of Orkney, Þorfinnr Sigurðarson (died 1064) and his nephew Rǫgnvaldr Brúsason (died 1045). Arnórr tells us in a strophe that he was married to a relative of Rǫgnvaldr. He was sadly grieved at the quarrel between his patrons, and he was on Þorfinnr's ship when they fought at Rauðuborg (Dunnet Head, c. 1045), but took no part in this battle. Arnórr followed Þorfinnr in many of his battles and raids in Scotland and in the Hebrides, and one of his chief poems is a Memorial Lay (Þorfinnsdrápa) made after the hero's death.[2] As history the Þorfinnsdrápa has unique value, for not only was the poet an eye-witness of many events, but he was well able to describe what he saw. As the viking Jarl marched through Scotland, homesteads were laid waste, and the red flames leapt in the smoking reeds of the roof-tops. It is instructive to contrast these lifelike descriptions of Þorfinnr's raids with those in which Sigvatr recorded the exploits of S. Ólafr in his viking days (see p. 44 above). The language of Arnórr is richer than that of Sigvatr, and he does not shrink from kennings in which allusion is made to pagan myth. Arnórr's poetry is the 'froth of Óðinn's malt', but he lacks the restraint characteristic of some of the best Icelandic poets, thinking no praise too great for his hero. In lines which recall the Vǫluspá he says that a nobler prince than Þorfinnr will not be born in Orkney before the Ragnarǫk:

> The fair sun will be swarthy,
> sink earth in the ocean
> black, waves hill-tops batter,
> break the load of Atlas—
> ere is born in Orkney
> a Jarl of nobler temper.
> Save, O Lord of peoples,
> the prince who fed his warriors.

---

[1] In the Skáldatal, published in Edda Snorra Sturlusonar, edition already quoted, p. 328.  [2] Skjald. B. i. 316–21.

Soon after the death of Rǫgnvaldr (1045), Arnórr was in Norway, where he won the patronage of both kings, Magnús the Good (died 1047) and Haraldr Harðráði (died 1066). Once, when these two kings were on fairly friendly terms, they were sitting together at table, and they sent a messenger to Arnórr, bidding him come to recite the *drápur* which he had made in praise of each of them. The poet was in the harbour, tarring his ship, but he hurried unwashed to the court and delivered his *drápur*. The one dedicated to Haraldr was called the *Blágagladrápa* (Blue-goose Lay, Raven Lay), and the one dedicated to Magnús is called the *Hrynhenda*.[1] The *Hrynhenda* is an unconventional poem, for Arnórr uses the measure *Hrynjandi*, and this was perhaps the first time that it had been used for a royal panegyric. I have already mentioned the ways in which this measure differs from the usual *Dróttkvætt* (see p. 33 above). Its octosyllabic, four-footed lines resemble those of popular hymns in Latin, and it was much used for religious poetry in Icelandic in the later Middle Ages. It has been said that expression in the *Hrynjandi* is less cramped than in the *Dróttkvætt*.[2] It is less jerky, and also less forceful. The following lines in the translation of William Morris and Eiríkr Magnússon[3] will give a fair idea of the rhythm of Arnórr's *Hrynhenda*:

> Thou, king's son, shalt hear in stave-lay
> how the war-shield unto Wendland
> bare ye. Then thou drewest, O happy,
> rimy boards off the smooth rollers.
> Heard I ne'er of king that ever
> more ships hosted to their heir-land.
> Then by ships was ploughed the sea-flood;
> wrought ye, king, once more Wend-sorrow.

The *Hrynhenda* resembles the *Þorfinnsdrápa* in many ways. In both poems, Arnórr shows his remarkable talent for visual description, and lavishes praise on his hero without stint. After Magnús, aided by the intercession of S. Ólafr, had routed the heathen Wends,

---

[1] Ibid., pp. 306–11.
[2] On the measure of the *Hrynhenda* see de Vries, op. cit. i. 258; L. M. Hollander, *The Skalds*, 1945, pp. 182–3.
[3] *The Saga Library*, v (= *Heimskringla*, iii), 1895, p. 32.

L

the piles of bodies stood so high that hungry wolves could not climb to the tops of them. The decorated fleet of Magnús putting out to sea was likened to the sun rising in a brilliant sky; as they sailed over the waves, the ships resembled a host of God's angels.

After the death of Magnús, in 1047, Arnórr made a lay in memory of him, and he retold many of the stories and used some of the same symbols which he had used in the *Hrynhenda*. He lived to make a Memorial Lay for Haraldr Harðráði, who was killed at Stamford Bridge in 1066.[1] The date of Arnórr's death is not known, but he lived to be an old man. The last of his poems of which we hear was a lay made in memory of the Icelandic chieftain Gellir Þorkelsson, who died in 1073 on the way back from a pilgrimage to Rome. None of this lay survives, but in it Arnórr described a noble church which Gellir had built at Helgafell.[2]

Although his style resembles that of the pagans in many ways, Arnórr was no less Christian than Sigvatr. His poems contain prayers for the salvation of the souls of his heroes, and in one strophe he describes the Archangel Michael, weighing men's good and evil deeds.

Þjóðólfr Arnórsson lived at the same time as Arnórr and, like Arnórr, he made poetry both for Magnús the Good and for Haraldr Harðráði. Þjóðólfr was reared in Svarfaðardalr in the north of Iceland. He was of no family and was the son of a penniless crofter,[3] but he grew up to be a court poet of refined and over-exclusive taste. About twenty strophes addressed by Þjóðólfr to Magnús the Good are preserved, and they probably belong to a lay composed about 1046. The poet praises the king in conventional terms, and lists his triumphs as they were listed by Arnórr.

Þjóðólfr was the favourite poet of Haraldr Harðráði, and the stories of his relations with the king help us to understand Haraldr's taste in poetry and show what he expected of his poets. He once detected, in a line by Þjóðólfr, a metrical fault which many a modern critic would overlook.[4] It is not difficult to see why

[1] *Skjald.* B. i. 322–6.
[2] *Laxdæla Saga*, ed. Einar Ól. Sveinsson, 1934, ch. 78.
[3] See especially *Flateyjarbók*, edition quoted above, iii, 1868, pp. 421–2.
[4] See *Morkinskinna*, ed. Finnur Jónsson, 1932, p. 248.

Þjóðólfr should be the favourite of Haraldr, for he was hardly surpassed in technical excellence. His chief surviving work is the *Sexstefja*,[1] which he made in honour of Haraldr shortly before his death in 1066. As the name *Sexstefja* implies, the poem must originally have contained six refrains, although only one of these can be detected now. Some thirty-five strophes and half-strophes of the *Sexstefja* are known, but it is clear that a great part of the poem has been lost.

The *Sexstefja* is equally interesting for its subject and its style. The poet speaks of Haraldr's travels and especially of his victories in the east. He tells a story, which he must have heard from the king himself, of how Haraldr put out both the eyes of the Emperor of Byzantium. He speaks later of Haraldr's return to Norway, of his wars with the Danes and his suppression of rebellious subjects in Norway. The tall roof-wolf (fire) taught them discipline, while the beams glowed over their heads. These passages of the *Sexstefja* are not unlike those in which Arnórr described the ravages of Jarl Þorfinnr in Scotland, but the language of Þjóðólfr is removed farther from that of daily speech. Þjóðólfr's kennings are often elaborate and far-fetched. They show that he was learned both in the poetry of earlier scalds and in legends. Like a scaldic poet of the ninth century, Þjóðólfr denotes 'fire' by an allusion to a viking story and calls it the 'bane of Hálfr'; the 'sword' is 'Óðinn's sickle' (*Gauts sigðr*); 'corpses' are the 'corn of the blood-swan'. The poet says: 'The King of the Hǫrðar brings the sickle of Óðinn to the corn of the blood-swan.' Similarly, Þjóðólfr alludes to the story of Hrólfr Kraki, and to the legendary battle of Fýrisvellir, calling 'gold' the 'seed of Yrsa's son', and the 'corn of Kraki'.[2]

A number of strophes which pass under the name of Þjóðólfr have been assigned to no sequence or lay, and some of them are occasional verses. An enlightening story is told about two of them. Þjóðólfr was once walking in the street with King Haraldr, and they passed a house where a tanner was brawling with a blacksmith. The

---

[1] *Skjald.* B. i. 339–46.
[2] Cf. *Edda Snorra Sturlusonar*, edition quoted, pp. 186–7.

king said: 'make a verse about this quarrel, Þjóðólfr.' Þjóðólfr answered that this was hardly a suitable subject for the king's chief poet, but the king told him to describe the ruffians as other than they were: the one must be Sigurðr and the other the dragon, Fáfnir. Þjóðólfr said:

> Hammer-Sigurðr the serpent,
> savage, egged to vengeance;
> the dragon, skin-scraping,
> scaled down from the boot-rocks.
> Dreaded was the dragon
> —dressed his claws in leather—
> till the long-nosed tong-king
> tore the ox-skin adder.[1]

Þjóðólfr followed his patron to the end, and must have died with him at Stamford Bridge. He left two strophes which he composed on the fateful battlefield.[2] He blames the king for this foolhardy invasion of England, while pledging his loyalty in death as in life. It has been said that the poetry of Þjóðólfr lacks personal interest and lyrical qualities, but that would not be a fair criticism of his last strophes.

Haraldr Harðráði was himself a poet, and many of the professional scalds of Iceland sought his patronage. Among them was Sneglu-Halli, also a man of northern Iceland.[3] Halli competed with Þjóðólfr for the favours of Haraldr and, in character as in poetry, he was the antithesis of Þjóðólfr. He was a plebeian, and his poetry is burlesque of a low order. He can be regarded only as a court fool.

Illugi Bryndœlaskáld is listed among the poets of Haraldr.[4] Little can be told of him, but four half-strophes of a lay which he made in honour of Haraldr are found in sagas and in tracts on prosody. These strophes show that Illugi's lay was a remarkable experiment in technique. In lines 1 and 4 of each half-strophe the poet praises Haraldr, but in lines 2 and 3 he tells the story of

---

[1] See *Morkinskinna*, pp. 235 ff. 'Hammer-Sigurðr' is, needless to say, the 'blacksmith', and the 'skin-scraping dragon' is the 'tanner'.

[2] *Skjald*. B. i. 353, Nos. 26 and 27.

[3] Cf. Finnur Jónsson, *ONOI*, i. 620–2.

[4] In *Skáldatal*, edition quoted above, p. 321; see *Skjald*. B. i. 354.

Sigurðr the Dragon-slayer and the Hunnish King Atli, and thus two stories are made to run concurrently:

> Many a wolf was merry
> —master of gold plunged the javelin
> deep in the fish of the forest—
> fled the hosts before Haraldr.

The *Skáldatal* (List of Scalds) contains the names of several Icelandic poets who worked for princes of Denmark and Sweden in the eleventh and early twelfth centuries. Little is known about them and few fragments of their work survive. Þorleikr Fagri[1] is named among the poets of Sveinn Úlfsson, King of Denmark (died 1074). Nothing can be told of his ancestry or career, except that he left Iceland about 1051. Some twelve strophes of a poem which he made for Sveinn Úlfsson are preserved. In the first of them, Þorleikr describes the battle of Hlýrskógsheiðr (1043), in which Sveinn had fought at the side of Magnús the Good against the heathen Wends. In other strophes, Þorleikr describes battles which Sveinn had fought against Haraldr Harðráði. In one strophe, Þorleikr shows some ability in describing a beaked ship dashed by the waves on a stormy sea, but most of his poetry is too conventional to have great interest.

Markús Skeggjason was among the most powerful chieftains of Iceland. He was Law-speaker from 1084 to 1107 and assisted Bishop Gizurr in drawing up the laws of tithe in 1096. He is named in the *Skáldatal*[2] as the poet of Ingi Steinkelsson, King of the Swedes (died 1111), as well as of Knútr the Saint, King of Denmark (died 1086). Few of his lines about these monarchs are preserved, but we possess some thirty strophes of a lay which he made in memory of Eiríkr the Good, King of Denmark (1095–1104).[3] Markús uses the measure *Hrynjandi*, which Arnórr had used in his *Hrynhenda*. The *Eiríksdrápa* is not the work of a master, but it is valuable as a source of history, for the poet runs through the triumphs of the late king, and alludes to his death in Cyprus, while on a pilgrimage to the Holy Land. Markús pays tribute to Eiríkr as the Prince who had persuaded the Pope to found the arch-see of Lund in 1104.

---

[1] *Skáldatal*, p. 328.     Ibid., pp. 318, 328.     [3] *Skjald.* B. i. 414–20.

The Icelanders and all the northern peoples were thereby released from the jurisdiction of the archbishops of Bremen.

The surviving verses of Markús, like those of Þorleikr Fagri, have little of the euphuism which is commonly associated with the scaldic style. This may be because the verses were designed to be understood by Danes, among whom the scaldic art was less highly developed than in western Scandinavia. But there are reasons for believing that the standards of scaldic poetry were now declining in Norway as well. Several of the poets patronized by the Norwegian princes of the first decades of the twelfth century sought to introduce simpler measures, using Eddaic verse-forms for panegyrics. This suggests that the rulers and courtiers of Norway now found it hard to appreciate the metrical complexity and the abstruse imagery of the classical scalds.

A story is told of Gísl Illugason, one of the poets of Magnús Bareleg (died 1103).[1] Gísl went to Norway about the year 1096, at the age of seventeen. To avenge his father, who had been killed in his childhood, Gísl killed one of the courtiers of Magnús. He was arrested and put in chains, but rescued by the Icelanders then in Niðaróss. Gísl pleaded his case before the king, and when he did so, recited a poem which he had made in the king's honour. He declaimed it boldly but, the saga-writer says, there was not much poetry (*skáldskapr*) in it. None of Gísl's 'Head-Ransom' is known now. It has been said that, by his criticism, the author of the saga implied that the verses were lacking in poetic uplift. But if we judge by the existing works of Gísl, it seems more probable that the 'Head-Ransom' was condemned on technical grounds. The saga-writer probably meant that Gísl did not show sufficient artistry, or practised workmanship, in the use of intricate measures and abstruse imagery. The most important surviving work of Gísl is a lay about Magnús, probably made soon after his death in Ireland in the year 1103.[2] Gísl here uses the Eddaic *Fornyrðislag* instead of the scaldic *Dróttkvætt*. The influence of scaldic diction can be detected in some strophes but, like the metre, the style and

---

[1] In *Borgfirðinga Sǫgur*, ed. Sigurður Nordal and Guðni Jónsson, 1938, pp. 329 ff.　　　　[2] *Skjald.* B. i. 409 ff.

vocabulary of the poem are, for the most part, Eddaic, and not scaldic. Gísl praises the romantic young king as if he were a hero of the viking age, but the poem has none of the freshness and vigour of the best lays of the *Edda*.

Several of the poets of this period used Eddaic verse-forms for panegyrics on the princes. The *Fornyrðislag* was used by Ívarr Ingimundarson to commemorate Sigurðr Slembidjákn, who was tortured to death in 1139, and by Halldórr Skvaldri (the Chatterer) for a poem on Sigurðr Magnússon's martial pilgrimage to the Holy Land.[1] Halldórr also made another lay about Sigurðr's voyage and his adventures in the Mediterranean. This is called the *Útfarar-drápa*. Its form is the *Dróttkvætt*, and it sounds like a weak imitation of the Viking Verses of Sigvatr. These attempts to simplify the scaldic style were not fruitful but, in adopting Eddaic verse-forms, the scalds show how much they admired and how deeply they studied the heroic poetry of the *Edda*.

Einarr Skúlason was the most influential poet of his age. He was born about 1090–5 and took clerical orders. He descended from the settler Skalla-Grímr, and lived a part of his life in western Iceland, for his name appears among a list of noble priests serving that area in 1143. Einarr travelled widely, and the stories in which he figures took place abroad. He was a professional scald of the kind familiar already in the pagan period, and made his living by praising and entertaining ruling princes. He made poems for Sørkvir Kolsson, King of the Swedes (died 1156), and for Sveinn Svifandi (Svíðandi), King of the Danes (died 1157). When the King of the Danes failed to pay him his due reward, Einarr made another poem, in which he complained that the generous king would rather listen to the fiddles and the pipes than to the scaldic strophes.[2] The scaldic poets were now being supplanted in Denmark by meretricious competitors from the south. The minstrels were replacing the scalds.

Einarr's surviving poetry is mostly addressed to the kings of Norway. In the *Sigurðardrápa*[3] he described how King Sigurðr sailed to the Holy Land and bathed in the Jordan. He used the

---

[1] Ibid., pp. 467–75, and pp. 457 ff.      [2] Ibid., p. 455, No. 3.
[3] Ibid., pp. 423–4.

difficult riming *Fornyrðislag*, the *Tøglag*, for a poem in praise of Haraldr Gilli (died 1136). He thanked a nameless chieftain for the gift of a jewelled axe in an unusually intricate sequence of verses.[1] In this poem, the *Øxarflokkr*, he gives many examples of the most abstruse form of kenning, the *ofljóst*. The 'jewelled axe' is the 'glorious child of Hǫrn' (*Hróðrbarn Hǫrnar*), for Hǫrn is a name for Freyja, and Freyja's daughter was called Hnoss, a name which means 'jewel'.

Stories told of Einarr, as well as the verses which he left, show that he was a master in the art of poetry. His reputation rests chiefly upon the *Geisli* (The Sunbeam),[2] with which he brought new motives and a new kind of symbolism into Icelandic poetry.

The *Geisli* is dedicated to S. Ólafr, and the poet declaimed it in the cathedral at Niðaróss beside the relics of the saint, probably in the year 1153. A few months earlier, the English cardinal, Nicholas Breakspear, as Papal Legate, had established the arch-see of Niðaróss.[3] The poet's audience included the newly created archbishop, Jón Birgisson, and the three kings who shared the throne of Norway, Sigurðr, Ingi, Eysteinn. As the poet ended his declamation, it is said, a sweet scent permeated the cathedral church.[4]

The *Geisli* is not among the most beautiful of Norse *drápur*, but it must be admired as a technical triumph, and is formally among the most perfect. Its metre is the *Dróttkvætt*, and it consists of more than seventy strophes, divided into three sections, Introduction, Refrain Section (*Stefjabálkr*), and Ending (*Slœmr*). The poet shows that he was learned both in the traditions of his pagan ancestors and in the symbolism of Christian Europe. He was, perhaps, the first Icelandic poet to use the 'light' or 'sun' symbolism, so typical of medieval Christianity. S. Ólafr is the 'Sunbeam' (*Geisli*); God is the 'Sun', and is born on earth of the 'Star of the Sea' (*flœðar stjarna*). While God is the 'Sun of Justice and of Mercy', S. Ólafr is his 'warlike ray'. The Heavenly Jerusalem is called the 'Vision of Peace' (*friðar sýn*).[5]

---

[1] *Skjald*. B. i. 425–6 and 449–51.     [2] Ibid., pp. 427–45.
[3] Cf. A. O. Johnsen, *Nicolaus Brekespears legasjon til norden*, 1945.
[4] *Morkinskinna*, edition quoted above, p. 446.
[5] Cf. F. Paasche, op. cit., pp. 72 ff.

Although well known in Europe, such expressions were new to
Icelandic poetry. Einarr drew no less liberally upon the imagery of
earlier scalds. He might be accused of incongruity when he speaks
of God as the 'highest of the Skjǫldungs' (*hæstr Skǫjldungr*), and
designates S. Ólafr by kennings better applicable to a pagan
warrior. Ólafr is the man who reddens the mouth of Óðinn's raven
(*munnrjóðr Hugins*). Like the princes of old, he is the one who
destroys the lair of the coiling fish—hurls golden rings to his
courtiers.

It is commonly said that, for a poet of Einarr's age, the kennings
which had pagan associations were no more than form. Indeed,
Einarr was a Christian, and he could not believe in the gods, but
he cherished their memory and knew the poetry in which they
figured. He proved in his *Øxarflokkr* that he was well trained in
pagan mythology, and that he knew the stories on which his kennings were based. His style was in one sense a revival, for it resembles that of the tenth-century poets more closely than that of
those who immediately preceded Einarr.

The subject of the *Geisli* is not less interesting than its diction.
After calling upon the Trinity to help him to make his poem, and
passing through the great moments in the life of Christ on earth,
the poet addresses the kings and the archbishop. He says little of
S. Ólafr's life, reminding his audience that it had been narrated
by Óttarr and Sigvatr and the poets who lived at the time of the
saint. Einarr concentrates on the miracles worked after S. Ólafr's
death. He was the northern Christ, for the sun was darkened when
he died, just as it was when Christ died on Calvary. A blind man
wiped his eyes with water in which the blood of the saint was mixed.
One who had lost his tongue recovered speech at the tomb of
S. Ólafr.

Many of the miracles took place in lands distant from Norway.
When Gutthormr, the nephew of the saint, was fighting against
superior forces off Anglesey, he called upon his uncle to intercede,
and won the victory. He had rewarded the saint with a crucifix,
worked in gold and silver, which he placed beside his shrine.

Miracles worked through the intercession of S. Ólafr were

recorded in Wendland and in Constantinople. His sword, Hneitir, had been taken from his dead body by a Swede, and was afterwards found among the Greeks. After its worth had been proved by miracles, the Emperor hung it over a jewelled altar. The Greek army was once put to flight by the heathen Patzinaks, and the Emperor would have lost most of his dominions had it not been for the Varangian guard. They invoked their patron and routed the heathen.

The sources of the *Geisli* are difficult to determine. Some of the miracles took place soon after the saint's death, and others within the poet's own time. Several of them are also recorded in the *Passio Sancti Olavi* and in other prose accounts of the saint (see ch. vii), but the stories told in the *Geisli* differ from these in detail. It is not impossible that a short list of the miracles of S. Ólafr had been written by the clergy of Niðaróss before the end of the eleventh century.[1] If so, we may suppose that Einarr used it as a source, although he probably treated the legends freely and retold them as he would have them. He names a certain Eindriði as a source for a part of his poem. Nothing is known about this man, but he was probably one of Einarr's oral informants, and it is likely that most of the sources were oral.

As a professional poet, Einarr closed the *Geisli* with an appeal for payment in gold, and it has been said that his poem is lacking in true religious sentiment and finesse. This could also be said of other poems of the period, and especially of the *Rekstefja*, the work of a certain Hallar-Steinn.[2]

Ólafr Tryggvason is the hero of the *Rekstefja*, and its author seeks to praise him as S. Ólafr was praised by Einarr. The poet lists the victories of Ólafr Tryggvason and describes his prowess as an athlete. He had burned down the heathen temples and won five lands for Christ, and now he lives in bliss with the Lord of the Sun. The *Rekstefja* has some value for the history contained in it, but as poetry it is interesting only for its form. Artistry is here carried to extreme lengths. The conventional *Dróttkvætt* is varied

---

[1] See *Heimskringla*, ii, ed. Bjarni Aðalbjarnarson, 1945, Introduction, pp. v ff.
[2] *Skjald*. B. i. 525–34.

and elaborated, so that lines 1 and 3 of each half-strophe begin with
three heavily stressed syllables, e.g.:

> Qrrjóðr allra dáða
> jartegnir gat bjartar
> —dvergregn dýrðar magnak
> dimmt—í sinn et fimmta.

This form is called *Tvískelft* (Double Shaken), as the poet informs
us at the end of the *Rekstefja*. The poem received its name because
the refrain (*stef*) is 'inlaid' or 'chased' (*rekit*), its lines being distributed among successive strophes. The poet takes especial pride
in the obscurity of his diction. His poetry is the 'dark rain of the
dwarfs' (*dimmt dverga regn*). Another poet of this age, whose name
is not recorded, made a *drápa* about Ólafr Tryggvason. This poet
appears to be influenced by the diction of Hallar-Steinn. His work
is conventional and of little interest.

During the second half of the twelfth century, many Icelandic
poets turned from transitory subjects to sacred ones. They sing less
of the kings of Norway than of God and His saints, and the eternal
truths of Christian teaching. I have already mentioned the *Plácítús-
drápa* (Lay of Placid), which is assigned by some critics to the
middle of the twelfth century, and is found in a manuscript dating
from about 1200.[1] Its author was perhaps the first to make a great
scaldic lay about a popular European saint.

The *Leiðarvísan* (Way-director) is also thought to date from the
middle decades of the twelfth century.[2] It is a *drápa* of forty-five
strophes and its subject is the observance of Sunday. The poet
retells the popular story of the 'Sunday Letter' which, he says, was
written in golden characters and found in Jerusalem.[3] It was found
on a Sunday, and God will punish those who do not keep Sunday
holy as he will punish those who defraud the clergy in their tithes.
The most memorable events in the history of the world have taken
place on Sunday. God created the angels on Sunday, and it was
on a Sunday that Noah stepped out of the Ark. The Jews crossed
the Red Sea on Sunday, the Ten Commandments were issued to

---

[1] Ibid. B. i. 606–22; cf. Paasche, op. cit., pp. 85–91.     [2] Ibid. 622–33.
[3] On this legend see Paasche, op. cit., pp. 101 ff.

Moses and the water flowed from the rock. Christ was conceived, born and baptized on a Sunday, and rose from the tomb on a Sunday. He will return to the earth on the same day of the week.

The *Leiðarvísan* may be interesting for those who study Christian legends and practices, but it has little value as poetry. The poet tells us that he was moved to write it by a priest called Rúnólfr. This man has been identified with Rúnólfr, the son of Bishop Ketill, who died in 1186. Rúnólfr made a poem about the cathedral church of Skálaholt, which was completed and consecrated about 1154. It has been suggested that the *Leiðarvísan* was declaimed before the huge crowd which assembled at Skálaholt for the ceremony of consecration.[1] The evidence is not conclusive, but the remarks about those who neglect to pay their tithes would be appropriate if uttered at a see in such grave financial straits as Skálaholt must have been after the cathedral was built.

Nikulás Bergsson (also called Bergþórsson and Hallbjarnarson) is remembered best for his essay on geography, the *Leiðarvísir* (Sign-post).[2] This is designed as a guide for Icelanders who visit Rome and the Holy Land, and is based upon a pilgrimage made by Nikulás himself about the year 1150. He points out features of traditional and natural interest on the way, as well as Christian monuments and relics. He identifies, in Germany, the supposed site of Gnitaheiðr, where Sigurðr slew the dragon, and he tells of a city in Switzerland which the sons of Ragnarr Loðbrók had destroyed. When Nikulás came to Sicily, he noticed that the mountains were volcanic, and the waters boiled as they do in Iceland. On the banks of the Jordan he measured the height of the pole-star by a simple but ingenious method. He lay on his back with his knee drawn up and his fist upon it with the thumb extended. He found that the pole-star was as high as his thumb.

It is recorded that Nikulás returned from his pilgrimage in the year 1154. Shortly afterwards he was appointed abbot of the newly founded Benedictine monastery of Þverá, in the Eyjafjǫrðr. He

---

[1] See Finnur Jónsson, *ONOI*, ii. 118–19.

[2] Ed. Kr. Kålund, *Alfræði íslenzk*, i, 1908, pp. 1–31. On Nikulás see also F. P. Magoun Jr., *Harvard Theological Review*, xxxiii, 1940, pp. 277–89; and the same scholar's paper in *Scandinavian Studies*, xvii, 1943, pp. 167–73.

died in 1159, and must have written, or rather dictated, the *Leiðar-vísir* in his last years. Nikulás was long remembered, both for many virtues, for his good memory and other intellectual gifts.[1] Few fragments of the poetry of Nikulás survive but, besides technical excellence, they have lyrical and spiritual qualities rare in the poetry of this age. Three strophes made by Nikulás in honour of S. John the Apostle are quoted in a late Icelandic life of that saint. The poet emphasizes the chastity of S. John, which he shares only with Mary. John was the best loved of God, who had permitted him to hear his words and to see his whole splendour.

A fragment of a lay which Nikulás made about Christ is even more interesting. It is quoted by the prosodist Ólafr Hvítaskáld (died 1259) as an example of *Parabola*.[2] If Ólafr had not explained the strophe, it would have little meaning for us. Nikulás said:

I think two seamen carried a berry between them on a pole.—The hour of life is not long in the Promised Land.—Both of them, the Jew and the Heathen, pressed the berry against the Cross. Faith preserves us, and thus has God repaid the fruit.

It would take long to explain the full meaning of this strophe. The poet draws his symbols from *Numbers* (xiii. 23 ff.). The messengers of Moses brought a sprig of vine and a grape from the Promised Land: 'absciderunt palmitem cum uva sua, quem portaverunt in vecte duo viri'. The grape on the twig represents Christ on the Cross. The Jew and the Heathen, pressing the berry, are seen as those who crucified Christ. It is the juice of the grape, the blood of Christ, which restores them to life. That was how God repaid mankind for the stolen apple.

Such mystical qualities as are found in the poetry of Nikulás are developed further by Gamli. Little is known of this man's life but that he was a canon of the Augustinian house of Þykkvabœr, in the south of Iceland, which was founded in 1168. Gamli probably worked in the last decades of the twelfth century, and was the author of a *Jónsdrápa* (Lay of S. John the Apostle).[3] Four strophes

---

[1] See *Postola Sögur*, ed. C. R. Unger, 1874, p. 509; *Biskupa Sögur*, i, 1858, p. 407; *Alfræði íslenzk*, i. 23.

[2] *Edda Snorra Sturlusonar*, ii, 1852, p. 186; *Skjald.* B. i. 547.

[3] *Skjald.* B. i. 547–8.

of this lay are preserved, and it is composed in the unusual *Hryn-hent*, the metre of Arnórr's *Hrynhenda* and of Markús's *Eiríks-drápa* (see pp. 149, 153 above). Verbal similarity may suggest that Gamli was influenced by Nikulás's lay on S. John, and similar sentiments are expressed by both poets. Gamli's poem is the more personal, and he calls on God to forgive his sins, that he may not be deprived of the blessings enjoyed by the apostle.

Gamli's *Jónsdrápa* is a good example of the Christian poetry of the late twelfth century, but it is insignificant beside his *Harmsól* (Sun of Sorrow).[1] The *Harmsól* is perhaps the finest Icelandic poem of its age, and its excellence is at once technical and aesthetic. Its form is the *Dróttkvætt*, and it consists of sixty-five strophes, ornamented with two refrains. In the opening strophes the poet calls on God to inspire him, and to send the Holy Spirit, for men can accomplish nothing without the help of God. He urges his hearers to tell their sins to the priests, and then begins to confess the sins of his youth. He had sinned against the 'Lord of the bright flame of the storm's roof' (*Dróttinn bjartloga hreggs hróts*) in word, deed, and thought. He had followed evil example, and had tasted the body of Christ with a sinful heart. The poet passes from his own transgressions to the life of Christ on earth. He was born of a Virgin; the 'mighty Prince of the sky's flame' was bound and beaten and nailed on a tree between two wicked men. The bad thief addresses Him in arrogant words, bidding Him climb down from the Cross in all His might, but the good thief begs His mercy humbly. Christ's resurrection is described in few words, as is His ascent into Heaven. Gamli has more to say about the second coming of Christ, and this is the climax of the poem. Gamli seems to share the medieval doctrine, expressed so forcefully in one of the Icelandic homilies,[2] that all the great events in this world, Christ's birth, passion, resurrection and Ascension, are nothing but preparation for the one fearful day, when the angels will awaken the dead and fire burst from the earth. Christ will appear in awe and dazzling light, and the angels will support the Cross bearing His wounded body and stained with blood. On that day, even the

---

[1] *Skjald.* B. i. 548–65.      [2] *Homilíu-Bók*, ed. Th. Wisén, 1872, p. 44.

angels will stand aghast with fear, and Gamli describes the dread-
ful scene almost as the *Ragnarǫk* was described in the *Vǫluspá*, a
poem which he must have known well:

> King of the moon's curtain
> comes again from Heaven
> —mild is He in mercy—
> men to call to judgement;
> fire breaks forth and fumes the
> fishes' land. From graveyards
> men rise up in millions,
> many groan in terror.

In a later passage Gamli describes the last judgement, but spares
few words for Hell, where sinners will suffer stench, fire, and frost.
In the ending of his poem *Gamli* derives comfort from considera-
tion of God's mercy, reminding his hearers of David, Peter, and
Mary Magdalen, who had sinned and were forgiven. He calls on
God to judge him in mercy rather than in justice and, finally, he
asks all who hear the *Harmsól* to pray for him.

Gamli shows how the artificial and highly complicated style of
poetry, devised by the pagan scalds, survived fundamental changes
in outlook and religious belief, and he put it to uses quite other
than those for which it was designed. No poet was more Christian
in sentiment, and yet his style was modelled on that of the pagans
of Norway and Iceland. His diction is derived from theirs. He calls
God *hlýrnis elds buðlungr*, although he must have known that
*hlýrnir* was, in legend, a name which the pagan gods gave to the
'sky'. When he designates men by names for Óðinn, and calls
women by valkyries' names, pagan associations must have lived in
his mind. It is misleading to say, as is generally said, that such expressions were lifeless form. Gamli did not believe in the gods, but
he was sufficiently learned in the poetry of the *Edda* and of the
scalds to know the legends about these gods. He could regard the
myths, on which his kennings were based, with the detached
interest of an antiquarian.

If we judge by the surviving monuments, Icelandic poetry of
the late twelfth century was concerned chiefly with religious

subjects. There are comparatively few important poems on profane subjects which can safely be assigned to this period, although much has undoubtedly been lost. I may mention the *Íslendinga Drápa*[1] (Lay of the Icelanders) of Haukr Valdísarson. Twenty-six strophes of this lay are preserved, and they have little but antiquarian interest. The poet names a number of famous Icelanders of the 'saga-age', including Egill, Brodd-Helgi, Hallfreðr, and Finnbogi the Strong, and he alludes to some of their great deeds. Haukr's style is stilted, and he delights in elaborate kennings. He calls the 'Icelanders' *hvals búðar húðlendingar*; for *hvals búð*, 'the whale's house', is the 'sea', whose 'skin' (*húð*) is 'ice'. The poet has only to add the syllables -*lendingar*, and the kenning is complete.

The *Nóregs Kongunga Tal* (List of the Kings of Norway) was mentioned in an earlier chapter (Ch. III). Like Haukr, the nameless author of this poem was interested in the heroes of the past, although he worked in a simpler poetic form.

Some of the poetry found in the family sagas and Kings' sagas, and ascribed by the authors of those works to heroes of the 'saga-age', must, in reality, have been composed by antiquarians of the twelfth century. It has been said, to take one example, that many of the verses ascribed to the hero of the tenth century, Gísli Súrsson, date from this period.[2] The authenticity of many verses found in the family sagas may be questioned, but it is not yet possible to say precisely which were composed in the twelfth century, and which in the tenth.

As was suggested in the introductory chapter of this book, some of the poetry of the *Edda*, mythological as well as heroic, probably dates from the eleventh and twelfth centuries. Much of it has been claimed in recent years for Lower Germany and for Denmark.[3] It is said to be influenced by ballads in forms older·than those in which we now know them. The early history of the ballad is ob-

[1] *Skjald*. B. i. 539–45.
[2] See *Vestfirðinga Sǫgur*, ed. Björn K. Þórólfsson and Guðni Jónsson, 1943, Introduction, §1.
[3] See W. Mohr, *Zeitschrift für deutsches Altertum*, vol. 75, 1938, pp. 217–80; H. Kuhn, *Beiträge zur Geschichte der deutschen Sprache und Literatur*, lxiii, 1939, pp. 178 ff.

scure, but before we assign lays of the *Edda* to countries other than Iceland, it is well to remember that some primitive form of *dans*, or ballad, was current in Iceland as early as the second decade of the twelfth century.[1] Such poems may have influenced the later lays of the *Edda*, and may have contributed to their romantic, sentimental tone.

It is not yet possible to see the development of Icelandic poetry in the eleventh and twelfth centuries as those who lived in that age would have seen it. At least, we can say that, while this was a preclassical age in prose, it was a silver age for poetry.

[1] *Biskupa Sögur*, i. 237; Cf. U. Brown in *Saga-Book*, XIII. ii, 1947–8, pp. 51–71.

# VII

# HISTORICAL LITERATURE OF THE LATE TWELFTH CENTURY

## 1. The Icelandic Synoptics

PROSE literature of several kinds was written in Icelandic during the latter decades of the twelfth century. This was stated plainly by the author of the 'First Grammatical Treatise' who probably wrote about 1170–80, although some would assign his work to a rather earlier date.[1] The author of this treatise devised a new system of spelling, whereby the sounds of Icelandic could be expressed more accurately than they could by the defective system then in use. He explained that the main branches of vernacular literature current in his day, and those for which his system of spelling was chiefly designed, were law, genealogy (*áttvísi*), renderings of Holy Writ (*þýðingar helgar*), and the learned works of Ari.

In this passage, the grammarian shows that, besides law, at least two kinds of narrative prose, written in the vernacular, were known to him. On the one hand were the renderings of Holy Writ, which would include lives of saints and other sacred literature discussed in Chapter V above, and on the other were the works of Ari discussed in Chapter IV. The term *áttvísi*, which I have translated as 'genealogy', must also imply historical literature of one kind or another, although its precise meaning is hard to determine. It might be better rendered as 'family history'. It would undoubtedly include the genealogical lists (*ættartǫlur*), such as those already mentioned, and probably works of wider scope as well. I refer especially to the *schedulae*, or summary lives of eminent men and their descendants. Some of these *schedulae*, whether written by Ari or by others of the twelfth century, must ultimately have been

[1] See *Den første og anden grammatiske Afhandling*, ed. V. Dahlerup and Finnur Jónsson, 1886, p. 2; A. Holtsmark, *En islandsk scholasticus*, 1936; E. Haugen, supplement to *Language*, xxvi. 4, 1950.

incorporated in the *Landnámabók*, and others were used as sources by men who wrote sagas of Icelandic heroes in the thirteenth century.[1]

History in the style which Ari had introduced with the *Íslendingabók* flourished in Iceland throughout the Middle Ages and, in this sense at least, Ari is the father of Icelandic prose. Those who followed him wrote synoptic histories rather than detailed biographies. At best, their work is the outcome of painstaking investigation and study, rather than of imaginative artistry.

The next book in this style, of which we have record, is the *Hryggjarstykki*, written by Eiríkr Oddsson.[2] This was an account of the kings who ruled Norway during a part of the twelfth century, but it no longer survives, and many problems about its form and scope remain unsolved. The name *Hryggjarstykki* is also obscure; it seems to mean 'Backbone piece', but no satisfactory explanation of it has been found.

Although the *Hryggjarstykki* is lost, excerpts from it may be found in existing books, and it is possible to form some ideas of its style and shape. It was used as a source by several later writers, and especially by the author of the *Morkinskinna*[3] and by Snorri in the later sections of the *Heimskringla*. Snorri more than once names Eiríkr Oddsson among his authorities,[4] and in one passage he gives a number of details about the *Hryggjarstykki* and its author:

Eiríkr wrote the book called *Hryggjarstykki*, and in it he told of Haraldr gilli and of two of his sons, as well as of Magnús the blind and Sigurðr slembi, right down to their deaths. Eiríkr was a wise man, and he spent a long time in Norway at this period. He wrote a part of his story according to the dictation of Hákon magi . . . and Eiríkr also names other wise and reliable men who told him of these events . . . but he wrote several passages according to what he had heard and witnessed himself.[5]

---

[1] See above, Ch. IV.
[2] On the *Hryggjarstykki* see especially Finnur Jónsson, *ONOI*, ii. 370 ff.; G. Indrebø, *Fagrskinna*, 1917, pp. 49 ff.; Bjarni Aðalbjarnarson, *Om de norske kongers sagaer*, 1937, pp. 159 ff.
[3] See *Morkinskinna*, ed. Finnur Jónsson, 1932, esp. p. 419.
[4] See *Heimskringla*, ed. Finnur Jónsson, 1911, esp. pp. 576, 578–80.
[5] *Heimskringla*, 1911, p. 579.

This description of the *Hryggjarstykki* can be interpreted in various ways, for the phrase 'right down to their deaths' (*allt til dauða þeirra*) is ambiguous. As shown in the translation, this could mean 'down to the deaths of Magnús the blind and of Sigurðr slembi', which, grammatically, is perhaps the most natural interpretation. It would imply that the *Hryggjarstykki* began with the year 1130, and covered only nine years of the history of the kings of Norway, for Haraldr gilli became king in 1130, and Magnús and Sigurðr died in 1139. Alternatively the phrase 'right down to their deaths' could mean 'right down to the deaths of the sons of Haraldr gilli' and, in that case, the *Hryggjarstykki* covered more than thirty years of history, from 1130 until 1161, when Ingi the son of Haraldr gilli died. On the whole, the second interpretation is the more probable, because several stories about events of the mid-twelfth century found in the *Morkinskinna* and the *Heimskringla* seem to derive from the *Hryggjarstykki*.[1] It is now generally held that Eiríkr wrote his book within a few years of the death of Ingi, probably about 1170. Snorri's assertion that Eiríkr had himself witnessed some of the events which he described hardly allows us to assign the book to a date later than that.

Eiríkr probably continued the history of the kings of Norway from the time where the *Konunga Ævi* of Ari's older *Íslendingabók* came to an end, and he must have learnt his methods chiefly from Ari. Like Ari, he had few, if any, written records and, as Snorri shows, he gathered his information from wise and reliable men, several of whom he named. One of these was Hákon magi, a bailiff of Haraldr gilli's sons, and another was Hallr Þorgeirsson, described as one of King Ingi's courtiers. Hallr had been present when Sigurðr slembi was tortured to death in 1139, and had described the grim scene for Eiríkr. The story of the capture and slaughter of Sigurðr, as it is told in the *Morkinskinna* and the *Heimskringla*,[2] is probably taken chiefly from the *Hryggjarstykki*. It is more detailed and vivid than any passage in Ari's work now known,

---

[1] Cf. Bjarni Aðalbjarnarson, op. cit., pp. 162 ff.

[2] *Morkinskinna*, ed. Finnur Jónsson, pp. 435 ff.; *Heimskringla*, 1911, pp. 580 f.

and shows how the art of narration had developed since Ari's day.

Since the foundation of the archbishopric of Niðaróss in 1152, relations between Iceland and Norway had grown closer. The literature of Norway was not so rich as that of Iceland, but for a time the two ran parallel, and they soon began to influence each other. Books written in Iceland were taken to Norway, and those written in Norway were brought to Iceland, where they were copied, and sometimes revised, while excerpts from them were included in the works of Icelandic historians.

## 2. The Norwegian Synoptics

The Norwegians did not begin to write history in their own language as early as the Icelanders did. Like the Icelanders, they compiled records of history in the twelfth century, but these were mostly written in Latin. The Norwegian works have many defects as literature, but they helped to preserve memories of antiquity, and had considerable importance for the Icelandic historians of the late twelfth and thirteenth centuries.

The oldest Norwegian historian whose name is known was the monk Theodoricus (Theodericus), whose surviving work has the title *Historia de antiquitate regum Norwagiensium*.[1] It is a synoptic history of the kings of Norway from Haraldr Finehair to Haraldr gilli (died 1136). Theodoricus dedicated his book to Eysteinn, Archbishop of Niðaróss (1161–88), and probably wrote it about 1180.[2]

Theodoricus says himself that he worked chiefly from oral sources, and he could hardly do otherwise, for the written sources of history available in Norway were few. Theodoricus did not know the 'History of the Kings of Norway' of Sæmundr, nor the notes about the kings contained in Ari's older *Íslendingabók*. The oral records, upon which Theodoricus largely relied, were transmitted to him, not by his own countrymen, but rather by Icelanders. He explained in his Prologue that he had undertaken his work because

---

[1] Published in *Monumenta Historica Norvegiæ*, ed. G. Storm, 1880, pp. 2–68.
[2] Cf. Sigurður Nordal, *Om Olaf den Helliges Saga*, 1914, pp. 8–9; Bjarni Aðalbjarnarson, op. cit., pp. 5 ff. and 49 ff.

he had been able to make inquiries among Icelanders, who preserved memories of antiquity in their ancient verses. The verses
to which Theodoricus refers can be no other than those of the
scalds, in which kings of Norway ever since Haraldr Finehair
had been eulogized. The scalds had commemorated the achievements of the princes, telling of their great battles and of how
they died. The authors of many of these poems, and especially of
the older ones, were Norwegian, but it was in Iceland, rather than
in Norway, that this ancient court poetry lived orally in the twelfth
century. Theodoricus was one of the first historians to use scaldic
poems scientifically as sources of history and, for the earliest period,
these were almost the only and certainly the most reliable sources
available.

In style, the Latin of Theodoricus is generally straightforward,
plain and efficient. When he writes of the pre-Christian period of
Norse history, his account is somewhat bare, and he concerns himself largely with chronology. Here and there he interrupts his narrative and devotes passages, sometimes of considerable length, to
quotations from classical authors, e.g. Pliny, Sallust, Lucan,
Horace. These quotations contribute nothing to the artistic value
of the book, but they show, as they were perhaps intended to show,
that Norwegian monks did not read less widely than their colleagues
in other lands. Theodoricus also quotes Fathers and early medieval
historians, such as Jerome, Eusebius, Paulus Diaconus, and Jor-
danes, and he makes interesting references to European scholars
of the twelfth century. These include the chronicler Sigebert of
Gembloux (died 1112), Hugo of S. Victoire (died 1141) and William
of Jumièges, author of the *Historia Normannorum Ducum*. Theodoricus says that he had read in the *Historia Normannorum* how
S. Ólafr was baptized by the Archbishop of Rouen (*Rothomagensi
metripolitano*), but he is evidently quoting from memory, for he
has corrupted the story told by William.[1] These references to
French authors may suggest that Theodoricus was inspired by
them to write his summary of the history of Norway;[2] it is not

[1] See *Monumenta Historica Norvegiæ*, ed. Storm, p. 22, footnotes *ad loc*.
[2] Cf. G. Storm, *Snorre Sturlassöns historieskrivning*, 1873, p. 20.

improbable that he had studied in the monastery of S. Victoire in Paris, and had done much of his reading there.[1]

Although he worked chiefly from oral sources, Theodoricus once alludes to a book about Norse history,[2] called *Catalogus Regum Norwagiensium*. He had read in it how long some of the kings of Norway had reigned, and it can hardly have been more than a chronological list. It is difficult to decide how great a period of history was covered by the *Catalogus*, but the chronological system followed in it differed from those of Sæmundr and of Ari, and it was evidently based upon Norwegian rather than upon Icelandic traditions. Theodoricus also mentions a written account of the translation and miracles of S. Ólafr, saying that he had not included details about these subjects in his book because they had already been committed to posterity by others.[3] In this passage, Theodoricus is evidently referring to a lost work, known to scholars as the *Translatio Sancti Olavi*.[4] Its age cannot be determined, but it is probable that the clerks of Niðaróss had begun to keep records of the miracles worked through the agency of their patron soon after his relics were translated in 1031.

Theodoricus had also read the so-called *Acta Sancti Olavi*,[5] a collection of tales in Latin about S. Ólafr and his miracles. The author of this collection was Eysteinn, Archbishop of Niðaróss (1161–88), and it is found in its fullest form in an English manuscript of the late twelfth century, preserved in Corpus Christi College, Oxford.[6] It was translated into the Norse language at an early date, and soon became popular reading.

Although the *Historia* of Theodoricus has no great value as literature, Theodoricus influenced abler writers than himself. His work was one of the chief sources for the *Ágrip* or 'Summary of the History of the Kings of Norway',[7] a book composed about the end

---

[1] Cf. A. O. Johnsen, *Theodoricus*, 1939, esp. pp. 50 ff.
[2] *Historia*, ch. xx.                                      [3] Ibid.
[4] Cf. Storm in *Monumenta Historica*, Introduction, p. xxxiv; Sigurður Nordal, op. cit., p. 10.
[5] Cf. Storm, op. cit., loc. cit.; also A. O. Johnsen, op. cit., loc. cit., pp. 18 ff.
[6] See *Passio et Miracula beati Olavi*, ed. F. Metcalfe, 1881.
[7] Cf. Sigurður Nordal, op. cit., pp. 18 ff.; Bjarni Aðalbjarnarson, op. cit., pp. 5 ff. The *Ágrip* was last edited by Finnur Jónsson, 1929.

of the twelfth century. The *Ágrip* is written in the vernacular, not in Latin, and is preserved only in one manuscript, written in Iceland early in the thirteenth century, of which several leaves are missing at the beginning and the end. Although this manuscript is Icelandic, the author of the *Ágrip* was probably a Norwegian, for his interests were in Norway, and especially in Trondheim, rather than in Iceland. Whatever his nationality, the author was a cleric.

The *Ágrip* resembles the work of Theodoricus in many ways. In its present form it extends from the beginning of the reign of Haraldr Finehair to that of Ingi the Hunchback (died 1161), but originally it probably continued down to the accession of Sverrir in 1177.[1] It is fuller and richer than the work of Theodoricus, and the author used sources of more varied kinds, although scholars do not agree what these sources were. In addition to the *Historia* of Theodoricus, he seems to have read the so-called *Historia Norwegiae*,[2] or rather an early synoptic in Latin which was itself the main source for the existing *Historia Norwegiae*. Besides these sources in Latin, the author evidently used a separate biography or saga of Hákon the Good, the foster-child of King Æþelstan, written in the vernacular. This *Hákonar Saga* no longer survives, although its existence can be proved from the *Egils Saga*, *Fagrskinna*, and *Heimskringla*, whose compilers made use of it. It was one of the oldest of the separate biographies of kings of Norway of which any record survives.[3]

The author of the *Ágrip* used oral sources as well as written ones. Like Theodoricus, he sometimes cited scaldic poems, one of which had the surprising title *Oddmjór* (Narrow Point). He quoted four lines of this poem, interpreting the scaldic expression *skeiðar brandr* ('warship', literally 'prow of a warship') as if it were the name and nickname of a king called Brandr. This led him to invent the story of a battle between the mythical King Brandr and Haraldr Finehair.[4] Mistakes of this kind support the prevailing opinion that

---

[1] Cf. Finnur Jónsson, Introduction to *Ágrip*, 1929, p. ix.

[2] Cf. Sigurður Nordal, op. cit., pp. 41 ff.; Bjarni Aðalbjarnarson, op. cit., pp. 6 ff.

[3] On the *Hákonar Saga* see Bjarni Aðalbjarnarson, op. cit., pp. 190 ff., G. Indrebø, *Fagrskinna*, pp. 127 ff.              [4] *Ágrip*, ch. ii.

the *Ágrip* was the work of a Norwegian, for an educated Icelander of that day would be sufficiently well trained in scaldic diction to avoid such obvious pitfalls.

Some of the most interesting passages in the *Ágrip* must be traced to popular tales of Norway, which this author was the first to write down. Among them may be counted that of Haraldr Fine-hair's marriage with the Lappish witch, Snæfríðr (*Snjófríðr*, Snow-Fair), whose peerless beauty bereft him of his wits.[1] This passage, rich in motives of wandering folk-tale,[2] was copied by Snorri almost word for word and included in the *Heimskringla*. It is not surprising that Snorri should admire its style for, mannered as it is, the mannerisms are used tastefully. The author delights in half-rhythmical and alliterative phrases:

festi ok fekk ok unni svá með œrslum . . . hugði af heimsku, stýrði síðan ríki sínu ok styrkði . . .

and in balanced sentences:

syrgði hann hana dauða, en landslýðr syrgði hann viltan . . .

and in epigrams:

bar inn sami reiði hans út, er boð hans hafði borit inn.

The influence of Latin syntax may sometimes be detected in this story of Snæfríðr, as in the striking use of the dative as if it were an ablative absolute:

þat mundi eigi vera nema honum nauðgum.

Phrases like these have been said to show that the author of the *Ágrip* translated the story of Snæfríðr from a version written in Latin,[3] but it would be rash to accept this conclusion, for the author's reading was mostly in Latin, and it is not surprising that its idiom should colour his style, most especially when he was writing a passage of such dramatic moment as this.

[1] Ibid., ch. iii.
[2] Cf. Bjarni Aðalbjarnarson in Introduction to *Heimskringla*, i, 1941, p. lix and footnote 3.
[3] See Jan de Vries, *Altnordische Literaturgeschichte*, ii, 1942, para. 193, and the same author's paper in *Beiträge zur Geschichte der deutschen Sprache und Literatur*, lxvi, 1942, pp. 85 ff.

The *Historia Norwegiae*[1] has already been mentioned, and it was also written by a Norwegian, although scholars do not agree about its age. Weighty arguments were given by S. Bugge[2] to show that, in its present form, it could not be older than 1211. It contains a detailed account of a volcanic eruption and of an earthquake in Iceland, which had occurred in the author's own time, and this account tallies with others given in the Icelandic annals of terrible natural disturbances which took place in 1211. But even though the *Historia Norwegiae* was probably written after that date, it is based largely on an older work in Latin, which was also one of the sources of the *Ágrip*. It is designed for foreign, rather than for Norwegian readers, and is dedicated to a certain Agnellus, whom some have identified with Thomas Agnellus, Archdeacon of Wells (*circa* 1170–90), and others with the Franciscan Agnellus, who was in Oxford in 1224.[3] The *Historia Norwegiae* is preserved in a manuscript written about the middle of the fifteenth century, probably in Orkney, and the text is incomplete. It begins with a description of Norway and of the neighbouring islands, Orkney, Faeroe, Iceland. This section also contains a valuable chapter in which the customs of the Lapps are described, and especially their sorcery, in which the author displays great interest. In this same chapter there is a description of the beaver, hunted by the Lapps, which resembles that given of the beaver by Giraldus Cambrensis in the *Itinerary through Wales*[4] so closely that the two most probably descend from a common source.

The geographical section of the *Historia Norwegiae* is followed by a summary of the history of Norway, which begins with the royal house of the Ynglingar, and ends with the return of S. Ólafr from England (1015). Because of the defective state of the manuscript, it cannot be said how far the story continued in its original form. It seems from the Prologue that the book must originally have contained a third section, in which the author described the

[1] Ed. G. Storm in *Monumenta Historica Norvegiæ*, pp. 69–124.
[2] In *Aarbøger for nordisk Oldkyndighed og Historie*, 1873, esp. pp. 32 ff.
[3] Cf. F. Paasche, *Norges og Islands litteratur indtil utgangen av middelalderen*, 1924, pp. 421–2.
[4] Book II, ch. 3.

struggle between paganism and Christianity,[1] but no trace of this is left now.

In style, the *Historia Norwegiae* is florid and rhetorical and, although not pleasing, this gives proof of the author's wide learning. In some passages, and especially in the Prologue, the influence of Adam of Bremen may be detected. When he traces the pedigree of the kings of England, the author is obviously following an English chronicle, known from the great compilation of Roger of Hoveden.[2] The *Historia* had little influence, and it is unlikely that it was ever known in Iceland, but several details of history told in it are important. Sometimes it preserves ancient and valid traditions, of which Icelandic saga-writers knew nothing.[3]

In form the Norwegian synoptics are based upon foreign chronicles, and their authors must consequently be regarded as collaterals, rather than as direct descendants of the Icelanders, Sæmundr and Ari. Theodoricus, who was the oldest of these Norwegian historians, used methods like those of Ari; he made inquiries among those who preserved oral traditions. But he was less careful or critical, and more credulous than Ari.

## 3. Sagas of S. Ólafr

About the same time as Theodoricus was writing his summary of the history of Norway, a nameless author in Iceland was compiling a biography of S. Ólafr in his own language. This biography is the oldest 'saga' known to us, if the word 'saga' is used in its most restricted sense, to mean a detailed biography of a Norse hero (or heroes) based on native tradition. The author of this 'First Saga of S. Ólafr' also followed the methods established by Ari, but he combined them with those of the foreign hagiographers, whose works were becoming ever more widely known in Iceland. Like Ari, the biographer of S. Ólafr worked from oral sources, consulting men who were learned in ancient tradition. But he was less discriminating than Ari, and considered wonder-tales and miracles

---

[1] Cf. Finnur Jónsson, *ONOI*, ii. 494–5; Bjarni Aðalbjarnarson, op. cit., p. 2.
[2] Cf. G. Storm, *Monumenta*, Introduction, p. xxi.
[3] Cf. Finnur Jónsson, *ONOI*, ii. 600 ff.

no less credible than the historical traditions which Ari had investigated and sifted with such scientific precision. Moreover, the
form into which the life of the native saint was cast bore no resemblance to that of the *Íslendingabók*. It was much more like
the life of S. Nicholas or of S. Martin, or of many other foreign
saints.

The 'First Saga of S. Ólafr' cannot be dated precisely, but it is
reasonably safe to say that it was written before 1180.[1] Six small
fragments of a transcript of it made early in the thirteenth century
are preserved, besides another fragment of a transcript made in the
fourteenth century.[2] These seven fragments alone would give a
very incomplete picture of the saga in its original form, but our
knowledge is supplemented by the so-called 'Legendary Saga of
S. Ólafr',[3] which is found in a Norwegian (Trondish) manuscript
assigned to the middle of the thirteenth century. The compiler of
the 'Legendary Saga' did not work directly from the 'First Saga',
but rather from a later redaction of it, which is now lost, and he
occasionally made interpolations from other sources. But these
additions to the 'First Saga' can generally be detected and, in most
chapters, the 'Legendary Saga' reproduces the text of the 'First
Saga' in somewhat shortened form.

It is thus possible, with the help of the 'Legendary Saga', to see
what the 'First Saga' was like before it was damaged. The author
sketched the career of his hero, describing the chief moments in
his life, his battles and political disputes in Norway and abroad.
Sometimes these descriptions were very detailed, and sometimes
they were summary, and the book was thus uneven in construction.
The saint's worldly victories were often attributed to divine favour.
While raiding in France, S. Ólafr was accidentally separated from
his companions, and captured a large number of Frenchmen with

---

[1] Cf. Sigurður Nordal, op. cit., pp. 53 ff.

[2] All these fragments were published in facsimile, together with a valuable
Introduction, by G. Storm, *Otte Brudstykker af den Ældste Saga om Olav den
hellige*, 1893.

[3] The 'Legendary Saga' was published by R. Keyser and C. R. Unger, *Ólafs
Saga hins helga*, 1849, and by O. A. Johnsen, *Ólafs Saga hins helga*, 1922.
References in this chapter apply to Johnsen's edition. See also Sigurður Nordal,
op. cit., pp. 55–68; G. Indrebø, *Fagrskinna*, 1917, pp. 93–101.

Fragment of 'First Saga of S. Ólafr' from a manuscript of early thirteenth century

the help of a host of heavenly knights (*guðs riddarar*).[1] On another occasion, sailing off the coast of France, S. Ólafr encountered a monstrous mermaid, whom the native inhabitants used to worship. He struck her with a spear and she burst.[2] He engaged his namesake, Ólafr, King of the Swedes, in battle in the Baltic. The saint was heavily outnumbered by the Swedish king, and was driven into a creek in the Mälaren, where he was cut off from the open sea by a strip of land called the Agnafit. He fell on his knees and prayed, and sailed his ship straight into the Agnafit, which sprang apart and allowed him to pass.[3] S. Ólafr's whole career was attended by miracles, but many more were worked through his intercession after death than during his lifetime. After his body had lain buried for a year and five days, it rose of its own accord from the earth. Lepers were healed at S. Ólafr's shrine, the blind received sight, and the dumb spoke.

The seventh fragment of the 'First Saga', like the later chapters of the 'Legendary Saga', consists of lists of miracles worked through S. Ólafr's agency after death. Some of these were said to have occurred in the first years after his death, and others as late as the middle of the twelfth century. Many were located in Norway, but others in distant lands, as far afield as Wendland, Anglesey, London, and Constantinople. Most of the miracles are conventional, and consist of standard motives, but some of them have historical interest. As an example the following miracle may be quoted. It is found in the seventh fragment of the 'First Saga', and is said to have taken place in the reign of the Emperor Kirjalax (Alexios, 1081–1118):

These wonderous events took place in Constantinople (Miklagarðr): the Bulgars designed to pillage the city and the Emperor dispatched a foreign force to resist them, and they met on the plains of Pezina, and there were sixty against one. First of all the Greeks rode forward, but they were not successful. Then the Franks rode forward, but they were not victorious. The Emperor bewailed his loss, and upbraided his troops. But they said to him: 'Deploy those wine-skins, your Varangian guards'. It had not been thought right to subject these fine men to such grave danger. Þórir of Helsingjaland, who was in command of the Varangians

[1] 'Legendary Saga', ch. xiii.    [2] Ibid., ch. xv.    [3] Ibid., ch. xvi.

in those days, said: 'Even though there were a flaming fire, we should
go through it, if that would bring you peace.' The Emperor said: 'Call
upon your King, S. Ólafr, to help you', and they promised to do this. Then
the Varangians drew themselves up in battle-array and charged the
heathens. The heathen King asked: 'how large is their force?', and they
told him it was but a handful of men. 'Then who', said the King, 'is that
glorious and noble man riding before their host on a white horse?' But
his men said they could see no one. But then panic and terror broke out
in their ranks, and they took to flight, while the Varangians pursued
them together with the Greeks and Franks, and they killed as many as
they wished. The heathen (?) King was blind, and he submitted to
baptism and told them of his vision. Afterwards a church was built for
S. Ólafr in Constantinople.

Before discussing the author's sources and methods in detail,
it may be helpful to consider his reasons for writing this biography of the northern saint. It need hardly be said that he wrote
it for the glorification of S. Ólafr, no less than as an historical
record, and it should be studied against the background of S.
Ólafr's cult.

The cult was very old by the time the 'First Saga' was written,
for S. Ólafr had been revered as a saint within a short time of his
death. Magnús the Good (died 1047), the son of S. Ólafr, who succeeded him as king, ordered that his father's feast day should be
observed throughout Norway, and this is recorded in a verse made
by the saint's favourite poet Sigvatr.[1] Two feast days (29 July and
3 August) are assigned to S. Ólafr in early laws of Norway.[2] I have
already mentioned the lost Translatio Sancti Olavi and suggested
that parts of it were written by clerks of Niðaróss soon after S.
Ólafr was dead. Before the middle of the eleventh century the fame
of Ólafr's sanctity had reached foreign lands. His death is recorded
in a text of the 'Old English Chronicle', probably written in
Abingdon about 1050, and the compiler adds that he wæs syððan
halig.[3] Adam of Bremen, writing about 1070, gives the feast day of

---

[1] Heimskringla, ed. Finnur Jónsson, 1911, p. 428.
[2] Cf. G. Storm, Introduction to Monumenta, p. xxxv.
[3] See Two Saxon Chronicles, ed. J. Earle and C. Plummer, 1892–9, i. 157.
On the cult of S. Ólafr in the British Isles see Bruce Dickins, Saga-Book, xii,
1940, pp. 53 ff.

S. Ólafr as 29 July, and speaks of the great crowds who used to flock to his tomb, and of the miracles worked at the shrine.[1]

Widespread as the cult was in these early days, the fame of the saint was greatly enhanced by events which took place in the middle of the twelfth century. In the year 1152, the English cardinal, Nicholas Breakspear, visited Norway as Papal Legate, and raised the episcopal see of Niðaróss to an archiepiscopal see, conferring new dignity upon the city and upon the bones of the saint resting in the cathedral church.[2] Iceland was made a part of the new province, and its importance for the civilization of that country cannot be over-emphasized.[3]

I have already alluded to the poem *Geisli* (The Sunbeam).[4] Its composition was one of the first results of the foundation of the new archbishopric and, as the Icelandic poet shows in his ninth strophe, his purpose was to honour, not only the saint, but also the see where his relics were kept.

Although the author of the 'First Saga of S. Ólafr' chose the same subject as Einarr had chosen for the *Geisli*, he chose a different medium. He commemorated the northern saint just as many a foreign saint had been commemorated, in hagiographic biography. He must have known lives of foreign saints in Icelandic or Norwegian versions, and these could help him to construct the work. The miracle chapters in the 'First Saga of S. Ólafr' are not unlike chapters in the 'Life of S. Martin', and the 'First Saga of S. Ólafr' is no more heroic than the 'Life of S. Ambrose'.

But, although lives of foreign saints might suggest a form for the biographer of S. Ólafr, they could not supply the material, for which the author must rely on native sources. The native sources could include both written and oral records. Sæmundr must have written something about S. Ólafr in his *History*, and Ari wrote a few sentences about him in the existing version of the *Íslendingabók*, and probably rather more in the lost version of that work. Some

---

[1] Adam of Bremen, *Gesta Hammaburgensis Ecclesiae Pontificum*, ed. B. Schmeidler, 1917, iv, p. 33.
[2] For a detailed account of Breakespear's visit to Norway see A. O. Johnsen, *Nicolaus Brekespears legasjon til norden*, 1945.
[3] See Chs. V and VI above.                     [4] See Ch. VI above.

of the miracles of S. Ólafr had been recorded in the Norwegian *Translatio*. It is possible that the author of the 'First Saga of S. Ólafr' used written records like these, but the existing text would not justify the conclusion that he did. The available evidence suggests rather that he relied on oral sources.

The method used by the biographer in assembling his material was like that of Ari. As the passages already quoted have shown, he was less critical than Ari but, like Ari, he consulted men who were learned in tradition and legend. In one passage he named a certain monk, Hallr, as his authority for a miracle tale.[1] Uncritical as he was, it is improbable that he repeated stories which he did not believe himself. He once alluded to stories about S. Ólafr which he had heard, but had not written, because he was not satisfied with the evidence upon which they were based.[2]

The oral records available to this author were of two kinds. On the one hand were popular and especially ecclesiastical tales about the viking saint, and on the other were scaldic poems of various ages composed in S. Ólafr's honour.

The tales about S. Ólafr were concerned chiefly with miracles, and they were, no doubt, cultivated most ardently in the city of Niðaróss. The fullest record of them, the *Acta Sancti Olavi*,[3] was probably written about the same time as the 'First Saga of S. Ólafr', although the two were independent of each other. Undoubtedly the miracles were famous in other parts of the diocese besides Niðaróss, and it is not necessary to suppose that the Icelandic biographer collected his material there. He might well have heard it in the bishoprics and monasteries of Iceland, which were now in close contact with the archbishopric.

As is well known, formless tales and legends quickly become corrupted and altered during oral transmission. It is improbable that tales about S. Ólafr which reached the first biographer 150 years after his death had any great value as history, although they were often interesting as folk-lore. But besides formless tales, the

[1] *Otte Brudstykker*, ed. Storm, p. 13.    [2] Ibid., p. 8.
[3] Cf. Sigurður Nordal, op. cit., pp. 133 ff.; F. Metcalfe, *Passio et Miracula beati Olavi*, 1881, Introduction.

biographer had access to scaldic verses and these, in their turn, were of two kinds. Some of them were of recent date, and had little value as history. The *Geisli* is the best known example of that class.

More valuable sources of history were verses made in the saint's lifetime, or within living memory of him, by scalds whom he had patronized himself. Stories or incidents in a king's life recorded in verses had much better chances of survival than those entrusted to story-tellers or to popular memory, for, unlike formless tales, verses may be preserved for many generations virtually uncorrupt. The nursery rimes of today, some of which are very ancient, provide evidence of this conservative tendency, and the traditional ballads of the Faeroe Islands, written down only in recent times, are examples more closely akin to the scaldic poetry.

The more complicated the form of the verse the greater its chances of survival. Poems in the *Dróttkvætt* and other intricate scaldic forms could be remembered and recited correctly even after their meaning had become obscure, for alliteration, internal rime and the syllabic line demanded that the right syllable should fall in the right place. This is one of the reasons why scaldic poetry survives in much greater quantity than does the Eddaic.

The technique of scaldic poetry was briefly described in an earlier chapter of this book, and its aesthetic qualities were mentioned. Its value as history should also be considered. It is well known that kings of Norway, even since Haraldr Finehair, had delighted in poetry, and that nearly all of them kept favourite poets whom they rewarded for their work. The chief function of the court poets was to entertain their patrons and especially to eulogize them. But they had another function as well, and this was to record and immortalize the achievements and chief events in the lives of their patrons. This was not unimportant in the days when written records were not kept, as may be illustrated by a story in S. Ólafr's life. Before his last battle, at Stiklastaðir, S. Ólafr summoned his poets and said to them: 'You must stay here and see what happens; I have no story to tell you, but you must tell the story and make verses about it afterwards.'[1]

---

[1] *Heimskringla*, ed. Bjarni Aðalbjarnarson, ii, 1945, *Ólafs Saga hins helga*, ch. ccvi.

As already said, the scalds who praised the earlier kings of Norway were mostly Norwegians, but towards the end of the tenth century a change set in, and those who worked at the courts of the later kings were mostly Icelanders.[1] Although this change has never been explained, it shows that, after the end of the tenth century, the scaldic art was practised more ardently and professionally by Icelanders than by Norwegians. Consequently, it is not surprising that early scaldic poetry, whether composed by Icelanders or Norwegians, was better remembered in Iceland in the twelfth century than it was in Norway.

Before deciding the historical value of a King's saga, or indeed of a saga of an Icelandic hero, it is generally necessary to consider how much of the story is based upon scaldic poetry, and how much upon popular tales. These remarks do not imply that sagas, or passages in them, which are based on scaldic verses are necessarily accurate historically, for the scaldic tradition is subject to several dangers. One of them is that a scaldic strophe may be falsely ascribed to an early poet although it is really the work of a much younger poet. It has been said, to take an extreme example, that most of the verses ascribed to Gísli Súrsson, who lived in the tenth century, were really made by a poet who lived in the twelfth, or even in the thirteenth century.[2] But even if the verses upon which a saga is based are really as old as the author of the saga asserts, or implies, they may have been transferred from one poet to another, and may have been made for an occasion other than the one which they are thought to describe. Another danger, closely linked with this one, is that the author of the saga may misunderstand the scaldic diction and kennings, just as the author of the Ágrip did in the example quoted above. Even Snorri, the most accomplished critic of scaldic poetry, sometimes failed to understand the historical content of the verses with which he dealt.[3]

The oral sources of the 'First Saga of S. Ólafr', and of the

[1] Cf. Sigurður Nordal, *Íslenzk Menning*, i, 1942, pp. 239 ff.

[2] Cf. Björn K. Þórólfsson in *Vestfirðinga Sǫgur*, 1943, Introduction, pp. v ff.; Guðbrandur Vigfússon and F. York Powell, *Corpus Poeticum Boreale*, ii, 1883, pp. 331 ff.

[3] See, e.g., *Heimskringla*, i, ed. Bjarni Aðalbjarnarson, 1941, p. 119.

'Legendary Saga', which follows it closely, are easier to detect than are those of most Kings' sagas. This is partly because of the great age of the 'First Saga', and because it is closer to oral tradition than other sagas are. Another reason is that the 'First Saga' and its descendant the 'Legendary Saga' are constructed with little skill, and the bare bones can be seen through the skin.

It is plain from the outset that the 'First Saga of S. Ólafr' consists of a mixture of history and fiction. This is best illustrated by stories about S. Ólafr's early life as a viking. This period of his career has been studied by many scholars, and in greatest detail by O. A. Johnsen.[1] The chapters in which these stories are related are not preserved in the fragments of the 'First Saga', but they are in the 'Legendary Saga', which in these passages may be regarded as a faithful representative of the 'First Saga', although abridged. It is interesting to notice that some of these stories about Ólafr's early years can be compared with foreign records written more than a century before the 'First Saga'.

Among S. Ólafr's favourite poets were Óttarr the Black and Sigvatr. Both of them had eulogized S. Ólafr for his achievements as a young man, when he travelled from land to land as a viking. Óttarr's memorial to the young king was called the 'Head-Ransom', and that of Sigvatr the 'Viking Verses'. Although he knew both of these poems, or parts of them, the author of the 'First Saga' (and consequently of the 'Legendary Saga') must have relied chiefly on the 'Viking Verses', and on tales which had clustered round them, in these early chapters.

In chapter ix of the 'Legendary Saga'[2] it is said that, at the age of twelve (i.e. in 1007), Ólafr set forth with two ships and fought his first battle in Vík, beside some rocks called Sóta Sker (Sóti's Rocks). These rocks were named after a viking called Sóti, who lay at anchor nearby with a fleet of ten ships. S. Ólafr attacked Sóti with

---

[1] *Olav Haraldssons ungdom indtil slaget ved Nesjar*, 1916; useful accounts of S. Ólafr's early life were also given by K. Maurer, *Die Bekehrung des norwegischen Stammes zum Christenthume*, i, 1855, pp. 507 ff.; and by Bjarni Aðalbjarnarson, *Heimskringla*, ii, Introduction, pp. xxi ff.

[2] References apply to O. A. Johnsen's edition of the 'Legendary Saga', cited above, p. 176, note 3.

his two ships, and defeated him by one of those ruses which made him famous as a seaman. He spared Sóti's life, and Sóti became his friend and follower.

The whole of this passage, including details not repeated here, appears to be based on a single strophe of the 'Viking Verses'. In that strophe Sigvatr says only that the 'long ship carried the young prince out to sea; men learnt to fear his wrath. . . . For the first time, in his anger, he reddened the wolf's foot, beside Sótasker'.[1] The poet does not say that the battle was fought in the Vík, nor that Sótasker was named after a man called Sóti, still less that Sóti brought ten ships against Ólafr's two. Snorri,[2] with better reason, placed Sótasker off the Baltic coast of Sweden, but he also said that Ólafr fought there against Sóti. This is probably due to folk-etymology.

Three battles in which S. Ólafr was engaged in the Baltic are recounted in chapter x of the 'Legendary Saga'. Sigvatr had devoted one strophe to each of them, and his strophes appear to be the only records of these battles which the author of the saga knew. After this the story grows more complicated. According to the 'Legendary Saga', Ólafr heard that Þorkell the Tall was in England, and went there to join him, and they fought side by side at Suðrvík in England. This is based mainly on the fourth strophe of the 'Viking Verses', where Sigvatr says that the prince fought a battle at Suðrvík, which is well known to the Danes. Snorri used the same strophe in the *Heimskringla*,[3] and he took the expression 'well known to the Danes' (*Dǫnum kunn*) to mean that Suðrvík was in Denmark. But the tradition that S. Ólafr collaborated with Þorkell the Tall recurs in Icelandic literature.[4] Since Þorkell is often mentioned in early English records, these may throw light on the story told in the saga.

According to the 'Old English Chronicle' an immense Danish

---

[1] Cf. *Heimskringla*, ed. Bjarni Aðalbjarnarson, *Ólafs Saga Helga*, ch. vi.
[2] *Heimskringla*, loc. cit.                    [3] *Ólafs Saga Helga*, ch. x.
[4] Cf. *Heimskringla*, loc. cit. The story is also supported by a verse of doubtful origin, which is ascribed to S. Ólafr himself, and quoted in the 'Legendary Saga' (ch. xi) and elsewhere (see *Den norsk-islandske Skjaldedigtning*, ed. Finnur Jónsson, A. i, 1912, p. 220.)

host landed at Sandwich early in August 1009,[1] and according to one text of the 'Chronicle' it was known as *Þurkilles here*. First the vikings went to Canterbury, and the people of Kent bought them off. They marauded during the following months and attacked London several times, but the Londoners withstood them. In the spring of 1010 the vikings attacked Ipswich. The defences of East Anglia were then in charge of a certain Ulfcytel and, according to Florence of Worcester, the Danes engaged him at Ringmere.[2] The result was disaster for the English.

S. Ólafr is not named in the English records of this period, but if it is true that he was allied with Þorkell while in England, it is likely that he took part in the Danish invasion of 1009. According to the 'Viking Verses', the sixth battle in which S. Ólafr was engaged consisted of an attack on London Bridge (*bryggjur*); he was fighting against the English, and a part of the viking host was encamped at Súðvirki or Southwark.[3] The poet does not suggest that Ólafr or his viking companions conquered London, and the little that he says is consistent with the assertion of the 'Chronicle' that the Londoners beat off their assailants.

This last strophe of the 'Viking Verses' is quoted in the 'Legendary Saga', and is there preceded by a detailed and circumstantial story. This story is far from clear, and it may be summarized as follows:

Six years after the death of Ólafr Tryggvason (i.e. 1006 or 1007), Sveinn Forkbeard died in England. By the time of his death, Sveinn had conquered the whole of England. S. Ólafr was now thirteen or fourteen years old,[4] but in spite of his youth, he played a leading part in restoring Ethelred to the throne.

[1] *Two Saxon Chronicles*, ed. J. Earle and C. Plummer, i. 139, cf. ii. 187; see also F. M. Stenton, *Anglo-Saxon England*, 1943, p. 377.

[2] *Two Saxon Chronicles*, i. 140, and notes in ii. 187.

[3] 'Legendary Saga', ch. xi; cf. *Heimskringla, Ólafs Saga Helga*, ch. xiii.

[4] The chronology of the 'Legendary Saga' is, at this point, confused. It is said there that Sveinn died six weeks (*vikum*) after Ólafr Tryggvason. But *vikum* must be a scribal error for *vetrum*, as shown in the following passage, where it is said that S. Ólafr was thirteen or fourteen years old when he restored Ethelred to the throne on the death of Sveinn. According to the 'Legendary Saga', S. Ólafr was seven years old when Ólafr Tryggvason died (A.D. 1000), and he was, therefore, born in 1093. But according to Snorri (*Heimskringla, Ólafs Saga Helga*, ccxlvi), who quotes the authority of Ari, S. Ólafr was born in 1095.

Three years after the death of Sveinn (i.e. 1009), Knútr, the son of
Sveinn, invaded England, and fought against Edmund (Ironside), the
son of Ethelred. Knútr now conquered the whole of England, except
for London. He ruled for twenty-four years.

After this it is described in the 'Legendary Saga' how Knútr besieged
London, but could not take the Bridge. He heard that S. Ólafr was in
England, and offered to pay him for advice. As his price, Ólafr stipu-
lated that Knútr should renounce any claims which he might have to the
Kingdom of Norway.

London Bridge was supported by props, and there were fortified
houses upon it. S. Ólafr approached the Bridge with a large fleet; he
attached chains to the props which supported the Bridge, and then
rowed downstream, dragging the Bridge and the buildings down
the Thames.

The chronology of this story does not bear investigation. The
author implies that Sveinn Forkbeard died in 1006 and, in that
year, or the following one, Ólafr, then thirteen or fourteen years
old, restored Ethelred to the Kingdom. In reality, Sveinn lived
until February 1014, and it was in that year that Ethelred returned
from exile in France and recovered his throne. Knútr was in England at the time of his father's death,[1] but it is improbable that
Ólafr, who is remembered as the adversary of Knútr, ever entered
an alliance with him.

Ólafr's seventh battle was fought at Hringmaraheiðr, according
to the 'Viking Verses', and it must be equated with the battle of
Ringmere, fought, according to English sources, in 1010. The battle
of Hringmaraheiðr is mentioned in the 'Legendary Saga', but
nothing is there added to the bare account given by Sigvatr.
Hringmaraheiðr is said by Sigvatr to lie in Ulfkell's Land. This is
plainly an allusion to Ulfcytel, who was in charge of the defences
of East Anglia, according to English records.[2]

Ólafr's eighth battle was at Canterbury, and it is recorded in the
'Legendary Saga' and in the 'Viking Verses', where it is made plain
that the city fell.[3] According to the 'Legendary Saga', Ólafr was now

---

[1] Cf. Stenton, op. cit., p. 381.
[2] *Two Saxon Chronicles*, i. 140, cf. notes, ii. 187; see also Stenton, op. cit.,
pp. 375 ff.
[3] 'Legendary Saga', ch. xiii; cf. *Heimskringla, Ólafs Saga Helga*, ch. xv.

fighting against the Danes, but Sigvatr gives no authority for this, and shows that Ólafr was among the assailants of Canterbury. The capture of Canterbury by Þorkell's army took place late in 1011, according to English records.[1] The vikings left Canterbury in April of the following year, taking Archbishop Ælfeah as a hostage. Shortly afterwards they murdered Ælfeah, whereupon Þorkell went over to Ethelred, perhaps because he was shocked at the unruly conduct of his army. It might be supposed that Ólafr had joined Ethelred at the same time, and for the same reason as Þorkell, but that is not likely, for it may be deduced from the next strophe of the 'Viking Verses' that Ólafr was still fighting against the English in his ninth battle. This battle was fought, according to the poem and the saga, at Nýjamóða,[2] but no allusion to it has been found in English sources.

Although they give fairly detailed accounts of the battles of the years 1009–12, the English chroniclers say nothing about Ólafr. The 'Viking Verses' and the Saga, on the other hand, give the impression that S. Ólafr was leader, or at least joint leader, of the viking host, although, in the year 1009, he can hardly have been more than fourteen years old. He was the son of a petty prince from eastern Norway, and must have served as a very minor officer in the great Danish army. It was not until several years later that he distinguished himself sufficiently to be named by a foreign chronicler.

According to the 'Viking Verses', Ólafr's tenth battle took place at Hóll, in Hringsfjǫrðr, where he destroyed a fortress held by some vikings. The battle of Hóll is also recorded in the 'Legendary Saga',[3] but nothing is there added to the story told by Sigvatr. Snorri, in the *Heimskringla*,[4] says that Ólafr went south over the sea before he came to Hringsfjǫrðr, which implies that Hringsfjǫrðr was in France. Consequently the battle of Hóll has been equated with one mentioned by William of Jumièges in the *Gesta Normannorum Ducum*, written about 1070. William says that Richard II,

---

[1] *Two Saxon Chronicles*, i. 141, and notes ii. 188; cf. Stenton, op. cit., p. 378.
[2] 'Legendary Saga', xiii; cf. *Heimskringla*, *Ólafs Saga Helga*, ch. xv.
[3] Ch. xii.  [4] *Ólafs Saga Helga*, ch. xvi.

Duke of Normandy, quarrelled with Odo, Count of Chartres. Richard enlisted the aid of two viking chiefs, who were in England. One of these was Lacman, Rex Svavorum, who cannot be identified, and the other was Olavus Rex Noricorum. The precise date of these events is not known, but they could well have taken place between the years 1012 and 1014.[1] According to William, the viking chiefs attacked and conquered a castle called Dol. William's record agrees substantially with Sigvatr's strophe and with the 'Legendary Saga', except that in the Icelandic poem the name Dol appears to be corrupted to Hóll. Evidence that Olavus, to whom William alludes, was in fact S. Ólafr may be found in a statement which William makes about him in a later passage. He says that Olavus afterwards returned to his own country, where he was betrayed and unjustly killed by his subjects.[2]

After further adventures and travels, recorded both in the 'Viking Verses' and in the 'Legendary Saga', Ólafr returned to France, and remained for a while in the region of the Seine. At this point William of Jumièges throws further light on his career, saying that he went subsequently to Rouen, where he was instructed in Christianity and baptized by Archbishop Robert.[3] This is inconsistent with the story told in the 'Legendary Saga', and in several Icelandic sources,[4] that S. Ólafr was baptized at the age of five, and that Ólafr Tryggvason stood godfather for him. It is more probable that S. Ólafr was still a pagan throughout his early career as a viking.

I have mentioned the Icelandic story that S. Ólafr helped Ethelred to recover his kingdom, and this story cannot be rejected lightly, if only because it is supported by a strophe of Óttarr's 'Head-ransom'.[5] If the chronology of the 'Legendary Saga' is followed, this must have been about 1007, or little later. But, according to English records, Ethelred fled to France in 1013, and in 1014 he

---

[1] *Gesta Normannorum Ducum*, ed. J. Marx, 1914, Bk. v, 10–11; cf. O. A. Johnsen, op. cit., p. 15. See also Stenton, op. cit., p. 396; and especially A. Campbell, *Encomium Emmae Reginae*, 1949, pp. 78 ff., and works to which reference is there made.          [2] Op. cit., v. 12.

[3] William of Jumièges, op. cit., loc. cit. See also p. 170 and note 1.

[4] 'Legendary Saga', ch. viii; *Heimskringla*, *Ólafs Saga Tryggvasonar*, ch. lx.

[5] Quoted in *Heimskringla*, *Ólafs Saga Helga*, ch. xiii.

returned to England and recovered his kingdom. If S. Ólafr helped him to recover it, this must have been the time when he did so. It is not improbable that Ólafr joined Ethelred at this time, since they were both in France, and Ólafr was a recent convert to Christianity. In 1014 Ólafr was nineteen years old, according to Ari's chronology, and sufficiently mature to take a leading part in military and political affairs. He returned to his own country at the age of twenty (1014–15).

In the foregoing pages some stories of S. Ólafr's youth, which are told in the 'Legendary Saga', have been considered in the light of trustworthy foreign records. This has shown that the early chapters of the 'Legendary Saga', and of the 'First Saga', from which it is derived, contained a remarkably high proportion of historical truth. This is especially interesting because hardly more than a century and a half had elapsed between the death of the saint and the time when the 'First Saga' was written. Such oral records of history could scarcely survive uncorrupt unless they were cast in a rigid form. The oral records of this period of S. Ólafr's career were preserved chiefly in the verses of Sigvatr and Óttarr; poets who knew S. Ólafr well while he was alive. These poets admired the king, and their first purpose was to praise him, and so they made him the leader of every army in which he served, and the centre of every scene which they described.

It must be admitted that, as records of the saint's early years, the verses of Sigvatr and Óttarr are somewhat bare. For this reason popular imagination had to supply details, and to complete the picture of a favourite hero. Stories such as those about the viking Sóti and the miraculous delivery of S. Ólafr in the Mälar Sea, could be explained in this way. It is to the credit of the first biographer of S. Ólafr that he preserved these interesting folk-tales, as well as genuine records of history.

The 'First Saga' was a source for later biographers of the saint, and ultimately for Snorri. When Snorri rewrote the story of Ólafr, he did so as a mature and masterly artist. He rearranged the material, pruned it, made it realistic and, above all, convincing. Snorri's life of S. Ólafr is the greatest of all Kings' sagas, and the picture which he draws is a true one, but its truth is of an artistic, not of a scientific kind. If considered as a work of scientific history, which it was not intended to be, it will be found no more reliable than the 'First Saga'.

I have said that the 'First Saga of S. Ólafr' is the oldest saga known to us, and it was probably the first ever written. None of these early works betrays the origins of Kings' sagas—and ultimately of sagas of Icelandic heroes—more plainly than this one. In form, the 'First Saga' owed most to European biography and hagiography, but the material was drawn largely, although not exclusively, from the native oral sources, from poetry and folk-tale. It was the native traditions to which the author gave expression and assembled as a permanent monument to the northern saint, but the form into which he cast them was a foreign one.

Although indigenous, many of the oral stories incorporated in the 'First Saga' must have flourished in clerical circles. But the verses were the heritage of the lay, rather than of the clerical tradition, and they provided the historical basis for this saga as for many later ones. As the classical period of Icelandic literature approached, the culture of the laymen grew stronger, or perhaps it would be more true to say that the lay and clerical cultures separated more widely. The lives of saints grew more verbose and more 'clerical', in style if not in content. But the lives of the Norse heroes were gradually shorn of their hagiographic covering.

## 4. SAGAS OF ÓLAFR TRYGGVASON

One of the next sagas to be written was about Ólafr Tryggvason, and its author was Oddr Snorrason, monk of Þingeyrar.[1] The Benedictine house of Þingeyrar was the oldest of Icelandic monasteries, and had been founded in 1133.[2] For three or four decades of the late twelfth and early thirteenth centuries it was the chief centre of intellectual activity in northern Iceland, if not in the whole country.

[1] Critical edition: *Saga Ólafs Tryggvasonar* (Oddr Snorrason), ed. Finnur Jónsson, 1932.
[2] See Bishop Jón Helgason, *Islands Kirke*, 1925, pp. 94 ff., and Janus Jónsson, *Tímarit hins íslenzka bókmenntafjelags*, viii, 1887, pp. 182 ff.

In writing the 'Saga of Ólafr Tryggvason', Oddr was probably inspired directly by the 'First Saga of S. Ólafr', and, in his Prologue, he gives some reasons for undertaking the work. He compares Ólafr Tryggvason with his namesake, and implies that Ólafr Tryggvason deserved a share of the honour which had been accorded to S. Ólafr. The two kings were distantly related. Ólafr Tryggvason had laid the foundations of Christianity in Norway, and S. Ólafr had raised the timbers and completed the work. It was generally believed in Iceland that Ólafr Tryggvason had stood godfather at the baptism of his namesake and, therefore, Oddr thought of Ólafr Tryggvason as John the Baptist; he was the forerunner of the saint, whom Oddr, like many others of his day, regarded as a symbol of Christ.[1] After his death the sanctity of S. Ólafr had been revealed in countless miracles. No miracles had been attested after the death of Ólafr Tryggvason, but this itself was one of God's mysteries, which must not be probed. Like his namesake, Ólafr Tryggvason was a saintly man, and the Icelanders held him in high regard, for it was he, and not S. Ólafr, who had converted their ancestors. He could be called the Apostle of Iceland.

Oddr wrote his 'Saga of Ólafr Tryggvason' in Latin, but the original text is lost, and the saga survives only in the vernacular. Two texts of the vernacular version are preserved, besides the fragment of a third,[2] and the best of these is contained in a manuscript (AM. 310, 4to, called *A*) written in Norway towards the end of the thirteenth century. Although defective, the lacunae in this manuscript can generally be filled from another, now in the Royal Library of Stockholm (18 mbr, 4to, called *S*), which was written in Iceland at a rather later date. This manuscript contains a shorter text of the saga. The latter chapters are also preserved in another manuscript, written in Norway about the middle of the thirteenth century, and now preserved in Uppsala. In spite of considerable differences, the instances of verbal similarity between the three texts are sufficient to show that they all descend from the same

---

[1] Cf. F. Paasche, *Kristendom og Kvad*, 1914, pp. 73 ff.
[2] The manuscripts are described by Finnur Jónsson in his edition of the saga, Introduction, pp. iii ff.

original translation of the Latin.[1] This translation must have been
made in Iceland early in the thirteenth century, for it was known
not only to Snorri (died 1241), but also to the compiler of the
*Fagrskinna*, as well as to the author of the *Laxdœla Saga*, and to
several later writers.[2]

Oddr used written sources more extensively than the author of
the 'First Saga of S. Ólafr' had done. One of them was Sæmundr's
lost 'History of the Kings of Norway',[3] but this book could supply
little more than a few chronological details and some summary
sentences about the kings. He also used Ari's *Íslendingabók* and,
according to one text (*S*), he alluded to that book by name. It is
plain that the *Íslendingabók* which Oddr used was fuller than the
existing text, and it can only be the lost version of that work.[4] There
can be little doubt that Oddr also consulted the *Historia* of Theodoricus[5] and this suggests that his saga is younger than that work.
Oddr devoted several chapters to the legend of the Irish princess,
Sunnifa, who had fled from a viking suitor, and lived a saintly life
with her followers on the Norwegian island of Selja, where she
suffered a martyr's death during the reign of Hákon Sigurðarson
(died 995). In the year 1170 the bones of S. Sunnifa were translated
from Selja and enshrined in the cathedral church of Bergen. Her
story was written in Latin in Norway, and has been published
under the title *Acta Sanctorum in Seljo*.[6] The translation of S.
Sunnifa was recorded in the *Acta* which must, therefore, have been
written after 1170. In his chapters about S. Sunnifa, Oddr has
followed the *Acta* closely, although he has rearranged the material
and added some minor details from oral sources. Oddr probably
wrote his saga towards the end of the twelfth century, perhaps
about 1190.

Although he made full use of the books available to him, Oddr's
chief sources were necessarily unwritten ones. The outline of

[1] Cf. Finnur Jónsson, loc. cit., pp. viii ff.; Bjarni Aðalbjarnarson, *Om de norske
kongers sagaer*, pp. 56 ff.      [2] Bjarni Aðalbjarnarson, op. cit., pp. 59 ff.
[3] Cf. Bjarni Aðalbjarnarson, op. cit., pp. 33–39, 68–69.
[4] Ed. Finnur Jónsson, p. 127.
[5] Cf. Sigurður Nordal, *Om Olav den helliges saga*, pp. 37 ff. Bjarni Aðalbjarnarson, op. cit., pp. 69 ff.
[6] Published by G. Storm in *Monumenta*, pp. 147–52.

Ólafr's career as a viking and as a king could be reconstructed from scaldic verses, for he had patronized several poets, of whom Hallfreðr the Troublesome Poet (*Vandræðaskáld*) is the most famous. Hallfreðr had immortalized the chief exploits of Ólafr Tryggvason, just as Sigvatr had immortalized those of S. Ólafr. But the events recorded by the scalds were not sufficient to make a complete biography of Ólafr; they had left no verses about his early years and his wanderings as a child in foreign countries.

The gaps were filled by popular tales, and Oddr used them without restraint. In his Prologue he had spoken disdainfully of 'stepmother tales', such as cowherds tell each other; he did not intend to fill his book with these. But if, by 'stepmother tales' (*stjúpmæðra sǫgur*), Oddr meant tales about trolls and Lappish magicians and shape-changers, it was in these that his work excelled. The story of the trolls in Naumudalr,[1] whose lugubrious conversations were overheard by two of Ólafr's courtiers, is one of the best of its kind in Icelandic. Some of these tales have been coloured by the stories of Scripture.[2] As an example may be quoted that of the aged Russian queen, who beheld signs of the birth of Ólafr Tryggvason[3] almost as the wise men had beheld the Star of Bethlehem. A number of Oddr's tales, such as those about the wiles of Óðinn, and about the jovial red-bearded Þórr,[4] rest upon ancient beliefs of the northern peoples.

Oddr has been little appreciated as a literary artist. This is partly because his work survives only in translation, and its style cannot be judged, but even more because his 'Saga of Ólafr Tryggvason' has been surpassed by that of Snorri, with which it is sometimes compared. This comparison is not altogether just. Snorri excelled especially in construction; he knew how to make his story progress, as if of necessity, to a climax, and how to bring his heroes to life. Snorri could do this, partly because he had carefully studied the older sagas, and such study was not possible when Oddr lived. Oddr's excellencies were other than those of Snorri. If his saga of

---

[1] Ed. Finnur Jónsson, pp. 174 ff.
[2] Cf. G. Indrebø, *Fagrskinna*, 1917, pp. 159 ff.
[3] Ed. Finnur Jónsson, p. 20.  [4] Ibid., pp. 173 ff.

Ólafr Tryggvason is compared with the 'First Saga of S. Ólafr', or with the 'Legendary Saga', his achievement can be appreciated better, and it can then be seen how saga-writing had advanced since the 'First Saga of S. Ólafr' took shape.

Gunnlaugr Leifsson, another monk of Þingeyrar, must have been a younger contemporary of Oddr, and the date of his death is recorded in the annals as 1218 or 1219. He was more ambitious, both as an author and as a scholar, than Oddr, and was considered the most lettered man of his day.[1] Among his works was another 'Saga of Ólafr Tryggvason', and this is a further indication of the high regard in which the 'Apostle of Iceland' was now held. Gunnlaugr's 'Saga of Ólafr Tryggvason' does not survive in full, but it is known that it was written in Latin,[2] and was subsequently translated into Icelandic. Long passages of the Icelandic version were incorporated in the so-called 'Greatest Saga of Ólafr Tryggvason'. This vast compilation was made early in the fourteenth century, and survives in the Flateyjarbók, as well as in several other manuscripts. It was constructed as a kind of encyclopaedia of Ólafr Tryggvason's life, and many passages in it can safely be ascribed to Gunnlaugr.[3] They give a clear idea of the quality of his work.

Gunnlaugr undoubtedly based his work largely upon that of Oddr, but Gunnlaugr's saga was a larger one. It was also more verbose, and the influence of hagiography was even stronger. The miraculous and legendary elements in Ólafr's life were given greater prominence, and the story was swelled with fulsome and often vapid speeches ascribed to the hero. The chapters in which Gunnlaugr described the adventures of Ólafr after the battle of Svǫlð are especially interesting. Many of the kings' admirers had refused to believe that he had perished in the battle, and said that he had escaped secretly, and was living in the Mediterranean lands (Suðrríki).[4] The contemporary poet, Hallfreðr, had heard stories like these, but placed little faith in them.[5] Oddr, on the other hand,

---

[1] See Biskupa Sögur, ii, 1878, p. 31.
[2] See Flateyjarbók, i, 1860, p. 516.
[3] See Bjarni Aðalbjarnarson, Om de norske kongers sagaer, esp. pp. 92 ff.
[4] See, e.g., Fagrskinna, ed. Finnur Jónsson, 1902–3, p. 131.
[5] Ibid., pp. 132–4; Heimskringla, ed. Bjarni Aðalbjarnarson, 1941, pp. 368–70.

was nearly convinced that Ólafr had eluded his enemies, and had ended his days in a monastery in Greece or Syria, doing penance for the sins of his youth.[1] Although Snorri and the compiler of the *Fagrskinna*, both of whom used Oddr's work as their chief source, alluded to these stories of Ólafr's escape, they rejected them. Whatever might be the truth, said Snorri, it was certain that Ólafr had never returned to his kingdom.[2] But Gunnlaugr would leave his readers in no doubt of Ólafr's escape from the battle, and he wrote several chapters about his subsequent life in holy lands. Five years after his supposed death, some English pilgrims had met Ólafr in Jerusalem, and he had entrusted them with a book, which they had to bring to King Ethelred of England. In this book, Ólafr's own adventures after the battle of Svǫlð were related, and it contained the lives of seven other saints. Many years later, a Norwegian pilgrim had come upon Ólafr living in disguise in a monastery near the Red Sea.[3] Gunnlaugr must have embroidered, or even invented, some of these stories, and it can hardly be said of such a romancer that he is lacking in critical sense.

It is not known precisely when Gunnlaugr wrote his 'Saga of Ólafr Tryggvason' but, according to a surviving passage, he named six of his oral informants.[4] They include three men and three women. One of the women was Ingunn (Arngunn, v. l.), who might be identified with Ingunn, the chaste virgin, who studied Latin in the school of Hólar in the days of Bishop Jón.[5] Ásgrímr Vestliðason, the third Abbot of Þingeyrar (died 1161), was another of Gunnlaugr's informants. Bjarni Bergþórsson is also named among them, and he was probably Bjarni the mathematician and computist, who died in 1173.[6] Bjarni was one of the students of Hólar. After he had drafted his work, Gunnlaugr submitted it to Gizurr Hallsson.[7] Gizurr kept the book for two years and then returned

---

[1] *Saga Ólafs Tryggvasonar*, ed. Finnur Jónsson, 1932, pp. 233–6 and 241–3.
[2] *Heimskringla*, ed. Bjarni Aðalbjarnarson, i. 368.   [3] *Flateyjarbók*, i. 501–6.
[4] Ibid., i. 517; cf. Oddr's *Ólafs Saga*, ed. Finnur Jónsson, p. 247.
[5] Cf. Bjarni Aðalbjarnarson, op. cit., p. 86 footnote.
[6] On Bjarni Bergþórsson see N. Beckman in *Alfræði íslenzk*, ii, 1914–16, Introduction, p. x.
[7] On Gizurr Hallsson see *Veraldar Saga*, ed. Jakob Benediktsson, 1944, Introduction.

it to Gunnlaugr, who 'emended' it as Gizurr had advised. Gizurr
was Law-speaker from 1181 until 1200, and he died in 1206 at the
age of eighty. He was renowned as a scholar, and especially as an
historian. Gunnlaugr's 'Saga of Ólafr Tryggvason' must have been
translated into Icelandic at an early date, and it was the chief source
of the *Kristni Saga*, in which the conversion of Iceland was described in detail. The *Kristni Saga*, as has recently been shown,[1]
was compiled by Sturla Þórðarson (died 1284). The author of the
*Njáls Saga* may also have referred to Gunnlaugr's saga when he
wrote his chapters about Þangbrandr and about the arrival of
Christianity in Iceland,[2] and the story of Þorvaldr the Far Traveller (*Þorvalds Þáttr*) is derived from it.[3] Snorri knew Gunnlaugr's
work, and consulted it occasionally when he wrote his 'Saga of Ólafr
Tryggvason', but it was too far removed from reality to be of great
use to Snorri.[4]

The purpose, both of Oddr and of Gunnlaugr, in writing sagas
about Ólafr Tryggvason was to demonstrate the moral worth of
their hero, and to show that the Icelanders had especial reasons for
devotion to him. But the need for a patron saint could not be satisfied by this Norwegian viking, however intimate his relations with
the Icelanders. The Icelanders must have saints of their own, just
as other nations had.

## 5. SAGAS OF THE BISHOPS

If they were to find saints among their own people, the Icelanders must look for them among their bishops. In the words of
an historian of the early thirteenth century, all the bishops of Iceland had been holy men,[5] and the holiest of them all was Þorlákr,
Bishop of Skálaholt (died 1193). He had not long been dead before
his sanctity was revealed in dreams.[6] So many miracles were

[1] See Jón Jóhannesson, *Gerðir Landnámabókar*, 1941, pp. 69 ff.
[2] Cf. Bjarni Aðalbjarnarson, op. cit., pp. 133-5; see also Einar Ól. Sveinsson, *Um Njálu*, 1933, pp. 67 ff.
[3] The *Þorvalds Þáttr* was published by B. Kahle, in *Kristnisaga*, 1905, p. 59 ff. There are several other editions.
[4] Cf. Bjarni Aðalbjarnarson, op. cit., pp. 124 ff.
[5] See *Guðmundar Saga góða* in *Biskupa Sögur*, i. 454.
[6] See *Biskupa Sögur*, i. 301 ff.

attributed to his intercession that his body was raised from the earth, and he was declared a saint by the *Alþingi* within six years of his death.

The members of the northern diocese of Iceland had a smaller choice of bishops, but the first of them, Jón Ǫgmundarson (died 1121) was greater and holier than those who came after him. About the end of the twelfth century, the sanctity of Jón was also made known through dreams,[1] and during a hard winter it was revealed that the weather would improve if his bones were raised from the grave. The formal translation took place in March 1200 and Jón was also declared a saint.[2]

Among the foremost of Jón's admirers was Guðmundr Arason, nicknamed the Good, a remarkable but eccentric man.[3] Although no more than a priest in orders at that time, Guðmundr was already famed for the miracles which he had worked throughout Iceland, and he was consecrated Bishop of Hólar, in succession to Brandr, in 1203. In time, the fanaticism of Guðmundr was to earn him many enemies, who included the monk Gunnlaugr and other eminent clerics. But at the beginning of the thirteenth century the monks of Þingeyrar regarded Guðmundr as nothing less than a living saint,[4] and it was at his instigation that Gunnlaugr wrote the 'Saga of Jón, Bishop of Hólar'.[5] He wrote it in Latin, but its fate was like that of most works written in Latin at that period; the Latin text is lost and the saga survives only in a translation into Icelandic. This translation is preserved in three versions, of which two have been published, a shorter and a longer one. The shorter and longer versions are both based upon the same translation from the Latin original and, despite the editor's arguments to the contrary,[6] there can be no doubt that the longer version represents the original translation more closely than the shorter one does.[7] To judge by

---

[1] Ibid., p. 459.  [2] Ibid., p. 186 and footnote 5.

[3] On Guðmundr see *Guðmundar Saga* in *Biskupa Sögur*, i. 407 ff., ii, 1878, pp. 1 ff.; also *The Life of Gudmund the Good*, translated by G. Turville-Petre and E. S. Olszewska, 1942.  [4] See *Biskupa Sögur*, i. 465.

[5] On the authorship of the *Jóns Saga* see *Biskupa Sögur*, i. 216; ii. 31.

[6] See *Biskupa Sögur*, i, Introduction, pp. xxxiv ff.

[7] Cf. Finnur Jónsson, *ONOI*, ii. 395 ff.; Sigurður Nordal in *Borgfirðinga Sǫgur*, 1938, Introduction, pp. cxlvii ff.

its stilted style, which betrays the influence of Latin syntax, this longer version of the *Jóns Saga* is a faithful rendering of the Latin text.

The date when the *Jóns Saga* was written can be determined with some precision. It was written after 1201, because the author's references to Bishop Brandr show that he was dead.[1] Allusion is made to Guðmundr Arason as Bishop of Hólar, which suggests that the saga was written after 1203, for Guðmundr took up his duties in that year.[2] Since Gunnlaugr wrote at the instigation of Guðmundr, he must have done so while they were still on friendly terms, but they had quarrelled before 1210.[3] The date when the translation from the Latin was made is more difficult to determine, but a clue may be found in the relationship between the *Jóns Saga* and the *Þáttr* of Gísl Illugason. Both in the *Þáttr* and in the saga, the same story is told, and many of the same words are used about Gísl, who was poet and courtier of King Magnús Bareleg (died 1103). Sigurður Nordal[4] has shown that the *Þáttr* was influenced by the Icelandic version of the *Jóns Saga*. This proves that the translation of the *Jóns Saga* can be hardly younger than the middle of the thirteenth century.[5]

Specimens of the *Jóns Saga* were quoted in an earlier chapter of this book,[6] and they may have given some idea of its flowery style. Since he was writing no less than eighty years after the death of Jón, Gunnlaugr must have had difficulty in assembling enough facts to make a biography for, unlike the kings of Norway, Jón had not been praised by contemporary poets. A few of the chief events of his life and work had been recorded by Ari, and Gunnlaugr made the fullest use of Ari's work. Moreover, written records of some of the miracles attributed to Jón had been made before Gunnlaugr compiled his saga, and he seems to refer to a book in which they were collected. This book had perhaps been put together under the instructions of Bishop Brandr, when the bones of the saint were washed in 1198, or when they were formally trans-

---

[1] *Biskupa Sögur*, i. 212, 250–1.     [2] Ibid. i. 485.
[3] Ibid. i. 465, cf. ii. 77.     [4] In *Borgfirðinga Sǫgur*, Introduction, ch. 22.
[5] Cf. Finnur Jónsson, op. cit. ii. 397.     [6] See above, pp. 112 ff.

lated in 1200.[1] But, for the most part, Gunnlaugr had to rely upon formless tales which had gathered around the figure of this saint. His saga helps to show what kind of tales used to be told in the religious houses, and probably on the farms of Iceland, at the beginning of the thirteenth century.

The *Jóns Saga* falls into two parts. In the first forty chapters an outline of the saint's life is given, and it is interspersed with miracles which Jón had worked during his lifetime. The remainder of the book is concerned with miracles worked through Jón's intercession after death. A great proportion of these were supposed to have occurred in the last years of the twelfth century, a period when many Icelanders were giving way to superstition and extravagance in their religious beliefs. This tendency was more pronounced in the northern than in the southern diocese, and was probably encouraged by the ascetic miracle-worker, Guðmundr Arason. Long before they elected him bishop, Guðmundr had exercised a powerful influence both on clergymen and laymen in the diocese of Hólar, although he really appears to be the expression rather than the cause of this fanatical movement. If the picture which Gunnlaugr draws of Jón and his followers is a faithful one, the germ of fanaticism was present in the Christianity of the northern Icelanders ever since the see of Hólar was established.

Gunnlaugr relates one of the earlier miracles of Jón on the authority of a woman called Oddný Knútsdóttir[2] and she had heard it from a certain Hildr, who had witnessed it herself. Hildr had been an anchoress while Jón was bishop, and had died about 1160. While still a young girl, she had fled to a lonely place near to Hólar, and had built a shed, intending to live alone with God. Afterwards Jón had a cell built for Hildr beside the cathedral, and consecrated her as a nun.[3] The miracle, of which Hildr told Oddný, concerned Guðrún, another woman of ardent piety, and it took place at Hólar when Ketill Þorsteinsson was bishop (1122–45). Guðrún had set up a kind of altar beside the church door, on which

---

[1] See *Biskupa Sögur*, i. 248 and 192.  [2] Ibid. i. 206–7 and 256–7.
[3] Ibid. i. 254–6.

she used to stand, crying: 'take me, Christ, take me quickly. . . .'
She would stay awake night after night beside the corpses awaiting
burial in the church. One night, a corpse, beside which she was
watching, rose from the bier and tried to grasp her. Guðrún fled
to the altar of the cathedral, and took hold of the box in which
the relics were stored. Meanwhile, Hildr, disturbed by the noise,
peered through the window of the choir, and saw the church filled
with terrible ghosts. Hildr invoked the help of Jón, and he appeared
on the steps of the choir in full regalia, and scared the wicked
spirits away.

Most of the miracles, worked through the intercession of Jón,
were of a homely kind. Lost property was recovered, mice driven
away, sufferers were cured of illnesses, and sailors weathered the
storms. Sometimes it was implied in the accounts of the miracles
that S. Jón was as holy or even holier than S. Þorlákr. Invocation
was once made to S. Þorlákr on behalf of a sufferer and, although
she got no better, S. Þorlákr appeared and advised that S. Jón
should be invoked. One man, who was deaf in both ears, invoked
Þorlákr for the right and Jón for the left. On the day when Jón's
bones were translated, the left ear was healed.

Although Gunnlaugr chose Latin as the medium for his
histories, he was also an accomplished student of traditional Norse
poetry. This is shown in his rendering into Icelandic verse of
Geoffrey of Monmouth's *Prophecies of Merlin*. The *Merlínússpá*,
as it is called in Icelandic, is composed in the oldest of the heroic
metres, the *Fornyrðislag*,[1] but, as Gunnlaugr uses it, the *Fornyrðislag* is smoother, and the lines show less variation in their syllabic
length than do most of those in the *Edda*. On the whole, Gunnlaugr follows the Latin text of the *Prophecies* closely, and this is
especially remarkable when it is considered that he was translating
prose into verse. For, although Geoffrey claimed that he was
following a 'British poem', he did not write the *Prophecies* in
metrical form. Here and there, as if to heighten the effect of the
poem, Gunnlaugr inserted strophes or half-strophes of conventional rhetoric, for which the Latin text gave no authority.

[1] Ed. Finnur Jónsson, *Skjald.* A. ii. 10–36; B. ii. 10–45.

Describing the battle between the wolf, the bear, and the fox, Gunnlaugr says:

> Hríð gerisk hjalma    hlífar klofna,
> eru ramliga    randir kníðar,
> gnesta geirar,    es guðr vakin,
> verðr víða lið    at vallroði (Strophe 33).

In such passages Gunnlaugr draws on well-established poetic diction. He was aware that Merlin's *Prophecies* had something in common with those of the Sibyl of the *Vǫluspá*, and, therefore, he often imitated that poem. Echoes of several other early lays may also be heard in the *Merlínússpá*, e.g. of the *Fáfnismál*, the First Lay of Helgi Hundingsbani, and especially of the *Grípisspá*.[1] If not in good taste, these passages are proof of Gunnlaugr's wide interests. The last strophe of the *Merlínússpá* closely resembles that of the *Hávamál*:

> Heilir allir    þeirs hlýtt hafa
> fleinvarpaðir    fræði þessu,
> geri gott gumar,    en glati illu . . .

Gunnlaugr is a scald, no less than a heroic poet, for he uses kennings such as the poets of the *Edda* would rarely use. Many of these kennings can be traced to earlier scalds, but a number of them were probably devised by Gunnlaugr himself.

The *Merlínússpá* is preserved only in the *Hauksbók*, a manuscript written early in the fourteenth century. It is there inserted in its correct place in the *Breta Sǫgur*,[2] the Icelandic version of Geoffrey of Monmouth's *Historia Regum Britanniae*. Strangely enough, the two sections of the *Prophecies* are inverted in the Icelandic text, although it is improbable that Gunnlaugr intended them to be given in that order, for, as they stand in the *Hauksbók*, the *Prophecies* are scarcely more than meaningless bombast. They are, at least, partially understandable as Geoffrey wrote them in the *Historia*.

It is believed that Geoffrey published the *Prophecies* about 1134,

---

[1] Cf. Finnur Jónsson, Introduction to *Hauksbók*, 1892–6, pp. cxii–cxiii; J. de Vries, *Altnordische Literaturgeschichte*, ii, 1942, pp. 228–9.

[2] *Hauksbók*, ed. Finnur Jónsson, pp. 271–83.

before he completed the *Historia*, and it is said that copies of the *Prophecies* circulated independently of the *Historia*,[1] At first sight, it might be supposed that it was one of these independent copies which reached the hands of Gunnlaugr. This is, however, unlikely, because the opening passages of the second section of the *Merlín-ússpá* suggest that the author knew the preceding chapters of the *Historia*. Gunnlaugr's knowledge of Geoffrey's work might have influenced his own taste in historical narrative. Like Geoffrey, he favoured the romantic and legendary, rather than the strictly factual.

It is doubtful whether the *Merlínússpá* could survive for long among people who did not know the *Historia*. This may suggest that the *Historia* itself was translated into Icelandic not, as is some-times said, in the fourteenth century, but early in the thirteenth, and perhaps by a contemporary of Gunnlaugr.

## 6. THE SCHOOL OF SKÁLAHOLT

A reader may turn with a sense of relief from the breathless hagiography of Gunnlaugr to the ecclesiastical histories written in the diocese of Skálaholt during the same period. The seeds of objective learning, which Sæmundr and Ari had planted in south-ern Iceland, bore fruit early in the thirteenth century, when three notable works of history appeared at Skálaholt or nearby. These are the *Hungrvaka*, the sagas of S. Þorlákr and of Bishop Páll.[2] It has been said that these three works were written by one author.[3] They have distinctive features in common, most especially the *Hungrvaka* and the 'Saga of Bishop Páll'. If not by the same author they were, at any rate, written in the same 'school'. The question of their authorship must be considered in another context.

---

[1] Cf. E. Faral, *La légende Arthurienne*, ii, 1929, pp. 8 ff. and 38 ff.

[2] All three of these texts were published in *Biskupa Sögur*, i, 1858; texts of a great part of them, together with translations into English, were given in *Origines Islandicae*, ed. G. Vigfússon and F. York Powell, i, 1905, pp. 420 ff. A critical edition of the *Hungrvaka* was published by Jón Helgason in *Biskupa Sǫgur*, i, 1938, pp. 72–115.

[3] See Guðbrandur Vigfússon in *Biskupa Sögur*, i, Introduction, pp. xxxi f., cf. *Origines Islandicae*, i. 420 ff.

The *Hungrvaka* is a synoptic history of the bishops of Skálaholt, from Ísleifr (1055–80) to Þorlákr Þórhallsson (1176–93), and reference is made to the bishops who held office at Hólar during the same period. The author begins with a Prologue, in which he states his aims. He thinks that young people ought to know how Christianity grew up in Iceland, how the sees were founded, and what remarkable men the bishops were. Another purpose was to induce young men to read books written in their native language, such as those on law, histories, and ancestral records (*lǫg eða sǫgur eða mannfrœði*).[1]

This author worked largely from oral sources, and he says something about his oral informants. Foremost among them was Gizurr Hallsson, to whom reference is made several times in the book. A great part of the *Hungrvaka* is based on Gizurr's words. No one was better acquainted with the lives of the bishops than he. He had spoken some words at the funerals of five bishops at Skálaholt, from Þorlákr the Elder (died 1133) to Þorlákr the Saint (died 1193).[2]

The author of the *Hungrvaka* was the direct descendant of Ari, for he followed Ari's example, both in assembling material and in presenting it. Ari would have written a book like the *Hungrvaka*, had he lived at a later period, and had better opportunities to learn his trade. It has often been said that the author of the *Hungrvaka* did not read Ari's *Íslendingabók*,[3] because the only sources which he named were oral ones. But it would be difficult to believe that an author so intimately concerned with Skálaholt had not read the *Íslendingabók*, most especially if his outspoken interest in literature in the Icelandic language is considered. At least one mistake in the *Hungrvaka* may, in fact, be traced to the *Íslendingabók*.[4] The chapter in the *Hungrvaka* on the introduction of tithes and the foundation of the diocese of Hólar closely resembles the corresponding chapter of the *Íslendingabók*.[5] It is another question whether the

---

[1] The precise meaning of *mannfrœði* is not known. See J. de Vries, *Altnordische Literaturgeschichte*, ii. 30.     [2] See *Biskupa Sögur*, i. 299.

[3] Thus Finnur Jónsson, *ONOI*, ii. 560; cf. B. Kahle, *Kristnisaga*, Introduction, p. xxvii.

[4] Cf. Björn Sigfússon, *Um Íslendingabók*, 1944, pp. 27 ff.

[5] See *Biskupa Sǫgur*, i, ed. Jón Helgason, pp. 86 ff.; cf. *Íslendingabók*, ch. x.

author of the *Hungrvaka* had read the *Íslendingabók* in its extant form. There are some reasons to believe that he knew the lost version of that book.[1]

It is possible that the author of the *Hungrvaka* used certain other histories in his own language besides the *Íslendingabók*. Short notes are appended to several chapters, in which memorable events, which took place during the lives of various bishops, are listed. These notes may be based on annals in a form older than that of the existing recensions.[2] It should, however, be remarked that the *Hungrvaka* exists only in transcripts of the seventeenth century, and some of these annalistic entries may have been interpolated.[3]

The author of the *Hungrvaka* shows a certain knowledge of foreign literature, quoting the *Cantilena* of S. Lambert.[4] He may also have been influenced, perhaps indirectly or through an oral medium, by Adam of Bremen's *Gesta Hammaburgensis*. Adam had written extensively about missionary bishops who preached in Scandinavia and in the Baltic lands, and some of the foreigners who worked in Iceland in the eleventh century have been identified among them.[5] Adam says of one of them, Johannes Scotus, that he was martyred by the Slavs:

Ille igitur pro confessione Christi fustibus caesus, deinde per singulas civitates Sclavorum ductus ad ludibrium . . . truncatis manibus ac pedibus, in platea corpus eius proiectum est, caput vero eius desectum . . .[6]

According to the *Hungrvaka*, some people said that the missionary Jón Írski (the Irishman) had gone to Wendland after he left Iceland, and his martyrdom there is described in the following words:

(Hann) var síðan tekinn ok barðr, ok hǫggnar af bæði hendr ok fœtr, en hǫfuð síðast, ok fór með þeim píningum til guðs.[7]

It is difficult to decide the date when the *Hungrvaka* was written.

---

[1] Cf. Björn Sigfússon, op. cit., pp. 116 ff., and passim.
[2] Cf. N. Beckman, *Alfræði íslenzk*, ii, 1914–16, Introduction, pp. cxxiv ff., and works cited there.        [3] Cf. Björn Sigfússon, op. cit., pp. 36 ff.
[4] Ed. Jón Helgason, p. 97.
[5] On the missionary bishops in Iceland see Ch. III above and works cited there.
[6] Ed. B. Schmeidler, 1917, bk. iii, 51.        [7] Ed. Jón Helgason, p. 80 (ch. 3).

It is probable that the author knew S. Þorlákr, of whom he writes with warm admiration, but the book was written after the canonization of Þorlákr (1199). The chief informant, Gizurr Hallsson, died in 1206, but it cannot be deduced from the author's references whether Gizurr was alive or dead when the book was written. The author speaks of Gizurr as a 'jewel among men' (manngersemi), and praises him in such terms that it is perhaps easier to believe that he had recently died.[1]

Although very short, the descriptions of the bishops given in the Hungrvaka are clear, and altogether free of that cloudy verbosity which characterizes the 'Saga of S. Jón'. The author speaks of the shortcomings as well as of the virtues of the bishops. He says of the older Þorlákr that he was not generally considered a handsome man, nor was he particularly outstanding, in the opinion of most people. When he went abroad to be consecrated bishop, people said there must be a poor choice of men in Iceland, and they did not think him fitted for such high office. Þorlákr was generous to the poor, but many found him close-fisted. One of his chief virtues was humility. Bishop Klœngr (1152–76) was another stamp of man, for his fault was extravagance, and he had the virtues which go with it. His first act as bishop was to build a new cathedral, for which he imported two shiploads of timber from Norway, and prudent men thought he was squandering the estate. When the building of the cathedral was sufficiently far advanced, it was ceremoniously consecrated amid pomp unparalleled in Iceland, and after the ceremony more than 800 guests sat down to dinner. The bishop, as the Hungrvaka says, acted 'rather in munificence than in full prudence'.[2]

The only bishop of whom the author of the Hungrvaka speaks with unmixed admiration is S. Þorlákr, who is said to be truly a saint, as no man in Iceland had hitherto been proved to be.[3] The career of S. Þorlákr is not described in the Hungrvaka, but instead, the Hungrvaka ends as if it had been designed as an introduction to

---

[1] Cf. Þorláks Saga (Biskupa Sögur, i. 98): svá mælir heilǫg ritning: 'eigi skaltu lofa mann í lífi sínu; lofa hann eptir lífit' (cf. Ecclesiastes iv. 2).
[2] Ed. Jón Helgason, p. 110.　　　　　　　　　　　　　　　[3] Ibid., p. 110.

the saga of that saint: 'Now we have come to the story which shall be told of the Blessed Þorlákr . . . who may rightly be called a bright ray or a jewel among saints, both in Iceland and elsewhere. He may truthfully be called the Apostle of Iceland, just as S. Patrick is called the Apostle of Ireland. . . .'[1]

In its best manuscripts the *Hungrvaka* is followed by the *Þorláks Saga* (Saga of S. Þorlákr), and these last lines of the *Hungrvaka* have been explained in various ways. If the author of the *Hungrvaka* wrote them, he must imply either that he was himself the author of the *Þorláks Saga*, or else that the *Þorláks Saga* was already written, and the *Hungrvaka* was intended to be an introduction to it. It has however, been suggested that the lines were not written by the same man as the rest of the *Hungrvaka*, but were added by the scribe who first put this book and the *Þorláks Saga* into the same manuscript. Those who hold this view say that, in style, these lines are too far removed from the rest of the *Hungrvaka* for it to be possible that they came from the same pen. It is also said that the *Þorláks Saga* itself is altogether unlike the *Hungrvaka*, and could not be the work of the same man.[2]

Such arguments are not conclusive. The author of the *Hungrvaka* admired none of the bishops as he admired Þorlákr. It would be strange that he should describe the careers of all of them except that of Þorlákr, unless the life of Þorlákr was already written and in his hands. The possibility that both the *Hungrvaka* and the *Þorláks Saga* were written by the same author cannot be ruled out. There are differences between them, but there are several features in which they resemble each other.

It is difficult to discuss the *Þorláks Saga* in any detail, because, while it exists in three versions, only two of these have been published, and the relationship between the three versions, and their various manuscripts, has not been finally established. It can, however, be said that, in the version which the editors designate as the 'Oldest', the form of the original is preserved better than in the

---

[1] Ed. Jón Helgason, p. 115.
[2] See Finnur Jónsson, op. cit. ii. 561, 564–5; cf. B. Kahle, op. cit., pp. xxvii–xxviii.

THE LATE TWELFTH CENTURY

so-called 'Younger' version. But it is probable that the 'Oldest' version has been shortened, in some passages at least.

Like the *Hungrvaka*, the *Þorláks Saga* was apparently written when Páll was Bishop of Skálaholt (1195–1211), and after Þorlákr had been declared a saint (1199). Reference is once made to a saying of King Sverrir (died 1202),[1] in a way which suggests that the king was dead when the saga was written. But the author wrote with personal memory of Þorlákr, and quotes words which he had heard him say.[2]

The tone of the *Þorláks Saga* is rather unlike that of the *Hungrvaka*. It is the life of a man whose sanctity had been proved, and his character is above criticism. In choice of expression, the *Þorláks Saga* shows certain affinities with the *Hungrvaka*,[3] although in most passages it differs considerably from it. On nearly every page the author quotes Holy Scripture. He was well versed both in the Old Testament and in the New.

It was remarked above that the author of the *Hungrvaka* had shown a certain moderation and restraint in his descriptions of the bishops. The author of the *Þorláks Saga* also tempered his praises of the saint, for Þorlákr was not blessed with all the gifts of God. He had not a beautiful voice, as S. Jón of Hólar had; he spoke haltingly, and it was a trial for him to preach. The author of the saga admired no quality in S. Þorlákr more than his temperance. He was not, like Bishop Guðmundr of Hólar, extravagantly ascetic. He ate little, and he never drank strong drink in such quantities that its effects were visible. He enjoined people of his diocese to observe Friday abstinence but, as an example to others, he allowed

---

[1] *Biskupa Sögur*, i. 100.                                                    [2] Ibid. i. 90.

[3] The following passages about Bishop Klœngr in the *Hungrvaka* and the 'Oldest' *Þorláks Saga* may be compared:

(a) Er hann tók at eldask, þá sótti at honum vanheilsa mikil, ok tók í fyrstu fœtr hans at opnask af kulða ok meinlætum ok óhœgindum þeim er hann hafði haft . . . (*Hungrvaka*, ed. Jón Helgason, p. 112);

Þá er Klœngr biskup gerðisk mjǫk aldri orpinn, þá tók hann vanheilsu mikla, opnuðusk fœtr hans ('Oldest' *Þorláks Saga*, ch. ix).

(b) Klœngr byskup fór til alþingis, ok sótti þá at hǫfðingja at maðr væri til biskups kørinn (*Hungrvaka*, loc. cit.);

Fór Klœngr biskup til alþingis þá, ok sótti at vini sína, at maðr yrði ráðinn til útanferðar (*Þorláks Saga*, loc. cit.).

himself some latitude when not in good health. He never spoke idle words, as others might do by cursing the weather or such inanimate things. S. Þorlákr's personal life is described in much detail. He enjoyed stories, poetry, and music, as well as conversation with thoughtful people, and elucidation of dreams.[1]

It is interesting to notice that the author of the 'Oldest' saga hardly considers Þorlákr except as a saintly and benevolent man. He does not dwell on his public life, and seems scarcely to remember how Þorlákr came into conflict with Jón Loptsson and other powerful chieftains.

The 'Younger' version of the *Þorláks Saga* is based on the 'Oldest', and was probably made about the middle of the thirteenth century. The compiler gives plain reasons for making this new version of the saga. The author of the 'Oldest' saga had not paid sufficient tribute to the sufferings which Þorlákr had endured at the hands of his adversaries.[2]

In the 'Younger' saga some chapters about Þorlákr's public life have been inserted. During the first years of his office, Þorlákr had pursued the policy laid down by Eysteinn, Archbishop of Niðaróss (1161–88). The archbishop represented the Universal Church movement and, in Norway, he asserted the claims of Church against State, just as Thomas of Canterbury did in England. Following Eysteinn's lead, Þorlákr challenged the right of laymen to own the churches on their estates. The foremost upholder of the laymen's rights was Jón Loptsson (died 1197), who was the most powerful man in Iceland in those days, and himself the owner of several churches. Jón had the force of tradition behind him, and successfully resisted the demands of Þorlákr.

Archbishop Eysteinn also complained of the lax morals of the Icelandic chiefs. In a letter addressed to Jón Loptsson and others, he wrote: 'You live the lives of cattle, and pay no heed to matrimony, or that holy union which must not be broken. . . .'[3] Þorlákr strove to raise the moral standard both of clergymen and laymen, dissolving marriages which he found invalid and condemning

---

[1] See *Biskupa Sögur*, i. 102–9.    [2] Ibid., p. 264.
[3] See *Diplomatarium Islandicum*, i, 1857–76, p. 262.

illicit unions. He met strong opposition, and, once more, tradition was against him. Þorlákr's chief adversary was Jón Loptsson, whose mistress, Ragnheiðr, was none other than Þorlákr's sister. The son of this union was Páll Jónsson, who succeeded Þorlákr as Bishop of Skálaholt. Since the 'Oldest' saga of Þorlákr was undoubtedly written with the knowledge of Bishop Páll, and probably under his supervision, it might be expected that these major episodes in the public life of S. Þorlákr would be passed over with delicate allusion.[1] They are related fully in the interpolated chapters of the 'Younger' saga.

In all versions of the Þorláks Saga the final chapters consist of stories about miracles which had been worked through the saint's intercession after death. In the 'Oldest' saga these miracle chapters are scarcely more than a list. Many of the miracles mentioned in the 'Oldest' saga took place in the neighbourhood of Skálaholt, but others occurred as far from the saint's relics as Faeroe, or even England. In the 'Younger' version of the saga the miracle chapters are fuller and contain more details.

These stories of S. Þorlákr's miracles have an interesting history, and a great proportion of them must be traced to records written before the canonization of the saint. Characteristically, the sanctity of Þorlákr was revealed first in the northern diocese, and accounts of his miracles were probably written first at Hólar. In December 1197 Þorlákr appeared in a dream to a priest in the northern diocese.[2] This vision was straightway reported to Bishop Brandr, who had it written down, and sent the record to Guðmundr the Good. In the following summer, Brandr sent his chaplain, Ormr, to the Alþingi with letters addressed to Bishop Páll. These letters contained the accounts of several miracles, which had been worked through the intercession of Þorlákr.[3] Bishop Páll was more cautious than Brandr and was, at first, reluctant to acknowledge the sanctity of his uncle. But Páll allowed himself to be persuaded, and authorized those who wished to invoke S. Þorlákr. Many more miracles

---

[1] See, e.g., 'Oldest' Þorláks Saga, Biskupa Sögur, i. 92, 107.
[2] Biskup Sögur, i. 114, 302, and esp. 451.
[3] Ibid., pp. 114–15, 303, 133.

occurred during the next weeks and, on 20 July 1198, the remains of the saint were translated. Meanwhile, a large miracle book was compiled, probably at Skálaholt, and Bishop Páll read it out at the *Alþingi* in the following year, when the feast of S. Þorlákr was made law.

The account of the miracles which Páll read out, or at least a part of it, survives in an early redaction. This is contained in MS. 645, 4to, which is believed to have been written about 1225.[1] It may conveniently be called the 'First Miracle Book'. The miracles related in it took place in the south of Iceland, mostly in the neighbourhood of Skálaholt. A few had been added after Páll had read the book at the *Alþingi*, and the latest mentioned in this 'First Miracle Book' took place in March, 1200.

It is plain that the author of the 'Oldest' saga abstracted stories of many miracles from Bishop Páll's collection, although he probably knew it in a form older than that which now survives. He also had access to other sources, probably written as well as oral ones, and he recorded a number of miracles which were not in the 'First Miracle Book'.

A few years after the 'First Miracle Book', a 'Second Miracle Book' was compiled, and this survives only in manuscripts of the seventeenth century.[2] None of the miracles recorded in MS. 645 are found in this book, and a large proportion of them are said to have occurred in the diocese of Hólar. Others are located farther afield, in Norway, Shetland, Lincoln, and Constantinople. The book ends with a short list of miracles which are said to have been recorded in Latin by the monk Gunnlaugr on the instructions of Guðmundr the Good.

Most of the miracles of Þorlákr were unpretentious, and a clear picture of life among simple people may be found in the records of them. S. Þorlákr sends food to those who are hungry, he cures illnesses, finds lost property, and helps the sailors to weather the storms. If S. Þorlákr is invoked when food is scarce, he sends a seal,

---

[1] Published in *Biskupa Sögur*, i. 333–56. There is also an edition in facsimile, *A Book of Miracles*, with an Introduction by A. Holtsmark, 1938 (= *Corpus Codicum Islandicorum Medii Aevi*, xii).

[2] Published in *Biskupa Sögur*, i. 357–74.

or perhaps a whale. If a jewel or even a hammer or hobble is lost, S. Þorlákr recovers it. He does not only heal the illnesses of men, but he even restores sight to a blind sheep. A few of the miracles are of a grander kind. The Varangian guards once promised to dedicate a church to S. Þorlákr in Constantinople in return for victory over heathen invaders. They were following the example of earlier Varangians, who had made the same bargain with S. Ólafr.[1]

The 'Saga of Bishop Páll' (*Páls Saga*) was probably written soon after Páll's death in 1211. Most scholars agree that it was written by the author of *Hungrvaka*,[2] and the two books resemble each other in so many ways, that this can hardly be doubted. In both of them, as indeed in the *Þorláks Saga*, greater interest is shown in the personal habits of church dignitaries than in their ecclesiastical policy. In the *Páls Saga*, as in the *Hungrvaka*, greater respect is shown for established truth than for legendary tales. They contain some of the same unusual words and phrases,[3] and in both of them far-fetched similes are used, such as are rarely found in Icelandic prose. The author of the *Hungrvaka*[4] says that his book is like a piece of unworked horn, from which a beautiful spoon could be fashioned. The author of the *Páls Saga*[5] compares the episcopate of Páll with a ship. Both the stern and the prow can be seen when the book is finished. When he comes to the end of Páll's life, the author gives a list of memorable events which took place while he was bishop.[6] Similar lists are given after the passing of each bishop in the *Hungrvaka*. Both in the *Hungrvaka* and the *Páls Saga* similar tributes are paid to Gizurr Hallsson.[7] In both texts the same passage is quoted, as it seems, from the lost version of the *Íslendingabók*.[8]

No Icelandic bishop, except perhaps Guðmundr the Good, was better portrayed than Bishop Páll. He represented the best in the traditional Christianity of Iceland, and belonged to the old school

[1] Ibid. i. 363–4; cf. p. 158 above.
[2] Cf. Finnur Jónsson, *ONOI*, ii. 562.
[3] Cf. Guðbrandur Vigfússon in *Biskupa Sögur*, i, Introduction, pp. xxxi f.
[4] Ed. Jón Helgason, p. 73.      [5] *Biskupa Sögur*, i. 146.
[6] Ibid., p. 147.      [7] Ibid., p. 137.
[8] Ibid., p. 145; cf. *Hungrvaka*, ed. Jón Helgason, p. 91; see also Björn Sigfússon, op. cit., pp. 121 ff.

rather than to the new. He did not pursue the aggressive ecclesiastical policy introduced by Þorlákr. Both by descent and training he was a chieftain rather than a cleric. As the son of Jón Loptsson, he came of the family of the Oddaverjar, and descended from Sæmundr the Wise. While a young man, he had stayed with Earl Haraldr in Orkney, and had later gone to school in England. He returned to Iceland one of the best educated men of his day. There were few to rival him in composing Latin verse, in reading(?) or in singing.[1]

Although ordained a deacon, it is plain that Páll had not at first intended to follow a clerical career. He was a *goði*, and settled down as a farmer. It was against his own intentions that he was elected bishop in succession to his uncle Þorlákr. He was remembered especially for his lavish hospitality and for the architectural improvements which he made at Skálaholt.

[1] *Biskupa Sögur*, i. 127-8.

# VIII

## EPILOGUE: THE CLASSICAL AGE

IN the foregoing chapters I have sketched the history of Icelandic literature before its classical age, the thirteenth century. Although much has been written about the great sagas of the thirteenth century, most English scholars have neglected the literature of the twelfth century. The classical literature can be appreciated better if that of earlier generations is also considered.

In this final chapter I shall say something about the great sagas of kings and of Icelandic heroes written in the thirteenth century, realizing that the subject is more suitable for a book than for a chapter. I shall attempt nothing more than to show how the literature of the thirteenth century developed from that of the twelfth.

The thirteenth century is commonly regarded as the classical age of Icelandic literature because it was then that the Icelanders discovered their full capabilities, and wrote prose on historical subjects which had no rival in medieval Europe.

In some branches of Icelandic and Norwegian literature the classical age was now over. In the tenth century Egill Skalla-Grímsson had composed poetry in scaldic forms which was never to be surpassed and, even earlier than that, the heroic poets, relics of whose verses survive in the *Edda*, had done much of their greatest work. The *Vǫluspá*, most beautiful of all the mythological lays, was probably composed about the end of the tenth century.

But prose develops later than poetry and, however important the poetry of the Icelanders, their greatest achievements were in prose. In earlier chapters of this book much fine prose has been described. Ari Þorgilsson was a conscientious and methodical historian, and his work had lasting value. The author of the *Hungrvaka* continued the tradition which Ari had established with the *Íslendingabók*. The monks of Þingeyrar, Oddr and Gunnlaugr, were both learned and gifted men. If Ari's work was a little dull, theirs was over-fanciful, and their flights of fancy were not always restrained by reason. In their works the adventure stories, the 'stepmother tales', sometimes gained the upper hand. Authors like Oddr and Gunnlaugr were influenced by the lives of European saints, such as those described in Chapter V above.

The authors of the twelfth century had lacked balance, for their work was either too pedantic to be enjoyable, or too romantic to be convincing. In neither case could living and realistic characters be created. It has been said that the masters of southern Iceland chiefly favoured scientific history, while those of the diocese of Hólar, and especially the monks of Þingeyrar, cultivated the hagiographic style. However that may be, it was probably at Þingeyrar that the balance between pedantry and fancy was first achieved, and the greatness of Icelandic literature lay largely in this.

The first of the great biographies was probably the 'Saga of King Sverrir' (Sverris Saga),[1] whose career provided a subject unusually suitable for a biographer. Sverrir, who was born about 1152, had been brought up in the Faeroe Islands, and ordained priest. When he was twenty-four years old, his mother told him that his father had been none other than Sigurðr Munnr, King of Norway (died 1155). This tale, whatever its truth, had a decisive influence on Sverrir's career. He went straightway to Norway, where he gradually fought his way from penury to power.

Like many of the works already mentioned, the Sverris Saga originated in the school of Þingeyrar, and the author of the first part of it, at any rate, was Karl Jónsson. Karl was twice Abbot of Þingeyrar, from 1169 to 1181, and again from 1190 to 1207. He died in 1215.

The Sverris Saga contrasts sharply with the early lives of S. Ólafr and of Ólafr Tryggvason. Karl was writing of a friend and a contemporary. He had been in Norway in the company of Sverrir from about 1185 to 1190, and must have written some chapters of the book during those years. The king himself sat by, and advised what Karl should write. The work was completed after Karl returned to Iceland, whether by Karl himself or, as some think probable,

---

[1] Sverris Saga, ed. G. Indrebø, 1920. See also Lárus Blöndal in Á Góðu Dægri, Afmæliskveðja til S. Nordals, 1951, pp. 173 ff.

by another hand. It was afterwards revised, to some extent, by
Styrmir Kárason, another learned clerk. It would be hard to decide
how closely the existing text resembles the original. There is little
in the text to show that it has suffered great alteration, or that the
beginning and the end of the story were written by different authors.

Since Karl was writing of a man whom he knew personally, he
could write in such detail as would have been impossible had he
been describing a saint or a king who had lived a century or two
before him. He admired his hero, but he could not idealize him in
the same way as S. Ólafr had been idealized. Nor could Karl de-
precate Sverrir's enemies in such terms as Oddr deprecated the
enemies of Ólafr Tryggvason. He wrote with respect and even with
sympathy of King Magnús Erlingsson, the chief antagonist of
Sverrir: this was the measure of his popularity, that, dangerous as
it was to follow him, he never lacked followers so long as he lived.
If little is made of Sverrir's moral defects, his physical ones are not
overlooked. He was a fine chieftain to behold sitting on the high
seat nobly dressed, because he sat high, but he was short in the leg.
In a word, the author (or authors) of the *Sverris Saga* could see not
only black and white, but also grey and the various shades between
the two extremes. It was partly because they could see faults in
those whom they admired, and good qualities in those whom they
disliked, that Icelandic authors of the thirteenth century were able
to depict and create characters which were something more than
lifeless types.

The 'Saga of the Orkney Earls' (*Orkneyinga Saga, Jarla Sǫgur*)
was written in the first years of the thirteenth century.[1] It shows
that Icelandic antiquarians were interested not only in the history
of Norway, but also in the history of the neighbouring lands where
the civilization of Norway had struck roots. This saga covers the
whole of Orkney history from the ninth century to the latter years
of the twelfth. It was one of the sources which Snorri used for his
'Saga of S. Ólafr', and for the *Heimskringla*. Like the *Sverris Saga*,
the *Orkneyinga Saga* is preserved only in later recensions, and it
is hard to know what it was like in its original form, although it is

[1] *Orkneyinga Saga*, ed. Sigurður Nordal, 1913–16.

plain that the author used sources of diverse kinds. The section on S. Magnús[1] is distinguished by its pious tone, and appears to be derived from a hagiographic life of S. Magnús written in Orkney some twenty years after the saint's death, when his bones were translated. Later chapters of the *Orkneyinga Saga* are based largely on scaldic verses, many of which are quoted in the text, and on the accounts of eye-witnesses. The most enjoyable passages in the *Orkneyinga Saga* are those in which the voyage of Rǫgnvaldr Kali (died 1158) to the Holy Land is described. These chapters contain many verses made by Rǫgnvaldr, as well as a number made by Icelandic poets who accompanied him on his voyage. Rǫgnvaldr was among the best of the later scalds, although poetry was for him an entertainment and a sport, rather than a serious pursuit or a profession.

Einar Ól. Sveinsson[2] gave reasons for supposing that the *Orkneyinga Saga* was composed in the south of Iceland under the auspices of the Oddaverjar, the descendants of Sæmundr the Wise. Members of this family had many dealings with the Orcadians during the first years of the thirteenth century. A party of Orkney merchants led by Þorkell Walrus, himself of noble birth, once spent a winter at Oddi, as the guests of Sæmundr Jónsson, great-grandson of Sæmundr the Wise. It was once proposed that Sæmundr Jónsson should marry Langlíf, daughter of the Orkney Earl, Haraldr Maddaðarson (died 1206), though nothing came of this in the end.

The 'Saga of the Faeroe Islanders' (*Færeyinga Saga*)[3] must also have been written early in the thirteenth century, and it was another of Snorri's sources for his 'Saga of S. Ólafr'. The state of the text in which this saga is preserved is no better than that of the *Orkneyinga Saga*. The *Færeyinga Saga* is found in disjointed chapters in late versions of the sagas of Ólafr Tryggvason and of S. Ólafr. The chapters which Snorri derived from the *Færeyinga Saga* in his 'Saga of S. Ólafr'[4] may represent it in a form closer to the

---

[1] Cf. Einar Ól. Sveinsson, *Sagnaritun Oddaverja*, 1937, pp. 19 ff.
[2] Op cit., pp. 16 ff.    [3] *Færeyinga Saga*, ed. Finnur Jónsson, 1927.
[4] On these chapters see Bjarni Aðalbjarnarson, *Heimskringla* II, 1945, Introduction, pp. xliii ff.

original than do the other texts. The character of Þrándr, the treacherous and independent Faeroe chieftain, who obstructed S. Ólafr's plans to gain control of the islands, is especially well described in Snorri's text, and with a certain restrained admiration, such as might be expected of an Icelandic author. As it is preserved in later compilations, the *Færeyinga Saga* is less realistic, but it has an added interest as folk-lore. One of the more remarkable scenes is that in which the dead hero, Sigmundr, appears before his murderers, carrying his head in his hands.

The *Morkinskinna* (Rotten Skin) was written about 1220, and its author continued the tradition established with the synoptic histories of kings of Norway. Earlier examples of synoptics were the *Ágrip* and the book of Theodoricus. The author, or perhaps we should call him the compiler, of the *Morkinskinna* could tell many secrets about the history of Icelandic literature. But scholars have not yet given this book the attention which it deserves, and little is yet known about the author's sources and methods.[1]

The *Morkinskinna* is preserved in a defective manuscript of the second half of the thirteenth century. The text in this manuscript has been interpolated, and has suffered considerable changes since the author left it. In its original form this book must have covered the history of the kings of Norway between S. Ólafr and Sverrir. One of the author's sources was the *Hryggjarstykki*.[2] Many scholars have also supposed that he also used separate sagas about kings whose lives he related. This would imply that, before the *Morkinskinna* was written, there were detailed biographies of Magnús the Good, Haraldr Harðráði, Magnús Bareleg, and of other kings.

In tone the *Morkinskinna* is quite unlike the early synoptics and, in style, it approaches the family sagas. When his sources allowed him to do so, the author described the adventures of his heroes in great detail. He delighted in anecdotes, and sometimes told them with humour which may be cruel or ribald according to circumstances. It is told in one passage how Magnús Bareleg captured his

[1] *Morkinskinna*, ed. Finnur Jónsson, 1934; see Bjarni Aðalbjarnarson, *Om de norske kongers sagaer*, 1937, pp. 135–73.
[2] See Bjarni Aðalbjarnarson, op. cit., pp. 159 ff.

antagonist Steigar-Þórir on an island off Hálogaland. Þórir died a
noble death and, as he was led to the gallows, he swayed in his gait
because his legs were weak. Þórir's enemy, Víðkunnr, who was
standing near, cried out: 'More to starboard, Þórir, more to port.'
Víðkunnr addressed Þórir in these words because Þórir had burnt
down his farm on Bjarkey, as well as his fine ship. And when the
swift vessel was in flames, Þórir had cried out: 'hold more to
starboard, Víðkunnr, more to port'.

The *Morkinskinna* contains many short stories (*þættir*) embedded in the lives of the kings. Most of these are concerned
with the adventures of Icelanders, who were associated with the
kings in one way or another. It is not known how these tales came
to be included in the *Morkinskinna*, or how many of them were
in it in its earliest form. In several cases it seems improbable
that the stories were written in the first place for the *Morkinskinna*, or by the same author as the main text. They probably
existed independently. The story of Hreiðarr the Foolish is one
of the best told of these tales and, linguistically, one of the most
archaic. It also gives an insight into popular medieval humour, so
different from the humour of today. Hreiðarr once insulted King
Haraldr Harðráði by striking a model of a sow in silver. This was
an allusion to the nickname of the king's father, Sigurðr Sýr (Sow).
In the story of Auðunn and the bear, it is told how Auðunn, a poor
man, sold all he had and bought a polar bear in Greenland, which
he brought as a present to King Sveinn of Denmark. This story
contains many motives drawn from international folk-lore.[1] Some
of the tales in the *Morkinskinna* appear to be very ancient, and they
are probably as close as any preserved to the oral tales of the medieval period. But it must be emphasized that the form in which these
tales are preserved is a literary and not an oral one. It is improbable
that they were told in words like those in which they were written.

The *Fagrskinna* (Fine Skin) was probably written soon after
1220,[2] and covers the history of the kings of Norway from Hálfdan
the Black (ninth century) to Magnús Erlingsson (i.e. 1177). Its

[1] See A. R. Taylor in *Saga-Book*, XIII. ii, 1947-8, pp. 78 ff.
[2] *Fagrskinna*, ed. Finnur Jónsson, 1902-3.

later chapters are based chiefly on the *Morkinskinna*, but the text of the *Morkinskinna* which the compiler of the *Fagrskinna* used was older and purer than that which is now preserved. The compiler chiefly followed Oddr in his account of Ólafr Tryggvason, copying long passages from the Norse version of Oddr's work, and he probably used Styrmir's life of S. Ólafr for his account of the saint's life. He must have had access to a well-stocked library, for he knew most of the sagas of kings written before his day. A number of these sagas are now lost, and the *Fagrskinna* helps to demonstrate their existence and to show what they were like. The chronological system applied in the *Fagrskinna* may be traced to that set forth by Sæmundr in his lost History.[1] Other sources used included a lost saga of the earls of Hlaðir, one of Hákon the Good, and another of the Jomsburg vikings. When he had no written sources, the compiler of the *Fagrskinna* used oral ones. The most valuable oral sources were scaldic verses, many of which he quoted in full. Some of the oldest scaldic strophes are preserved only in this text.

It is commonly agreed that the author of the *Fagrskinna* was an Icelander, for his education was that of Iceland. But it is equally clear that he wrote his book in Norway, and it was preserved in Norwegian manuscripts. As literature the *Fagrskinna* falls far below the *Morkinskinna*. The compiler had little appreciation of anecdotes, such as the author of the *Morkinskinna* used to bring his characters to life. The stories told in the *Fagrskinna* are badly proportioned and often dull. But as a record of history, and especially of literary history, the *Fagrskinna* is of great value.

Styrmir Kárason has already been mentioned for his work on the *Landnámabók* and on the *Sverris Saga*. A few incidents in his career are recorded in the *Sturlunga Saga*, the annals, and in diplomatic documents. He was twice Law-speaker (1210–14 and 1232–5), and was a friend of Snorri, although an older man. During his latter years Styrmir was prior of the monastery of Viðey, in Reykjavík, and died in 1245. Styrmir's name is associated with one of the family sagas, the *Harðar Saga*, but it cannot be told whether he wrote that saga, and if so in what form. More is known about

---

[1] Cf. G. Indrebø, *Fagrskinna*, 1917, pp. 43 ff.

Styrmir's 'Saga of S. Ólafr'. Sigurður Nordal[1] showed that Styrmir
revised and enlarged the version of the *Ólafs Saga* which was current in his day. The version of the *Ólafs Saga* from which Styrmir
worked was not the same as the 'First Saga', and not quite the same
as the 'Legendary Saga', but somewhere between these two. Both
the 'Legendary Saga' and Styrmir's version were based on this
'Middle Saga'. Therefore, Styrmir's 'Saga of S. Ólafr' resembled
the 'Legendary Saga' in many ways, but it contained a number of
tales not to be found there. Styrmir's *Ólafs Saga* no longer survives
as a separate work, but it has been incorporated in the 'encyclo-
paedic' sagas of S. Ólafr compiled in the fourteenth century. The
best known example of these conflated sagas is that preserved in
the *Flateyjarbók* (Book of Flatey).[2] It is easy to see that Styrmir
developed the hagiographic style devised by the monks of Þingeyrar. He discriminated as little as they and was as little critical. No
miracle was too improbable to be included in his book, no example
of S. Ólaf's benevolence too insignificant to be recorded. The chief
importance of Styrmir's *Ólafs Saga* was that it was a source for
Snorri's saga of the saint.

Snorri Sturluson was the author of literature of many different
kinds. He was born at Hvammr in western Iceland in 1179, and
was the son of a chieftain of that neighbourhood. At the age of
three, Snorri was brought to Oddi, where he was fostered by Jón
Loptsson (died 1197), grandson of Sæmundr the Wise. Jón was
the most powerful chieftain in Iceland in those days, and among
the best educated, for he had inherited the traditions of learning
established by Sæmundr at Oddi. He was a deacon in orders and
well known for his proficiency in the clerical arts. At the same time
he was ambitious, worldly, and rather licentious. As already remarked, Bishop Páll of Skálaholt was his natural son.[3] Jón's
mother was acknowledged as the natural daughter of King Magnús
Bareleg (died 1103), and Jón took an especial pride in his royal
descent. The poem *Nóregs Konunga Tal* (Sequence of the Kings of

---

[1] *Om Olaf den Helliges Saga*, 1914, pp. 69–133.
[2] *Flateyjarbók*, ii, ed. G. Vigfússon and C. R. Unger, 1862.
[3] See Ch. VII above, also Einar Ól. Sveinsson, op. cit., p. 5.

Norway) was made in Jón's honour about 1190, and in it the poet traced Jón's descent from the kings. The native and foreign cultures seemed to be combined in Jón more thoroughly than in any other chieftain of the period. He was at once a learned cleric and a chieftain of Iceland.

Much of Snorri's learning, and especially his interest in ancient poetry, history, and mythology, may be traced to his early years at Oddi. The works of Sæmundr and of Ari must have been kept and copied there, and the poems of the scalds and the Eddaic poetry, whether they lived orally or in writing, must have lived at Oddi. Snorri's education, unlike that of his foster-father, Jón, was the education of a layman. It is not recorded that he learned Latin, and literature in Latin does not appear to have influenced his work directly. Before Snorri's time the education of Icelandic chiefs had generally been that of clerics, for the chieftains had often taken orders and, on occasion, had officiated as clergymen. But a change had now set in. The aim of the ecclesiastical authorities, in Iceland as elsewhere, was to make the Church independent of the temporal rulers. Jón Loptsson himself engaged in bitter quarrels with Bishop Þorlákr over questions of patronage. In 1190, Archbishop Eiríkr of Trondheim formally forbade the Icelandic bishops to confer orders on the Icelandic goðar unless they renounced their title. The policy of the Church led to the separation of Church from State, and to a sharper distinction between the ecclesiastical and temporal leaders. If the chieftains were educated, they were not necessarily educated as clergymen, and they turned their attention to the native traditions rather than to the southern culture.

The incidents recorded in Snorri's career show that he was a child of his age, who strove for wealth and for power. At the age of twenty he had married a rich woman, and quickly came to own extensive properties in south-western Iceland. He was Lawspeaker from 1215 to 1218 and again from 1222 to 1231. His career was turbulent, and he was involved in most of the quarrels and feuds of his time.

It is not known precisely when Snorri wrote the various works which have been assigned to him. While still comparatively young he had won a reputation, in Norway as well as in Iceland, for his poetry. It was recorded that he made a poem about King Sverrir, and another about Earl Hákon Galinn (died 1214), which he sent to the earl, and received fine presents in exchange. It is generally supposed that Snorri's 'Prose Edda' was, for the most part, an early work, and that he wrote his lives of the kings of Norway in later life. He visited Norway in 1218 and won the favour of King Hákon, and especially of Earl Skúli. In the following year he went to Gautland, a province of modern Sweden. There he visited Kristína, the widow of Hákon Galinn, in whose honour he made a poem called *Andvaka* (Wakefulness). Snorri's travels must have stimulated his interest in the antiquities of Norway. It can be seen in his stories of the kings that he had examined some of their burial mounds and other historic scenes.

It is likely that Snorri was encouraged by Skúli and other Norwegian chieftains to write his lives of the kings of Norway. He probably began them after he returned to Iceland from Norway in 1220. Snorri's life of S. Ólafr is the chief of his sagas of the kings, and it was the first that he wrote. It is the greatest of all Kings' sagas, and was never surpassed in Icelandic prose except by the best of the family sagas. It has been shown, not only that Snorri wrote his 'Saga of S. Ólafr' before the sagas of other kings, but also that he designed it as a separate work independent of the others. It survives both as a distinct work and as a part of the *Heimskringla*. There are few major differences between the two versions.

Modern scholars have been able to show the sources which Snorri used for his *Ólafs Saga* with some precision, and consequently Snorri's methods can be appreciated fairly well.[1] Although Styrmir's version of the *Ólafs Saga* was his chief source, Snorri broke with the clerical tradition. The earlier lives of S. Ólafr had been written as lives of a saint. They were tendentious and unconvincing as lives of saints generally are. But as Snorri described him, Ólafr was, in the first place, a viking and a king. He became a saint gradually as he faced the trials of this life. Some of S. Ólafr's earlier

---

[1] See especially Sigurður Nordal, op. cit., and Bjarni Aðalbjarnarson, Introduction to *Heimskringla*, ii.

miracles, such as that of the mermaid off the coast of France, were ignored by Snorri. He rationalized others; Ólafr did not split the isthmus Agnafit in two by the force of his prayers, but he and his men dug a channel through it. But when the king drew near to death, signs of his sanctity appeared. Before he set off from Russia on his last journey to Norway, a boy was brought to S. Ólafr, sick with a septic throat. The king stroked the boy's throat, and gave him bread in the form of a cross, and he was healed. As Ólafr passed through eastern Norway, bound for his last battle, at Stikla-staðir, he had a strange vision. First of all he saw the whole of Trondheim, and then the whole of Norway, and after that the whole world. Ólafr's sanctity was shown even more clearly in the miracles worked after his death.

Snorri used other written sources for his *Ólafs Saga* beside the work of Styrmir. These included sagas of the Orkney earls and of the Faeroe islanders, and the lost version of Ari's *Íslendingabók*, on which he based a part of his chronology of S. Ólafr's life. Scaldic strophes were also an important source for him. He used them in greater numbers and deduced more from them than most of his predecessors had done. He said in the Prologue to the *Ólafs Saga* that he regarded the verses of contemporary poets as the most trustworthy of all his sources.

Using such diverse material, Snorri was able to give a complete picture of S. Ólafr, not only as a saint, but also as an ambitious and ruthless prince. One of Ólafr's aims, as Snorri describes his career, was to break the power of the chieftains, and to centralize government under the king. The reader is allowed to appreciate the motives of those who opposed him, and to sympathize with them as well as with the king. The story of Þórir Hundr, one of those who killed S. Ólafr at Stiklastaðir, is told with understanding. He had cause for vengeance, because his nephew, Ásbjǫrn, had been killed by Ólafr's men. Þórir had been incited to violence by Ásbjǫrn's mother. She had used words and symbols similar to those which Hildigunnr had used, when she incited Flosi to take vengeance against the sons of Njáll.[1]

---

[1] See below, pp. 251–3.

Snorri surpasses the authors of the earlier Kings' sagas, not only in describing character, but also in the structure of his work. The story of S. Ólafr progresses step by step to the climax at Stiklastaðir, when the sun is eclipsed and Ólafr falls as a martyr. Snorri was perhaps the first of Icelandic authors to master the double and triple stranded story. Stories of S. Ólafr's quarrels with his namesake, Ólafr, king of the Swedes, are interwoven skilfully with stories about internal politics, the revolt of the Uppland kings against S. Ólafr. However complicated the structure, Snorri never loses sight of his main theme.

In the *Ólafs Saga* Snorri gives a personal interpretation of history. He did not attempt, as Ari and the annalists did, to record events of the past in a scientific manner. His aim was rather to reconstruct the past. Like many medieval historians, he believed that the course of history was determined by outstanding men and not, as many have since believed, that the leaders of men are shaped by history. The character of those who made history was, therefore, of chief importance in understanding it. Snorri constructed his characters largely from the written and oral records. But since these records were incomplete, he had to supplement them from his own imaginative and creative genius. He should not be condemned because he did not write history of the kind which scientific historians of today would wish that he had written. His story is true in the same way as many pictures of historic events may be true, e.g. pictures by old masters illustrating the life of Christ, or those by more modern artists illustrating battles at Glencoe and Trafalgar.

As Snorri first wrote the *Ólafs Saga* it was preceded by a few introductory chapters, in which the lives of Haraldr Finehair and of others who ruled Norway before S. Ólafr were given in outline. At a later date, Snorri incorporated the *Ólafs Saga*, with small alteration, in the *Heimskringla* (Orb of the World). The *Heimskringla* consists of fairly detailed biographies of rulers of Norway from Hálfdan the Black to Magnús Erlingsson. It thus combines the value of the short synoptics, like the *Ágrip*, with that of the detailed biographies like Oddr's 'Saga of Ólafr Tryggvason'. The *Heimskringla* is dominated by the 'Saga of S. Ólafr', which is the

central piece, and covers about one-third of the whole text. Snorri
compiled the lives of earlier kings from diverse sources, such as those
which the compiler of the *Fagrskinna* had used. Superficially the
*Heimskringla* bears a close resemblance to the *Fagrskinna*, although
it is very different in style. When possible, Snorri used written
sources for his lives of the kings, and a large number of these are
preserved. Snorri described the career of Ólafr Tryggvason more
fully than that of any ruler before S. Ólafr, and this was only to be
expected, because much had been written about Ólafr Tryggvason
before Snorri's time. The chief source which Snorri used for his
'Saga of Ólafr Tryggvason' was Oddr's saga of that king,[1] but he
used many others as well, including the *Ágrip*, the lost saga of the
earls of Hlaðir, one of the Jomsburg vikings, and perhaps the
*Hallfreðar Saga*. Sometimes Snorri introduced tales from oral
sources which had not been written before. He did not follow his
sources slavishly, but exercised judgement. He corrected inconsis-
tencies, and omitted or rationalized episodes which he found improbable. He thus varied his methods according to circumstances.
The story of Haraldr Finehair's marriage with the Lappish woman
Snæfríðr is one of the finest passages in the *Ágrip*, and Snorri
copied it almost word for word in the *Heimskringla*.[2] In other cases
Snorri would alter his sources slightly, as if he intended to make
the picture more vivid. In the *Morkinskinna* the events leading to
the last battle and death of Magnús Bareleg (1103) in Ireland are
described as follows:

In the summer Magnús prepared to sail to Norway, and he appointed
bailiffs and deputies in Dublin. And he was now quite ready for his
voyage with all his host, intending to sail from there north to the
islands. But King Magnús thought that he needed some cattle for
slaughter.[3] King Myrkjartan was to send it down from Connacht, and
King Magnús waited a while. But since the consignment was delayed,
Magnús sent men to fetch it, and it so happened that they returned
rather later than he had expected. So then King Magnús went ashore
himself with the greater part of his force, intending to search for the
men who had failed to return with the spoil. This was on the eve of the
feast of S. Bartholomew. But by the time he found his men, he had

---

[1] See Ch. VII.                                    [2] See p. 173.
[3] Icelandic *strandhǫgg*, 'cattle seized for provisions'.

gone far inland, and the men met him with the spoil which they intended to bring to him, and so the king turned his force back. Now this was the lie of the land through which they were passing. In parts there were scrub-bushes and marshes, and deep bogs between the scrub-bushes here and there, and there were planks laid across the bogs. But by now an army of Irishmen had assembled in front of the king, and had come very near to his force by the time they were discovered, and they stood between them and their ships.[1]

This is how Snorri describes these same events:

Then King Magnús made his ships ready for sea, intending to sail eastward to Norway. He appointed some of his men to garrison Dublin, and himself lay off Ulster with all his forces, and they were now ready to sail. They thought that they needed some cattle for slaughter, and so King Magnús sent emissaries to King Mýrkjartan, asking him to despatch it. He decided the day on which it should arrive; this was to be the day before the feast of S. Bartholomew, if the messengers were not molested. But on the eve of the feast, the messengers had not returned, and at sunrise on the feast day itself, the King went ashore with the greater part of his host, and left his ships, intending to look for the messengers and the spoil. There was no wind that day, and the sun was shining; the road passed through marshes and bogs, over which sawn planks were laid, and there was scrub on either side. As they pressed forward, they came to a very high hill, from which they could see a long way. Farther inland they spied a large cloud of dust thrown up by the hooves of horses, and they debated whether this could be an Irish army, but some said it must be their own men returning with the spoil. They took their stand there.

Then Eyvindr Elbow said: 'King' said he 'how do you intend to conduct this expedition? People think you are acting incautiously. You know that the Irish are treacherous. Now think out some plan for your men.' The King answered: 'Let us draw up our men in battle order, and be ready, in case this is a trap.' Then the force was drawn up, and the King and Eyvindr were in the forefront. King Magnús was wearing a helmet and he carried a red shield enamelled with a golden lion. He wore a sword on his girdle, called 'Leg-biter'; its hilt was of ivory and the grip was ornamented with gold. It was a magnificent weapon. He held a halberd in his hand, and was wearing a doublet of red silk over his shirt, with a lion, embroidered in golden silk front and back. This was what people said; that they had never seen a more valiant man, nor a nobler. Eyvindr was also wearing a doublet of red silk, and was attired like the King; he was also a big man and fine, and most warlike.

[1] *Morkinskinna*, pp. 333–4.

But when the dust from the horses' hooves drew near, they recognised their own men, and they were driving a great herd of cattle, which the King of the Irish had sent, for he had kept all his promises to King Magnús. Then they turned seaward to their ships, and it was now about noon. But when they came on to the marshes, they made slow progress through the bogs. And then Irish soldiers rushed forward from every protruding bush and made to attack them. The Norwegians were scattered, and many of them were soon killed.[1]

Throughout the *Heimskringla* Snorri quoted scaldic verses, and these, as he explained in his Prologue, were the most trustworthy of his sources. Many of them were composed during the lives of those princes whose deeds were celebrated in them. There were few other sources available for the earliest period of the history, but, in the light of them, Snorri was able to construct a fairly detailed account of the career of Haraldr Finehair, the first king of all Norway, about whom only scraps had hitherto been written. The opening chapters of the *Heimskringla* are called the *Ynglinga Saga* (Saga of the Ynglingar). The ancestry of the kings of Norway is there traced to the kings of Sweden, and ultimately to the gods. The chief source was the poem *Ynglingatal*, composed by the poet Þjóðólfr of Hvin, a contemporary of Haraldr Finehair.

It was said in his own day that Snorri was good at everything to which he put his hand.[2] His versatility is shown in the different kinds of literature ascribed to him. His 'Prose Edda'[3] is no less interesting than his sagas of the kings, and no less popular today. The 'Prose Edda' was designed as a handbook for the use of poets, and especially for those who used scaldic forms. It may be surmised that Snorri feared that the technique of the ancient poets was falling into disuse. After two centuries of Christianity, the pagan kennings and allusions to pagan mythology were not fully understood. New and less 'precious' verse forms, introduced from Europe, were threatening the existence of the traditional ones.

Snorri's *Edda* is divided into three sections. The first section is called the 'Beguiling of Gylfi' (*Gylfaginning*). Snorri relates in it

---

[1] *Heimskringla*, ed. Finnur Jónsson, 1911, pp. 530–1.

[2] See *Sturlunga Saga*, ed. Jón Jóhannesson and others, i, 1946, p. 269.

[3] See Snorri Sturluson, *Edda*, ed. Finnur Jónsson, 1926; *Edda Snorra Sturlusonar*, ed. Guðni Jónsson, 1935.

how Gylfi, wishing to know the secrets of the gods, came in disguise to their citadel, Ásgarðr, where he found three gods, High, Equally High, and Third, sitting on the high seat. He asked them questions, and they told him about the beginning of the world, the fates of gods and men and the fall of the gods during the *Ragnarǫk*. In the end, Gylfi heard a loud crash, and looked round, and saw that there was no hall, and nothing but a level plain.

Snorri's first purpose in telling these stories of the gods was to help his readers to understand the early poetry, and especially the kennings in which allusion was made to myths. His sources were chiefly lays about the gods, such as those preserved in the *Edda*, e.g. *Vǫluspá, Vafþrúðnismál, Grímnismál*. Snorri seems also to use popular tales about the gods, and some of these must have survived in Iceland in his time. But although the first purpose of the *Gylfaginning* was didactic, it is read today chiefly for the tales which Snorri tells about the gods. They have the charm of fairy-tales. But Snorri was more sophisticated and more satirical than most of those who tell and write fairy-tales today.

The second section of the 'Prose Edda' is called the *Skáldskaparmál* (Speech of Poetry). This has greater technical interest than the *Gylfaginning*, though rather less value as art. Snorri attempts, with numerous examples, to define the meanings of the word *kenning*, and of other technical expressions. While quoting his examples, Snorri retells the stories, whether from myth or legend, upon which they were based. The stories which he tells include many heroic ones, such as those of Sigurðr and the Niflungar, and of Hamðir and Sǫrli at the court of Jǫrmunrekkr. Many of these legends are told admirably in the *Skáldskaparmál*, and Snorri's versions of them have great value for the study of these legends.

The third section of the 'Prose Edda' is called the *Háttatal* (List of verse-forms), and consists of a poem, which Snorri composed himself in honour of Earl Skúli and King Hákon Hákonarson. The poem is divided into three sections, and contains over a hundred strophes. Each strophe is composed in a different verse-form, and a detailed commentary is added. The *Háttatal* has much technical interest, although little value as poetry. It shows that Snorri knew better how to interpret poetry than to compose it. It may also show that by Snorri's time the scaldic style had had its day, although this was not what Snorri intended to show. The chief purpose of Snorri's *Edda* was to revive a literary technique which was dead. Although he was not successful in this, Snorri saved much fine literature, and many myths and tales from oblivion. He also showed that he was one of the best story-tellers of the Middle Ages.

Another major work, the *Egils Saga* (Saga of Egill), has long been associated with Snorri's name. Since Sigurður Nordal published his edition of this saga,[1] most scholars have regarded it as Snorri's work. It can hardly be doubted that the *Egils Saga* was written in the neighbourhood of Borg, where Snorri lived for several years (*circa* 1201–6). The saga appears to have been written during the best years of Snorri's life, and it is hard to see who but Snorri could have been its author. The methods used in composing the *Egils Saga* closely resembled those which Snorri used in composing the *Heimskringla*, and some of the same sources were used in composing both books. The differences between the *Egils Saga* and the *Heimskringla*, which J. de Vries has emphasized,[2] are not such as to make it impossible that one author wrote both books.

The *Egils Saga* is one of the family sagas, and it is among the finest of that class, but it is unlike most family sagas because a great part of its action takes place outside Iceland. The hero is the poet Egill Skalla-Grímsson.[3] The first thirty chapters form an introduction to the story of Egill, and the political state of Norway during the time of Haraldr Finehair is there described. Kveldúlfr, Skalla-Grímr, and Þórólfr, the grandfather, father, and uncle of Egill, were independent chieftains of western Norway, and they came to grips with Haraldr while the king was consolidating his authority on the west coast. Haraldr is here depicted as the first emigrants to Iceland must have seen him. He is the cruel and selfish tyrant, unlike the wise ruler depicted in works based on the Norwegian tradition, such as the *Ágrip*, the *Fagrskinna*, and even the

---

[1] *Egils Saga Skalla-Grímssonar*, 1933.
[2] See *Beiträge zur Geschichte der deutschen Sprache und Literatur*, vol. lxvi, 1942, pp. 80 ff.     [3] See Ch. I, pp. 40 ff.

*Heimskringla.* It was because of the tyranny of Haraldr that Skalla-Grímr, the father of Egill, migrated to Iceland and settled in the Borgarfjǫrðr.

Egill was born and reared in Iceland, but he lived his greatest moments abroad. His life was that of a viking of the tenth century. He spent much time in Norway, Vermaland, and the Baltic lands, and came to England twice. On the first occasion he visited the court of King Aeþelstan (924–39), and fought for that king in a battle which has been identified as that of Brunanburh (937). On his second visit to England, Egill went to York, where he made the poem *Hǫfuðlausn* (Head Ransom) in honour of Eiríkr Blood-axe. Egill is not a pleasing person, but no poet is described so realistically as he. He was avaricious, often unscrupulous and ill mannered, although capable of deep affection. Poetry had been the strongest of his interests ever since his childhood, and in times of adversity it was his solace.[1]

The family sagas hardly fall within the scope of this book. But this short account of Icelandic literature before its classical age may help the inexperienced reader to see how they developed. Although they may be of less significance as sources of history than the Kings' sagas are, since they deal with subjects of less importance for Europe, the family sagas are Iceland's chief contribution to the literature of the world. They resemble the Kings' sagas in form and in style, but differ from them in subject. Whereas the Kings' sagas treat of the kings of Norway, and their aim is to depict political and social developments in Norway and in the neighbouring lands in past ages, the family sagas are concerned with the lives of Icelanders. The native heroes lived in the tenth or early eleventh centuries. Many of them visited Norway and more distant lands and, like Egill, they became involved in the affairs of foreign princes. The adventures of the Icelandic heroes abroad are generally no more than light relief. They are often romanticized, and chapters in which they are told lack the detailed realism which characterizes the best passages in the family sagas.

Much has been written about the origin of the family sagas. It

[1] *Egils Saga,* ch. 78.

has been said that they are the most ancient form of Icelandic prose. They were composed in the eleventh century, soon after the events which are described in them. Their authors were men who did not read or write, and the sagas were handed down orally, almost without alteration, until they were written down by attentive scribes in the thirteenth century.[1] Such theories as these must imply that the family sagas were a branch of literature altogether different from the Kings' sagas, or from other prose described in this book. But the similarity between Kings' sagas and family sagas is too close to allow such a sharp distinction. It is partly because the Kings' sagas have been studied in much detail during the present century that the family sagas have come to be better understood. The studies of the native Icelandic scholars, Björn Magnússon Ólsen,[2] Sigurður Nordal,[3] Einar Ól. Sveinsson,[4] and of several others, have contributed much to the appreciation of the family sagas, although this is not to belittle the monumental work of Finnur Jónsson.[5]

The researches of recent years seem to suggest that the family sagas originated under the influence of the Kings' sagas, just as the Kings' sagas originated under the influence of hagiography and of other learned writing. This suggests that the family sagas were based on sources of many different kinds, on written records and genealogies, on the *Landnámabók*, works of Ari and other historical literature such as that discussed in earlier chapters of this book. It is widely agreed that the authors also used oral records, preserved both in prose and in verse.

It need not be doubted that Icelanders of the eleventh and twelfth centuries used to tell stories for entertainment, and that story-telling became a practised art among them. It is likely that some of the stories which they told were concerned with Icelandic family traditions, although the oral stories described in existing records were about subjects other than these. It is told in the

---

[1] See especially A. Heusler, *Die Anfänge der isländischen Saga*, 1914; K. Liestøl, *The Origin of the Icelandic Family Sagas*, 1930.

[2] *Um íslendingasögur*, 1937–9.

[3] See especially his Introduction to *Egils Saga*, 1933, Section 5.

[4] See especially his *Á Njálsbúð*, 1943, ch. i.                    [5] *ONOI*, i–iii.

*Morkinskinna* that an Icelander once came to the court of Haraldr Harðráði (1047–66), and told a number of stories. The only one of these described was about Haraldr's adventures in the Mediterranean lands. The Icelander told a little of this story each night, and it took a fortnight to tell it all. He had learnt it at the Assembly (*Alþingi*) in Iceland from Halldórr, the son of Snorri Goði, who had told him a little of it each year.[1]

In the year 1119 a marriage feast was held at Reykjahólar, in western Iceland, and at least two stories were told.[2] One of them was about a champion called Hrómundr Gripsson, who must have lived, if he ever did, in the eighth century. This story was apparently about a mythical or heroic subject, which would have little to do with the heroic traditions of Iceland. The other story told at this marriage feast was about Ormr the poet of Barrey. Ormr may have lived in historical times, and a scaldic strophe preserved in Snorri's *Edda* is assigned to him. But it is not stated that Ormr was an Icelander, and there is little to show what kind of story this was.

Attempts have been made to study the Icelandic family sagas by comparing them with certain family tales collected in Norway during the nineteenth and twentieth centuries.[3] But, interesting as the study of these Norwegian traditions is, they have contributed little to the understanding of the Icelandic family sagas. The tales collected by folk-lorists in Norway bear little resemblance to Icelandic sagas.

Something might be learnt about the oral traditions of Iceland by the analogy of the traditions of Ireland, although the two cultures were very different, and have not yet been compared in such detail as they deserve. It has been said that texts contained in the earlier Irish pergaments are no more than tale-summaries.[4] As they were told, these tales would be much longer and more verbose than they are on the pergaments. The story-tellers had not the

---

[1] *Morkinskinna*, edition quoted above, pp. 199 ff.
[2] See Ursula Brown in *Saga-Book*, XIII. ii. 51 ff.
[3] See K. Liestøl, op. cit.
[4] See M. Dillon, *The Cycles of the Kings*, 1946, pp. 2–3; cf. J. H, Delargy, *The Gaelic Story-teller*, 1945, p. 9.

same need for economy as the scribes. The style of the tales in the early Irish manuscripts, in its rigid economy, has something in common with the styles of some Icelandic family sagas, e.g. *Víga-Glúms Saga* and *Hrafnkels Saga*. The Irish and Icelandic styles both appear to be 'literary', rather than oral; they have both been developed through long practice on parchment. But it would not be correct to say that the family sagas were summaries of oral tales.

Every family saga, if studied in detail, seems to bear the individual stamp of an author; it shows something of the author's personal interests and of his artistic taste. Several attempts have been made in recent years to discover who these authors were. It is reasonable to suppose that the more proficient authors wrote more than one saga each. The *Egils Saga*, as already said, is ascribed with good reason to Snorri Sturluson. But other attempts to name the authors of family sagas have been less successful. It is even difficult to know to which classes of the population they belonged. Finnur Jónsson believed that a large proportion of the family sagas were written by clergymen.[1] Some of them, and especially those which are considered to be the oldest, appear to have been written in monasteries. Although the subjects of the family sagas were not religious ones, some of them could quite well have been written by monks. The history of Irish literature shows how monks could devote themselves to profane subjects.[2] If they could do this in Ireland, where monasteries were large and highly organized, how much more could they do it in Iceland, where communities consisted of about half a dozen monks, who must have been in close touch with the laity and have shared their interests? Nevertheless, the family sagas belong to the lay, and not to the clerical culture. The division of Church from State at the end of the twelfth century helped to promote a class of educated laymen, of which Snorri was the foremost example. If monks wrote family sagas, they wrote them as educated laymen, and not as servants of the Universal Church.

[1] *ONOI*, ii. 276 ff.
[2] Cf. R. Thurneysen, *Die irische Helden- und Königsage*, 1921, i. 11 ff.

It has often been said that the oldest of all family sagas is the *Heiðarvíga Saga*.[1] This has the defects of a primitive work. Its theme is tortuous and its style clumsy, but it has also the rugged beauty of a primitive work. Sigurður Nordal, who last edited the *Heiðarvíga Saga*, showed that it was probably written about 1200. He maintained that its author was a monk of Þingeyrar, working under the influence of the early sagas of S. Ólafr and of Ólafr Tryggvason, which must have been kept in that monastery. The *Heiðarvíga Saga* is a story of blood-vengeance, carried out by a group of men against another group whom they hardly knew. The climax of the saga is a famous battle which took place on a desolate moor in 1018. The saga falls into two distinct parts, joined by a thread which an unpractised reader may find difficult to follow. The story is told in great detail, but the characters are not complete, although several of them leave a mark on the memory. The cruellest and most arrogant is Víga-Styrr, who dominates the first chapters. The reader may rejoice when Styrr is struck down by a young boy, whose father he had slaughtered unjustly. Certain women also stand out among the people of the *Heiðarvíga Saga*. One of these is Þuríðr, mother of Barði, who is hero of the second half of the saga, and of Hallr who had been killed by his own countrymen in Norway. Þuríðr cannot rest until Hallr is avenged by blood. Years after Hallr's death she gives her sons stones to eat, telling them that they had swallowed meat as hard as that in failing to take vengeance for their brother. The sources for this saga must largely have been oral ones, traditions preserved in prose and verse. Considering how much of the *Heiðarvíga Saga* depends on the topography of northern and western Iceland, it may be suspected that these traditions were of a very local kind. It is probable that the author of the saga also used genealogical lists, which might contain summaries of events which he related. This saga was read widely in the Middle Ages, and the authors of such famous sagas as the *Eyrbyggja Saga* and *Njáls Saga* were influenced by it. But it is only by a lucky chance that the *Heiðarvíga Saga* has come down

---

[1] Edited with Introduction by Sigurður Nordal and Guðni Jónsson in *Borgfirðinga Sǫgur*, 1938.

to the present day. The second half of it is found in a manuscript now kept in Stockholm, part of which must have been written soon after the middle of the thirteenth century. The first half of this manuscript was burnt in Copenhagen, where it was on loan, in 1728. The first half, but not the second, had been read by a certain Icelander, called Jón Ólafsson, who rewrote it from memory after the fire. This story may help to show how much valuable literature has been lost since the Middle Ages.

The *Fóstbrœðra Saga* must be among the oldest of the family sagas, and, like the *Egils Saga*, it is closely associated with the Kings' sagas. The great age of the *Fóstbrœðra Saga* can be appreciated when it is realized that it was known to the compiler of one of the oldest sagas of S. Ólafr, the so-called 'Middle Saga'.[1] This implies that the *Fóstbrœðra Saga* cannot have been written later than the first decade of the thirteenth century. It is an adventurous and rather romantic story. Two young men, Þormóðr and Þorgeirr, swear oaths of foster-brotherhood. Soon afterwards they quarrel for trivial reasons, and later Þorgeirr is killed by a certain Þorgrímr trolli. In the following chapters of the saga it is told how Þormóðr wrought vengeance for his erstwhile foster-brother. He struck down Þorgrímr at a public assembly in Greenland. Þorgrímr was at that moment the centre of interest. He was sitting on a chair, encircled by an admiring crowd, telling them about his fight with Þorgeirr. Passages of exceptional interest follow the death of Þorgrímr. It is there described how Þormóðr lived as an outlaw in the wastes of Greenland. When he left Greenland, Þormóðr joined S. Ólafr in Norway, and died with him at Stiklastaðir.

Þormóðr was famous as a poet. Thirty-five strophes are assigned to him in the saga. Although these verses have no great appeal for modern readers, they must have supplied much of the material for the author of the saga, whether they are really the work of Þormóðr or of a later poet.

The *Fóstbrœðra Saga* is more advanced than the *Heiðarvíga Saga* in structure as well as in style. But it is somewhat episodic,

---

[1] See Sigurður Nordal's note in *Vestfirðinga Sǫgur*, ed. Björn K. Þórólfsson and Guðni Jónsson, 1943, Introduction, pp. lxx–lxxvii.

and its structure is not comparable with that of the most finished family sagas. The style of this saga underwent remarkable changes during scribal transmission. As it is preserved in the *Hauksbók*, a manuscript written early in the fourteenth century, the style of the *Fóstbrœðra Saga* is smooth and sparing. But in the version of the *Flateyjarbók* and the *Mǫðruvallabók* it contains numerous digressions, together with much extravagant commentary and simile, which are unusual in the classical prose of Iceland. It is said of Þorgeirr:

His heart was not like the crop of a bird; it was not so full of blood that it would tremble with fear, but it was tempered in every valour by the highest of great craftsmen . . .

and of a Greenland thrall:

All the bones in his body trembled; there were two hundred and fourteen bones. His teeth chattered; there were thirty of them. All the veins in his flesh quivered; there were four hundred and fifteen veins.

In the past these digressions have been regarded as interpolations, made in the post-classical period, showing a decline of taste. But comparison of the different manuscripts of the *Fóstbrœðra Saga* has shown that such passages as these were present in the saga in its original form.[1] The redactor who made the version of the *Hauksbók* left them out for aesthetic and stylistic reasons. This conclusion accords well with the evidence of changes of style, which may be gathered from the textual history of *Víga-Glúms Saga* and of some others. The textual history of the *Fóstbrœðra Saga* also suggests that, like the Kings' sagas, the family sagas, in their earliest form, bore a certain resemblance to the lives of the saints and to learned literature of that kind.

In many of the earlier family sagas, the lives of poets are related. The stories told in them often appear to be based on verses composed by those poets, and handed down orally. Even though these verses may not always be correctly assigned to the poets of the tenth and eleventh centuries, whose names they bear, they are in most cases older than the sagas themselves.

[1] See Sigurður Nordal's note quoted above.

Like Þormóðr of the *Fóstbrœðra Saga*, Bjǫrn Hítdœlakappi was associated with S. Ólafr. The saga of Bjǫrn (*Bjarnar Saga*)[1] has some of the romantic interest of the *Fóstbrœðra Saga*, but in form, and especially in its clumsy style, it resembles the *Heiðarvíga Saga*. The *Bjarnar Saga* is a love-story, and probably the oldest of its kind in Icelandic. It is told how the poet Bjǫrn was betrothed to a beautiful woman called Oddný 'Island Candle'. He went abroad to prove his valour, leaving his bride to wait for him. In Russia he overcame a champion called Kaldimarr. He served under Knútr in England, and slew a flying dragon. His adventures in Iceland were of a more realistic kind, and were occasionally grotesque. When Bjǫrn returned to Iceland, Þórðr Kolbeinsson, another poet, had spread the rumour that he was dead, and had married Oddný himself. Attempts were made to reconcile the two poets, but without success, and they continued to insult each other in bitter, satirical verses. In one series of them, Bjǫrn insulted Þórðr by describing how his mother, walking by the sea-shore, had devoured a stranded skate, and thus became pregnant with Þórðr. In the end, Þórðr with many others surprised Bjǫrn. Bjǫrn's last moments were his greatest. He fought wounded on his knees, defending himself with a pair of shears.

The story of Hallfreðr, the Troublesome Poet (*Hallfreðar Saga*),[2] has already been mentioned. This is also thought to be an old saga, but it is much better constructed than the *Bjarnar Saga*. The traditions about Hallfreðr were closely associated with those about Ólafr Tryggvason, and some of the stories about Ólafr Tryggvason were preserved in the verses of Hallfreðr. Although weak in the faith, Hallfreðr was the especial friend and godson of Ólafr. The *Hallfreðar Saga* appears to be influenced by one of the sagas of Ólafr Tryggvason, most probably that of Gunnlaugr,[3] and it contains a strong hagiographical element. It is told at the end of the saga how Hallfreðr died of sickness at sea. His coffin drifted to the Holy Island (Iona), and his body was buried in the church there.

[1] Ed. Sigurður Nordal and Guðni Jónsson, *Borgfirðinga Sǫgur*, 1938.
[2] Ed. Einar Ól. Sveinsson, *Vatnsdæla Saga*, 1939. Cf. Ch. II above.
[3] Cf. Einar Ól. Sveinsson's edition, Introduction, sect. 9.

Since Hallfreðr came of a family living in Vatnsdalr, the neighbourhood of Þingeyrar, it is widely held that the saga was written
in that monastery.

The *Víga-Glúms Saga*[1] is probably rather younger than the
sagas just mentioned. It is believed that it was written about 1230–
40. This saga may lack the freshness of the older ones, but it shows
how consciousness of form and construction had developed. Víga-
Glúmr was a poet of some distinction, although it is not recorded
that he made poetry for the entertainment of foreign chieftains.
He was a typical peasant, and had comparatively little to do with
foreign lands. He visited Norway in his youth, but lived the rest of
his life as a farmer in the Eyjafjǫrðr. The *Víga-Glúms Saga* must
have been written by one who lived in that neighbourhood, as is
shown by the detailed geographical knowledge of it. Glúmr was
ambitious and ruthless, and at first successful, but his downfall was
determined by fate. Fate is symbolized by three objects, a cloak,
a sword, and a spear, which Glúmr had received from his grandfather in Norway. So long as he kept them he was invincible, but
as soon as he gave them away, his enemies closed in and crushed
him. The saga contains interesting memories of pre-Christian
religion, and especially of the worship of Freyr, and of the fatalistic
philosophy which was a dominant feature in Scandinavian paganism. The *Víga-Glúms Saga* bears some resemblance to the Kings'
sagas, but it is nearly devoid of the hagiographical element which
was so noticeable in some of the earlier sagas. The saga-writers
were now beginning to forget how much they owed to their clerical
predecessors.

Some of the people of the *Víga-Glúms Saga* appear also in the
*Ljósvetninga Saga*,[2] which was probably written at a later date.
This saga, unlike the *Víga-Glúms Saga*, is poorly constructed, but
its characters are drawn realistically and, although disjointed, the
stories in it are well told. The surviving texts are probably somewhat corrupt. The chief character in the first part of the *Ljósvetninga Saga* is Guðmundr the Mighty. Few leading characters of any

[1] Ed. G. Turville-Petre, 1940.
[2] Ed. Björn Sigfússon, *Ljósvetninga Saga*, 1940.

saga are described with such contempt as he. He is rich and powerful, but cruel, cowardly, and immoral, and he earns the hatred of his
neighbours. The passage in which Guðmundr's death is described
is one of the most memorable in the lesser family sagas:

It is told that, when Guðmundr's life was drawing to its close, there was
a man living in the Eyjarfjǫrðr, called Þórhallr, a good husbandman.
He dreamed a dream, and went north to see Finni. Finni was standing
in the doorway, and Þórhallr said: 'I would like you to read a dream that
I have dreamed, Finni.' Finni said: 'Be off with you at once. I do not
want to hear your dream.' And he slammed the door, saying: 'go and
tell Guðmundr at Mǫðruvellir about your dream, otherwise you will
be driven off with arms.' Then Þórhallr went to Mǫðruvellir. Guðmundr had ridden down the Eyjarfjǫrðr that day, and he was expected
home in the evening. Einarr, the brother of Guðmundr, lay down and
fell asleep, and he dreamed that an ox was walking up the Eyjarfjǫrðr.
He was very fine and had large horns. The ox came to Mǫðruvellir, and
went to every building on the farmstead, and last of all to the high seat,
where he fell down dead. Then Einarr said: 'Such a dream must be the
presage of great events, and such things must be men's fetches'. Then
Guðmundr came home, and it was his practice to go into every building on the farm, and when he came to the high seat he sank back and
talked to Þórhallr. Þórhallr was telling Guðmundr about his dream.
Then Guðmundr sat up, and the food had now been brought in. There
was some warm milk, with hot stones in it. Guðmundr said: 'it is not
hot'. Þorlaug (his wife) said: 'that is strange', and she heated the stones
again. Then Guðmundr drank, and he said: 'it is not hot'. Þorlaug said:
'I do not know, Guðmundr, what has become of your feeling for heat.'
He drank again, and said: 'it is not hot'. And then he fell back, and he
had breathed his last. Then Þorlaug said: 'these are great tidings, and
they will be talked of far and wide. Let no one touch him. Einarr has
often foreseen lesser events than these.' Einarr came, and performed the
obsequies, and laid Guðmundr out. Einarr said: 'your dream had no
little force, Þórhallr. Finni could see by the look of you that the person
to whom you told it would die, and that was what he intended for Guðmundr. Guðmundr must have been cold inside when he could not feel.'[1]

The scenes of a small number of sagas are laid in eastern Iceland, a district which, even today, has irregular communications
with the north and west. Although some of these sagas cover long
periods of history and a wide range of events, all of them are

[1] Edition quoted, ch. xi.

concise, and the reader might be tempted to think of them as the product of a distinct literary school. The oldest of the eastern sagas is perhaps the *Droplaugarsona Saga*.[1] Some critics have supposed that its author was a certain Þorvaldr Ingjaldsson, who is named in the text as a source, but it would be difficult to decide when this man lived. The *Droplaugarsona Saga* contains some striking passages, but it is disjointed in construction, and uneven and unpolished in style.

The *Vápnfirðinga Saga*[2] is more highly developed. It is a tale of tragedy, in which a curse, uttered in the first chapters, is worked out. A family feud develops and continues through two generations, ending in reconciliation. At the beginning of the story Brodd-Helgi and Geitir are fast friends, but they soon quarrel. When Geitir was away in the north of Iceland, he was once asked what he thought of Helgi. With loyalty characteristic of an Icelandic hero, he spoke well of his former friend. When asked if Helgi was not a very unjust man, Geitir said: 'his injustice has chiefly been manifest to me in this way, that he is not content that I should always have the sky above me, as he has it himself.'

After Geitir had killed Brodd-Helgi, Helgi's son, Bjarni, was induced by his wicked stepmother to kill Geitir. The manuscripts of the saga have a gap at this point, but enough remains to show how well the scene was described:

Bjarni spoke few words. Kolfinnr left home with him. He began to speak, ill foreboding, and said, looking up into the sky: 'now the weather is very changeable; I thought that it was rather squally and cold as well, but now it begins to look as if it will thaw'. Bjarni said: 'then it will always thaw, if this is to be a thaw'. Bjarni stood up and said: 'my foot is numb'. 'Then lie still' said Geitir. Then Bjarni struck at Geitir's head, and he died on the spot. But as soon as he had struck Geitir, Bjarni repented. He placed Geitir's head on his lap, and Geitir died on Bjarni's knees.[3]

The story ends with the reconciliation between Bjarni and Þorkell, the son of Geitir.

The most perfect of the shorter sagas, in structure and character

[1] Ed. J. Jakobsen, *Austfirðinga Sǫgur*, 1902–3.
[2] Ibid., in *Austfirðinga Sǫgur*.    [3] Edition quoted, ch. 13, pp. 56–57.

drawing, is the *Hrafnkels Saga*,[1] which also belongs to eastern
Iceland. The hero, Hrafnkell Freyr's priest, settled in Hrafnkels-
dalr, a remote valley stretching into the interior of the island. He
lived at Aðalból, the chief farm of that valley, dividing the rest of
it among his dependents, and was soon a mighty chief. Hrafnkell
loved Freyr more than any other god, and shared his most treasured
possessions equally with him. Among his treasures was the stallion
Freyfaxi (Freyr's maned one), and Hrafnkell swore that he would
be the death of any one who should ride the horse without his
leave. Malevolent fate led Hrafnkell's shepherd Einarr to ride the
horse, and Hrafnkell killed him to fulfil his ill-considered oath.
When Einarr's poor father protested, Hrafnkell offered generous
payment as damages, but because of overbearing pride he would
not submit to arbitration. Einarr's relatives prosecuted Hrafnkell
at the *Alþingi* and, with the help of powerful men from the western
districts, they obtained the outlawry of Hrafnkell. Hrafnkell was
now driven from his lands in disgrace, and his place was taken by
Sámr, the cousin of Einarr. Hrafnkell founded a new farm in a
neighbouring district, and soon grew as rich and powerful as he had
been before. When the time came, he took his revenge. He waylaid
and killed Sámr's powerful brother, Eyvindr, as he was returning
home from Byzantium, laden with the decorations of the Emperor.
Then Hrafnkell expelled Sámr from Aðalból as ignominiously as
he had himself been expelled six years earlier.

The doctrine expounded in the *Hrafnkels Saga* differs in emphasis from that of some others. Fate causes Einarr to ride the
forbidden horse, but it is because of his unchastened pride that
Hrafnkell refuses to submit to arbitration and suffers humiliation.
It is because Hrafnkell is a chieftain by nature, and Sámr a man of
inferior birth and character, unfit for the position in which accident
had placed him, that Hrafnkell must triumph over Sámr in the end.

In recent years the *Hrafnkels Saga* has been the subject of much
learned and interesting discussion.[2] It was formerly supposed that

[1] *Hrafnkels Saga Freysgoða*, ed. F. S. Cawley, 1932.
[2] See especially Sigurður Nordal, *Hrafnkatla*, 1940; K. Liestøl in *Arv*, 1946,
pp. 94 ff.

it was one of the most faithful of all sagas to historical fact. It was also said to be one of those sagas which had lived orally, and were complete unities before they were written down; it had been little altered by the scribe who put it into writing. But Sigurður Nordal has shown that the *Hrafnkels Saga* can have little basis in history. Some of its leading characters can never have existed at all. It is rather to be regarded as an historical novel, written by an experienced author late in the thirteenth century. The author had perhaps read the *Landnámabók*, as well as the *Íslendingabók* of Ari, and other historical literature. Although guilty of anachronisms, he knew a good deal about life in Iceland in the tenth century, but it was not his aim to record historical facts. If he had attempted to do so, the *Hrafnkels Saga* could never have been so realistic and convincing as it is.

The scenes of many sagas are laid in western Iceland, and especially around the Breiðafjörðr. One of the most interesting of them is the *Eyrbyggja Saga.*[1] This has none of those excellencies of construction which are admired in many sagas. It is a series of scenes and stories, which follow the disordered course of life itself. The *Eyrbyggja Saga* has no hero, but in it those who lived on the southern shores of the Breiðafjörðr from the end of the ninth to the beginning of the eleventh century are described. The chief character in a great part of the saga is Snorri the Priest (*goði*), who died in 1031. Snorri was described in several sagas besides this one, and it is interesting to notice that his character is everywhere the same. He is calculating, cold, and cynical, gifted with cunning rather than with bravery, but at the same time wise, prudent, and sometimes generous. It was told in the *Kristni Saga* (ch. xii) that Snorri took part in the deliberations at the Assembly in the year 1000, when the Icelanders decided to adopt the Christian religion. The pagan party, hearing that a volcano was in eruption, said that this was a sign that the gods were angry. In reply, Snorri asked them what the gods had been angry about when the lava on which they were standing at Þingvellir (the place of the Assembly) had erupted. It is this same Snorri who confronts us in the *Eyrbyggja*

[1] Ed. Einar Ól. Sveinsson, 1935.

*Saga* and in other records. This shows how vividly his memory lived in tradition, as long as two centuries after his death.

The author of the *Eyrbyggja Saga* writes as an antiquarian, and probably did not recognize himself as the artist he was. He was interested in the ritual and practices of pagan religion, and his descriptions of a temple and of sacrifice are among the most detailed preserved. He retold ghost- and wonder-tales, which he must have heard from the peasants of his own time. A cloud rains blood, and dead men haunt their home until it is exorcized. There is also an interesting tale of metempsychosis in the *Eyrbyggja Saga*. The wicked Þórólfr Crook-leg seems to be born again in the bull-calf, Glæsir.

As well as oral tales, the author of the *Eyrbyggja Saga* used a large number of scaldic verses, which probably reached him in oral form, and it is largely these which give the saga its great value as an historical source. Some of the verses quoted in the *Eyrbyggja Saga*, particularly those of Þórarinn the Black, are among the best of the humbler scaldic poetry preserved.[1]

The author of the *Eyrbyggja Saga* had read widely in Icelandic. Among his written sources was a short note by Ari (*Ævi Snorra goða*), in which the chronology of Snorri's life was given, and his children were named. This document is still preserved, and it is generally held that it was an independent *scheda*, rather than a part of the lost *Íslendingabók* or of the *Landnámabók*.[2] The author of the *Eyrbyggja Saga* alludes directly to the *Heiðarvíga Saga*, in which Snorri had played a notable part. He also summarized a passage in the *Gísla Saga*, which shows that the *Eyrbyggja Saga* must be younger than that saga. It is even more surprising to notice that the *Laxdœla Saga* is mentioned by name in the text of the *Eyrbyggja Saga*. Were it not for this, the *Eyrbyggja Saga* would probably be considered an older saga than the *Laxdœla*. Indeed, the last editor of the *Eyrbyggja Saga*, Dr. Einar Ól. Sveinsson,[3] believed that the allusion to the *Laxdœla Saga* was interpolated, and

---

[1] See above, Ch. I, pp. 45 ff.

[2] Cf. Einar Ól. Sveinsson in *Eyrbyggja Saga*, Introduction, sect. 2; and the same scholar's work in *Laxdœla Saga*, 1934, Introduction, sect. 3.

[3] Edition of *Eyrbyggja Saga*, Introduction, sect. 6.

that the *Eyrbyggja Saga* must have been written about 1220. But the reasons which Dr. Einar gave for assigning the *Eyrbyggja Saga* to such an early date have not been widely accepted.[1] Although the *Eyrbyggja Saga* is archaic and apparently dependent, for a great part, on oral sources, it is not necessary to conclude that it was written before the middle of the thirteenth century.

The author of the *Eyrbyggja Saga* had an intimate knowledge of the district of which he was writing. Its centre was Helgafell (Holy Hill), which was the home of Snorri during a great part of his life. Helgafell was venerated as a holy place in pagan times, and after 1184 it was the site of an Augustinian monastery. It is tempting to suppose that the author of the *Eyrbyggja Saga* was an inmate of this monastery, but if so, he worked in the native, and not in the clerical tradition. His reading was chiefly in the vernacular, and not in Latin literature. The *Eyrbyggja Saga* was far removed from the hagiography of the monks of Þingeyrar.

Several of the characters known from the *Eyrbyggja Saga* appear also in the *Gísla Saga*,[2] but the *Gísla Saga* is a work of very different purpose and form. At first sight it might be supposed that the *Gísla Saga* was a younger work than the *Eyrbyggja Saga*. The author of the *Gísla Saga* shows a conscious artistry and a constructive power, of which there are no signs in the *Eyrbyggja Saga*. But, as already said, the author of the *Eyrbyggja Saga* knew the *Gísla Saga*, and this suggests that the *Gísla Saga* was written at a comparatively early date, or at any rate not later than the middle of the thirteenth century.

The *Gísla Saga* is not, like the *Eyrbyggja Saga*, the history of a district, or even of a family. Like the *Víga-Glúms Saga* and the *Hallfreðar Saga*, it is the biography of a single hero, whose life-story is told from beginning to end. The hero is the outlaw poet, Gísli Súrsson, who probably died about 980. Gísli was a noble person, and unusually pious for one who lived in pagan times, but the fates were against him. The story of Gísli's life is a tragedy and, unlike the sagas already mentioned, the *Gísla Saga* bears a

---

[1] See Jón Jóhannesson, *Gerðir Landnámabókar*, 1941, p. 136.
[2] Ed. Björn K. Þórólfsson in *Vestfirðinga Sǫgur*, 1943.

strong resemblance to the tragedies told in some of the heroic lays of the *Edda*. It contains nearly forty verses in scaldic form, which are ascribed to Gísli himself. If all of these verses are correctly ascribed to Gísli, Gísli must himself have been influenced by the heroic traditions and sentiments. In one of the verses he alludes to the legend of the Niflungs, and seems to contrast his own fortunes with those of Gunnarr, whom Atli slew. Gunnarr was avenged by his sister, Guðrún, whose first husband, Sigurðr, Gunnarr had himself caused to be murdered. Gísli had struck down Þorgrímr, the first husband of his sister, Þórdís, and Þórdís had betrayed him.

The authenticity of the verses in the *Gísla Saga* has been questioned, and few critics in recent times have accepted all of them as Gísli's work. Some have supposed that they were composed by the author of the saga, or even that they were inserted by a later hand.[1] Others have compared them with the great Christian poems of the twelfth century, and concluded that they were of similar age. If these verses are older than the text of the saga, they must be among the chief sources for the saga itself and, in that case, much might be learnt from them about the preservation and growth of oral tales before they were written.

Whatever their age, the verses of the *Gísla Saga* are unique in Icelandic literature. The Eddaic and scaldic traditions, together with Christian and pagan sentiments, blend in the mind of the poet, and an unusual wealth of simile and allusion is achieved. In a number of the verses, the poet describes visions, which he had seen in his dreams. Two spirits in the form of women appear to him, one good and the other evil. They have been associated with the good and bad angels of Christian legend. They make prophecies in symbols, and the fate determined for Gísli is seen, as if through a mist.

Loyalty of one man towards another, and the love between man and woman are dominant motives in this saga. Gísli was made outlaw because he killed his brother-in-law, Þorgrímr, in order to

[1] See Björn K. Þórólfsson, Introduction, sect. 1; my paper in *Modern Language Review*, xxxix, 1944, pp. 374 ff.; I. L. Gordon in *Saga-Book*, xiii, 1949–50, pp. 183 ff.

avenge his foster-brother, Vésteinn. Throughout his thirteen years
of outlawry, Gísli was supported by the steadfast devotion of his
wife, Auðr. The *Gísla Saga* lacks the cold detachment found in
many sagas. It is less austere than many of the others, and for this
reason it may appeal more readily to modern readers.

The *Laxdœla Saga*[1] is, in some ways, the richest of all the family
sagas, and it contains elements of very different kinds. Superficially
it resembles the *Eyrbyggja Saga*. Many of the people who appear
in the *Laxdœla Saga* are also known from the *Eyrbyggja Saga*.
Most of the action of the *Laxdœla Saga* takes place on the northern
shores of the Breiðafjǫrðr, and the story of the *Laxdœla Saga* covers
four or five generations, from the settlement of Dalir in the ninth
century to the first decades of the eleventh century. But the
*Eyrbyggja Saga* and the *Laxdœla* differ in tone, and the tastes and
interests of their authors must have differed widely. The author of
the *Laxdœla Saga* was not, in the first place, an antiquarian. It was
not his aim to save the memories of past ages from oblivion, but
he used these memories as the material for his art. The author of
the *Laxdœla Saga* was learned in antiquity. He had read a great
part of the Icelandic literature known now, and a good deal which
has since been forgotten. One of his sources was an early version
of the *Landnámabók*, most probably the one which Ari wrote. The
*Laxdœla Saga* has thrown much light on the textual history of the
*Landnámabók*.[2] When he described the conversion of his heroes
to Christianity, the author of the *Laxdœla Saga* referred to early
Kings' sagas, notably to Oddr's 'Saga of Ólafr Tryggvason'. Needless to say, he had also read a number of family sagas, such as the
*Heiðarvíga Saga* and the *Egils Saga*. There are several points of
similarity between the *Laxdœla Saga* and the *Vápnfirðinga Saga*.
Both of them tend to be sentimental, and in both of them a tragic
quarrel between intimate friends is described. Geitir, in the *Vápnfirðinga Saga*, declined to speak ill of his former friend, Brodd-
Helgi. Similarly, when others spoke ill of Kjartan, in the *Laxdœla
Saga*, his former friend Bolli would pretend not to hear, or else con-

---

[1] Ed. Einar Ól. Sveinsson, 1934.
[2] Cf. Jón Jóhannesson, op. cit., pp. 212 ff.

tradict them. Bolli, egged on by his wife, Guðrún, waylaid Kjartan
and killed him, just as Bjarni killed Geitir under the incitement of
his wicked stepmother. As soon as he had struck the mortal blow,
Bolli repented, and Kjartan died on Bolli's lap, just as Geitir died
on the lap of Bjarni. This quarrel ended in reconciliation between
the sons of Bolli and the relatives of Kjartan, just as the *Vápnfirðinga Saga* ended in reconciliation between the two parties.

The *Laxdœla Saga* is concerned largely with tragic conflict.
The hero and heroine in a great part of the saga are Kjartan and
Guðrún. The character of Kjartan is not well described, but
Guðrún is perhaps the best drawn of all women in the family sagas.
Early in the saga, she and Kjartan are informally betrothed.
Kjartan and his foster-brother, Bolli, go to Norway. Bolli returned
to Iceland first. He spoke of intimate relations between Kjartan
and Ingibjǫrg, the sister of King Ólafr Tryggvason, and by the
time Kjartan returned, Bolli had married Guðrún himself. Kjartan
then married Hrefna, an unlucky woman who was little more than
the plaything of fate. It is made plain that Kjartan and Guðrún still
loved each other, or perhaps it should be said that Guðrún's love
was turned to hatred, and she was cruelly jealous of the innocent
Hrefna. After Kjartan and Bolli had quarrelled, traces of their
former friendship remained, for theirs had been the deep friendship of youth. When he was attacked by Bolli in his last fight,
Kjartan threw down his weapons, saying: 'I should much rather
get my death-blow from you, cousin, than give you such a blow.'

Critics have often called attention to the similarity between the
story of Guðrún and Kjartan, and that of Brynhildr and Sigurðr.
Bolli and Hrefna seem to play the part of Gunnarr and Guðrún
of the Niflung legend. As W. P. Ker[1] put it, the *Laxdœla Saga* 'is
a modern prose version of the Niblung tragedy, with the person-
ages chosen from the life of Iceland in the heroic age, and from
the Icelandic family traditions'. Guðrún of the *Laxdœla Saga* resembles the Brynhildr of certain Eddaic lays, because, defrauded
of the man she loves, she compels her husband to slaughter him.
In the *Laxdœla Saga* the chief interest is in Guðrún, just as, in the

[1] *Epic and Romance*, 1922, p. 209.

*Sigurðar Kviða en Skamma* and in some other lays of the *Edda*, it is in Brynhildr. Kjartan resembles Sigurðr; he is the glorious, spotless hero, whom no author could describe. It would be difficult to know how far the author of the *Laxdœla Saga* was influenced by the heroic lays when he moulded his story and chose his phrases. Legends about Guðrún and Kjartan might have been influenced by the heroic concepts before the *Laxdœla Saga* was written.

The author of the *Laxdœla Saga* shows an unusual interest in visual beauty. Authors of classical sagas seldom paused, as this one did, to describe the beauty of dress, or of furniture or of ornamented weapons. It is said of Ólafr the Peacock, the father of Kjartan, that he had a 'parlour built at Hjarðarholt, and it was larger and grander than any seen before. Famous tales were carved on the wainscoting and on the roof, and they were so well worked that the parlour looked its best when the tapestries were down.' The author even remembers to describe how Guðrún was dressed on the day when her husband, Bolli, was killed:

Guðrún was dressed in a tunic of foreign cut with a close-fitting bodice of fine-woven cloth, and she wore a curved headdress. She had fastened a veil about her, on which were figures embroidered in blue, and a fringe at the end.

Bolli once offered to give Kjartan a stallion, which was 'white with red ears and a red forelock, and there were three mares with him, all of the same hue as he'. These horses were of the same colour as the cows from the elf-mound, described in the Irish story of Fróech.[1] The most detailed of the visual descriptions comes towards the end of the saga. Helgi Harðbeinsson was one of those who killed Guðrún's husband, Bolli. Many years afterwards, Guðrún incited her sons and her suitor, Þorgils, to take vengeance on Helgi. Helgi was in his sheiling, and before his assailants arrived, he heard his shepherds describe them one by one. Helgi knew from the description who each one was. It is not likely that this story was based on Icelandic tradition. It has been suggested that the author of the *Laxdœla Saga* was, on this point, following one of the romantic sagas (*riddara sǫgur*), whose author, in his turn,

[1] See *Táin bó Fraích*, ed. M. E. Byrne and M. Dillon, 1933, pp. 1 ff.

would have borrowed the motive from a foreign romance.[1] The
motive is especially common in Irish tales.[2] The *Mesca Ulad*
(Drunkenness of the Ultonians) and *Fled Bricrend* (Bricriu's Feast)
both contain good examples.

There is evidence of post-classical taste in the *Laxdæla Saga*.
We might suppose that the author had read some of the continental
romances, perhaps in Norwegian or Icelandic versions. It may be
remembered that a version of the story of Tristram was made for
King Hákon Hákonarson in 1226, and it was based on the French
poem of Thomas of Brittany. Other romances of this kind appeared
in the Norse language soon afterwards. In the end, the influence
of these romances greatly altered the course of Icelandic literature.
But it would be wrong to over-emphasize the strength of continental influence on the *Laxdæla Saga*. It is based, for the most
part, on historical records preserved in Iceland, whether orally or
in writing. The author writes as a man from Breiðafjǫrðr, and his
knowledge of the geography of that district was so exact that he
must have spent a great part of his life there. *Courtoisie* played a
minor part in his thoughts. It is safe to say that the *Laxdæla Saga*
was written about the middle of the thirteenth century, or perhaps
rather before that date.

One of the youngest of the family sagas, and the greatest of them
all, is the *Njáls Saga*.[3] It is commonly believed that this saga was
written towards the end of the thirteenth century, and probably
by an author who lived in southern, or rather in south-eastern Iceland. The greatness of the *Njáls Saga* lies partly in the wealth and
diversity of its material and motives, and this could not have been
achieved until many sagas and much literature of other branches
had become known in Iceland. The influence of a whole library of
earlier sagas can be detected in the *Njáls Saga*. These sagas include
the *Heiðarvíga Saga*, *Eyrbyggja Saga*, and *Laxdæla Saga*, as well
as sagas about foreign history, such as a lost saga about King
Brian and the battle of Clontarf, and probably one about Ólafr

---

[1] See Einar Ól Sveinsson's edition of the saga, Introduction, sect. 1.
[2] Cf. R. Thurneysen, op. cit., p. 61.
[3] *Brennu-Njálssaga*, ed. Finnur Jónsson, 1908.

Tryggvason. The author of the *Njáls Saga* must also have consulted genealogical lists, and books about early Icelandic law. The
influence of the 'Dialogues' of Gregory and of other religious
literature can be detected in the style and motives of the saga.

The *Njáls Saga* has two heroes, and falls naturally into two
parts, although these two parts are closely knit. The hero of the
first part of the story, if the introductory chapters are disregarded,
is Gunnarr Hámundarson. Gunnarr is the youthful hero of un-
stained honour, and he bears some resemblance to Kjartan of the
*Laxdœla Saga* and to Sigurðr of the heroic legends. But he is described more fully than these. He is not only brave and honourable,
but also athletic and generous. Like Kjartan and Sigurðr, Gunnarr
is guileless, and his misfortunes are caused by a woman. Gunnarr's
wife, Hallgerðr, stands with Guðrún of the *Laxdœla Saga*, among
the most memorable women in Icelandic literature, and she is one
of the most complicated. She is beautiful, but embittered, and was
subject to evil influences in early youth. She was proud, but so ill-
controlled that her dignity was nearly lost. She was guilty of theft,
the basest of all crimes in the eyes of a peasant people, and her theft
led to Gunnarr's death. The death of Gunnarr and his last stand
were famous in the history of Iceland before the *Njáls Saga* was
written. He was attacked by a strong force when he was in his house
with no companions but his wife and mother. When his bow-string
was cut, Gunnarr asked his wife to replace it with two locks of her
hair. All the bitterness of Hallgerðr's life was concentrated in her
refusal to grant Gunnarr's last wish. She remembered the day
when Gunnarr had struck her, and had exposed her as a thief.

Njáll, the hero of the second part of the saga, was the friend of
Gunnarr. Their friendship was all the more remarkable because
they were unalike, and because they remained friends despite the
endeavours of Hallgerðr to create a feud between their families.
Gunnarr was the conventional hero, whose character could have
no great depth. Njáll was a wise and thoughtful man. He was a
counsellor, rather than an active man. He was not only astute and
learned in law, but he could see into the future by virtue of prophetic gifts. It was in keeping with his character that his beard

never grew. It was once said of him in derision that those who saw him hardly knew whether he was a man or a woman. But despite physical peculiarities, Njáll is depicted as one of the foremost chieftains of his day. His character was a blend of many elements. Like the traditional Icelandic chief, he was noble and upright, and uncompromisingly loyal to his friends and relatives. But he also had many Christian virtues. He was generous to those in distress, and faced death submissively like a martyr. Since he could see into the future, he must be a fatalist, but he also believed in retribution, and in reward and punishment after death.

Much that has been said of Njáll could also be said of the saga itself, and it must reflect its author's views on ethics and philosophy. His tastes and opinions were chiefly the traditional ones which were older than Christianity in Iceland. But at times the Christian outlook dominates in the *Njáls Saga*; forgiveness triumphs over vengeance. One of the most tragic episodes is the death of Hǫskuldr, the foster-son of Njáll. Hǫskuldr was killed by the sons of Njáll, who had been incited by a slanderer to do this dastardly crime. As he was struck down, defenceless and alone, Hǫskuldr said: 'God help me and forgive you', words far removed from northern paganism. When Njáll heard of Hǫskuldr's death, he said that he would rather have lost two of his own sons, or even all of them, than Hǫskuldr. The sweetest light of his eyes had been quenched. But yet, morality demanded that Njáll should stand by his sons, and suffer a terrible death by burning at the hands of Hǫskuldr's relatives.

Hildigunnr, the wife of Hǫskuldr, contrasts with her husband. She was the tragic, vengeful woman of northern tradition, rather like Guðrún in the *Hamðismál*, who incites her sons to take vengeance on Ermanaric for their murdered sister. In the following passage[1] it is described how Flosi, her uncle, visited Hildigunnr after Hǫskuldr had been killed:

From there Flosi rode to Ossabœr. . . .
Hildigunnr was outside the door and she said: 'Now all my workmen must be standing outside when Flosi rides into the yard, and the women

[1] Ch. CXVI.

must sweep the house and hang the tapestries, and put up a high seat for Flosi.'

And then Flosi rode into the home meadow. Hildigunnr turned to him and said: 'Welcome and blessed, cousin. My heart rejoices in your coming.' Flosi said: 'We shall stop here for dinner, and then ride on.' Then their horses were tethered, and Flosi walked into the parlour. He sat down and knocked the high seat on to the dais saying: 'I am neither a king nor a prince, and there is no need to put up a high seat for me, and no need to mock me.'

Hildigunnr was standing near, and she said: 'I am sorry if you are offended, for we did this in all sincerity.' Flosi said: 'If you act in sincere good will towards me the result will speak for itself, if all goes well, and stand condemned if things fall out ill.' Hildigunnr laughed an icy laugh, and she said: 'This cannot be told yet, we two shall draw nearer to each other before the end.' Hildigunnr sat down beside Flosi, and they talked in undertones for a long time. Now the tables were set up, and Flosi washed his hands, and so did his followers. Then Flosi looked at the towel. It was nothing but rags, and one end had been torn away. He threw it on the bench, and would not wipe his hands on it, but cut a piece off the table-cloth, and dried his hands on that, and then threw it to his men. Then Flosi sat down to table and told his men to eat.

Then Hildigunnr came into the parlour, and she swept her hair back from her eyes and wept. Flosi said: 'You are sad at heart now, cousin, but it is right that you should weep for a good husband.' 'What will you do to bring this case to justice,' said she, 'and what help can I expect from you?' Flosi said: 'I shall prosecute this suit to the full extent of the law, or else bring it to such a settlement that honest men will see that we are fully recompensed in every way.' Hildigunnr said: 'Hǫskuldr would have taken vengeance for you, if he were in charge of a case after your death.' Flosi said: 'You do not lack ruthlessness, and you have shown what you want.' Hildigunnr said: 'Arnórr Ǫrnólfsson of Forárskógar had done less injury to your father, Þórðr Freysgoði, and yet your brothers, Kolbeinn and Egill, killed him at the Skaptafellsþing.'

Then Hildigunnr went into the outer hall and opened her chest. She took out the cloak which Flosi had given to Hǫskuldr, and he was wearing it when he was killed, and she had kept it with all the blood wrapped in it. She walked into the parlour, carrying the cloak, and went silently to Flosi. By now Flosi had finished his dinner, and the table had been cleared. Hildigunnr threw the cloak over Flosi's shoulders, and the blood crackled all around him. 'Flosi', she said, 'you gave this cloak to Hǫskuldr, and now I wish to give it back to you. He was wearing it when he was killed. I call upon God and good men to witness that I enjoin you in the name of all the miracles of your Christ, and in the name of your manhood and valour, that you avenge every one of the wounds which Hǫskuldr had on his dead body, or else be loathed and despised of all men.'

Flosi cast the cloak from his shoulders, and threw it into her arms, saying 'You are a most cruel monster, you would like us to do such things as will bring most evil upon all of us. Cruel is the counsel of women.'

And this is how Flosi was moved; his face was at one moment the colour of blood, and at another pale like grass, and then black like death. . . .

It has often been said that the *Njáls Saga* is a compilation, made up chiefly of two older sagas, one about Gunnarr and another about Njáll. But, since Einar Ól. Sveinsson published his detailed study of the *Njáls Saga*[1] it has been judged differently. This scholar showed how improbable it was that the separate sagas of Gunnarr and Njáll had ever existed. As already suggested, the author of the *Njáls Saga* used sources of many different kinds, but he used them with discretion, sometimes following them closely and sometimes taking incidents freely from them. He thus created a new and altogether independent work. His methods had much in common with those which Snorri used when he composed his 'Saga of S. Ólafr'. Snorri gave the saga its artistic form, and created the character of S. Ólafr, although much had been written about him before. The author of the *Njáls Saga* treated his sources more freely than Snorri did. The saga may have great value as a source of history, but this is incidental. It was not the author's purpose to write a work of history, but rather to use an historical subject for an epic in prose.

The *Njáls Saga* is the culmination of Icelandic literature. In no saga can we detect the influence of so many different kinds of literature, foreign as well as native.

[1] *Um Njálu*, i, 1933.

# INDEX